# Failing Grades

## The Quest for Equity in America's Schools

H. Roy Kaplan

D0770265

*Second Edition*

Rowman & Littlefield Education
Lanham, Maryland • Toronto • Plymouth, UK
2007

Published in the United States of America
by Rowman & Littlefield Education
A Division of Rowman & Littlefield Publishers, Inc.
A wholly owned subsidary of The Rowman & Littlefield Publishing Group,
Inc.
4501 Forbes Boulevard, Suite 200, Lanham, Maryland 20706
www.rowmaneducation.com

Estover Road
Plymouth PL6 7PY
United Kingdom

British Library Cataloguing in Publication Information Available

**Library of Congress Cataloging-in-Publication Data**

Kaplan, H. Roy.
  Failing grades : the quest for equity in America's schools / Roy Kaplan. —
2nd ed.
     p. cm.
  Includes bibliographical references and index.
  ISBN-13: 978-1-57886-648-9 (hardback : alk. paper)
  ISBN-10: 1-57886-648-0 (hardback : alk. paper)
  ISBN-13: 978-1-57886-649-6 (pbk. : alk. paper)
  ISBN-10: 1-57886-649-9 (pbk. : alk. paper)
  1. School violence—Prevention. 2. Conflict management—Study and
teaching. 3. Underachievers—Education. I. Title.
  LB3013.3.K364 2007
  371.7'82—dc22

                                                        2007014038

For my teachers who kindled in me the desire to learn,
and Zoey, Keeley and Nia . . .
May they be fortunate enough to have such educators.

# Contents

# Preface

Someone once said that life is what happens to you while you're making other plans. I never planned to write this book, but I decided that the public needed to learn about the experiences I was having in the nation's schools. This book is not intended to be a diatribe against our educational system or a critique of efforts to reform it. Indeed, in the following pages, readers will see many examples of outstanding leadership and dedication among teachers and administrators: people who are striving to improve the lot of children and who are desperately seeking to survive and achieve in the face of substantial social and cultural forces that can be formidable obstacles to their success.

It is my hope that the stories within, gathered from a decade and a half of work in the nation's schools, will help the public—and some of the people who staff our schools—realize the nature and extent of the sources of conflict that impede academic success. For many children, getting money for the next meal and finding a safe place to stay at night takes precedence over passing standardized tests. Children can't learn when they are hungry, in need of health care, clothes, and validation as human beings.

As our nation struggles with its increasing diversity, so, too, do our schools, which often become flash points where cultures clash and struggles for power and privilege pit one group against another. These stories need to be told because many people, including some educators and administrators, do not know about them, despite the fact that they are played out countless times everywhere, every day.

If there is one redeeming theme throughout this volume, it is that we can make our schools safe and successful learning environments for all children. The methods for accomplishing this are simple, but they must be acknowledged by parents, students, and staff and integrated throughout our schools. We cannot afford to ignore these lessons—our children deserve better, and our future depends on it.

## PREFACE TO THE SECOND EDITION

The themes emphasized in this book have dominated the news since the publication of the first edition in 2004. More attention is being focused on the nation's schools than ever before, thanks to the implementation of the federal No Child Left Behind (NCLB) legislation, with its emphasis on accountability. Every state now uses standardized tests to determine the adequate yearly progress (AYP) of students in reading and math. Despite enormous expenditures of time and money to improve student performance, 1,750 schools in the United States were ordered into radical "restructuring," including teacher and administrator firings, closure, and state takeovers in 2006 for failing to show improvements in student performance for five consecutive years.

One former U.S. Department of Education official predicted that more than ten thousand of the nation's fifty-three thousand schools would fall into the "restructuring" category as the nation continued to grapple with the challenge of narrowing the achievement gap between White children and their Black and Latino peers. Indeed, the situation might be dire; the Associated Press reported that schools were deliberately not counting the test scores of nearly 2 million students, mostly minorities (*St. Petersburg Times* 2006a).

It is generally believed that having competent teachers trained in their field of specialization is essential for quality instruction. One goal of NCLB was that all teachers would be required to have a bachelor's degree, state license, and proven competency in every subject they teach by 2005. This was not achieved and the deadline was moved to the end of the 2006–2007 school year, but not a single state had a highly qualified teacher in every core class at the start of school in 2006, and nine states along with Puerto Rico and the District of Columbia were so deficient that they faced penalties (*St. Petersburg Times* 2006b). Secretary of Education Margaret Spellings believes that "[m]any states took this very seriously, recognizing that good teachers make all the difference in whether or not our children succeed in their studies" (*St. Petersburg Times* 2006c).

The effects of these deficits on student achievement can be devastating. Nationwide, there is a persistent achievement gap between White students and their African American and Latino peers. This is apparent in lower reading and math scores of African American and Latino students on state and national standardized tests, for example, the Florida Comprehensive Assessment Test (FCAT) and the National Assessment of Educational Progress (NAEP). The 2005 NAEP national reading data for twelfth-graders was disappointing: their scores were lower than those of students in 1992, and the gap in scores between White versus Black and Latino students has not changed since 1990.

NAEP (2007) data for 2005 reveal that among fourth-graders, only 13 percent of Black and 19 percent of Hispanic students, compared to 47 percent of the White students, performed at the "proficient" level in mathematics. Among eighth-grade students, just 9 percent of Blacks and 13 percent of Hispanics, compared to 39 percent of White students, performed at the "proficient" level in mathematics. Florida's FCAT consistently reveals that African American and Latino students score thirty points lower than White students, and the NAEP indicates they are nearly four grades behind White students. Even more discouraging is that, despite an enormous effort under NCLB, states have not been able to appreciably close the gap, as Lee (2006) has documented for the Civil Rights Project at Harvard University.

The achievement gap is also reflected in high school graduation rates — the percentage of students who graduate with their class in four years. In recent years there has been a spate of reports analyzing the disparity in graduation rates (Greene & Winters 2002; Hall 2005; Civil Rights Project 2005; *Education Week* 2006). These reports demonstrate significant differences between the graduation rates of White and Asian high school students versus African American and Latino students. Only half of African American and Latino students graduate from high school, compared to three-quarters of White and Asian students, with Asians having the highest graduation rates. While there are some state and regional differences in these rates, the graduation rate for African American males is lower than 40 percent in many states, for example, in Florida it is 37 percent. (Using a different method of data collection Mishel and Roy [2006] contend otherwise, but even the rates they cite reveal disparities and their conclusions are derived from self-reports of individuals in home surveys versus district and state data.)

Although NCLB has increased awareness of the need to improve the quality of education for all students and strives to make states accountable to the standards, the bottom line is that the goal of attaining educational progress and parity for the poor and minorities (except Asians) is still more of a promise than reality. The pace of improvement has been slow, and some estimates indicate it could take nearly half a century to narrow the gap.

This book attempts to make the case that the achievement gap cannot be bridged without implementing comprehensive interpersonal activities (cultural competency training, multicultural workshops, and dialogues for students, teachers, administrators, staff, and parents) to improve school climate so *all* students feel safe and respected. Despite references to the importance of school climate in NCLB and concurring assertions and affirmations by school administrators, the major focus in the nation's public schools has been on teaching to the mandated standardized tests at the expense of substantive areas (e.g., art, music, literature, social studies, critical thinking, and ethics) that fall beyond the scope of the NCLB core areas of reading, math, and science.

This preoccupation with testing is having several devastating effects on our nation's schools. First, teacher morale is very low. While a number of factors such as low pay, insufficient resources, student discipline problems, lack of parental support, and an aging teacher population marking time until retirement affect the state of teacher morale, many teachers complain that the exaggerated emphasis placed on standardized tests required by NCLB is creating an even more stressful working environment for themselves and their students. For example, a recent survey of teachers in Hillsborough and Pinellas counties in Florida—two of the nation's largest school districts—revealed that 52 percent of the teachers said they had thought about leaving teaching in the past year. More than 60 percent in Pinellas County stated that morale had declined in the past year. More than two-thirds of the teachers felt that Florida's standardized test was not a good measure of student performance: they spent too much time preparing students for it, and it hindered their ability to teach subjects not covered in the test (Tobin & Ave 2006).

Second, some educators fear that the emphasis on standardized testing is pushing students, especially minorities, into nontraditional diplomas like the general education program and alternative courses of study (e.g., vocational/technical). This may be occurring because a disproportionate number of minority students, especially African Americans and Latinos, have difficulty meeting state standardized test requirements and do not qualify for regular graduation. Some are offered certificates of attendance after taking the tests numerous times, while others opt into other programs or drop out altogether, as reflected in the high dropout and low graduation rates of African American and Latino students (50 percent and 55 percent, respectively, according to *Education Week* 2006). Faced with the prospect of enduring endless drills in remedial classes to increase their scores and that of their schools to satisfy AYP—and the stigma of being assigned to them—it is understandable why some students opt out of school.

Third, and perhaps most devastating, are data that indict the very system and concept of education in the United States. NCLB was enacted to improve the quality of education in the United States, narrow the achievement gap between White children and children of color, and infuse a system of accountability as measured by goals, for example, having qualified teachers in all classrooms, and passing standardized tests of school and student achievement. While these are admirable goals, there is reason to believe that the means have become more important than the ends. No one disputes the importance of these objectives, but there are increasing indications that the emphasis on standardized testing is not having the desired effect. Indeed, while more high school seniors are taking and passing advanced placement tests (14.1 percent of the class of 2005 compared to 13.2 percent in the previous year and 10.2 percent in 2000), far fewer African American students than Whites are taking the exams, and their overall scores have remained behind those of White students ("More High School Seniors Pass" 2006). The academic success of students in college who took advanced placement tests prompted President George W. Bush to fund a $122-million initiative in FY 2007 to increase the number of students enrolled in Advanced Placement–International Baccalaureate programs (U.S. Department of Education 2006).

A look at state-by-state reports of the percentage of students who pass standardized tests is even more revealing. While NCLB mandates that states must test students in math, reading, and science, the federal government does not provide a uniform standardized test. Hence, every state has its own version and standards, and what qualifies for passing in one state may not in another. The 2006 American Federation of Teachers report "Smart Testing: Let's Get It Right" reveals how some states are gaming the system by adjusting their standards of acceptable work to persuade the federal government that they are making adequate progress.

Fortunately, the NAEP provides us with a uniform representative measure by which we can compare students across the nation. Commonly referred to as "The Nation's Report Card," this annual assessment, made by the commissioner of education statistics for the U.S. Department of Education, assesses the performance of students in grades 4, 8, and 12 in reading, math, science, writing, history, civics, geography, and the arts. While state tests and the NAEP methods of assessing proficiency differ, a comparison of the two reveals some startling disparities.

In a state-by-state analysis of NAEP data for thirty-two states between 2003 and 2005, Hall and Kennedy (2006) found that overall achievement gains in math and reading were most consistent in elementary grades; math achievement in middle schools improved, but reading scores actually declined in six states and remained the same in five; and high school math scores increased in twenty of twenty-three states analyzed, but reading results decreased in five. While the achievement gap was narrowed in most states in elementary grades, the authors noted that "the middle and high school results are cause for concern."

Even more discouraging is the general low level of student achievement. According to NAEP, only 29 percent of the nation's eighth-graders are proficient in math and reading. This finding conflicts with state standardized-testing data that show much higher levels of proficiency. The discrepancy may be explained by the variation in state testing standards, which in some states are clearly more liberal than the NAEP. For example, while the percentage of "proficient and above" in Alabama's state assessment of elementary reading in 2005 was reported at 83 percent, the NAEP "proficient and advanced" rate for grade 4 reading for Alabama was reported to be 22 percent, and the percentage of students at the "basic and above" NAEP grade 4 reading level was still only 53 percent. The state "proficient and above" number for Mississippi was 89 percent, compared to 18 percent for the NAEP "proficient and advanced" and 48 percent at "basic and above" in reading. Florida reported that 71 percent of its students in elementary school were "proficient and above" in reading, but only 30 percent scored "proficient and advanced" on the NAEP grade 4 reading level, with 65 percent in the NAEP "basic and above" category.

In fact, students in every state failed to achieve the NAEP's "proficient and advanced" rating for reading at grade 4. Missouri came closest, ranking 35 percent of its students in this category, compared to 33 percent on the NAEP. Middle school results were similar, showing wide disparities between the state and NAEP levels. And while differences between the two tests were not as pronounced in math scores, there were still numerous instances of widely divergent results, causing the authors to conclude, "[T]hat should send a warning signal to educators, policymakers and the public" (Hall & Kennedy 2006, 19).

In light of these data, one cannot but wonder about the credibility of AYP in districts and states claiming extraordinarily high rates of proficiency. For example, three-quarters of Florida schools, including 87 percent of Florida's middle schools, earned an A or B on the state's standardized test. Yet the U. S. Department of Education contended that 1,983 Florida schools failed to make adequate yearly progress, putting some in jeopardy of reorganization.

The situation is even more sobering when we consider the content of what is being offered in schools. Since the implementation of NCLB, there has been an increasing emphasis—even obsession—with those subjects the government deems most crucial for academic success: reading, math, and science. The preoccupation with these subject areas to satisfy state and federal mandates has had a numbing effect on students and teachers. Now, a disproportionate amount of time is being spent on drills to sharpen test-taking skills at the expense of other subject areas, most notably the humanities and social studies, for example, art, music, history, and civics. Even physical education requirements have been scrapped, despite the rising epidemic of childhood obesity.

And what has been the result of this infatuation with "hard science" and standardized testing? First, we're still graduating only about two-thirds of our high school students. The graduation rate has not significantly improved since the passage of NCLB, and the graduation rate for students who are poor and minorities still hovers around 50 percent (closer to 40 percent for African American males).

Second, comparisons between the United States and other countries on reading, math, science, and adult literacy indicate some room for improvement. While fourth-graders in the United States had higher average reading literacy scores than the international average and higher scores than students in twenty-three of thirty-four participating countries in 2001, they showed no measurable change in mathematics performance between 1995 and 2003. Indeed, during the early years of NCLB, U.S. fourth-graders failed to keep pace with improved scores of children in fourteen other countries participating in the math assessment (National Center for Education Statistics 2006, 13).

Looking at fifteen-year-olds, United States students had lower average mathematics literacy scores than their peers in twenty of the twenty-eight participating countries in 2003. This finding is particularly crucial because the test is designed to measure students' ability to apply their mathematical knowledge to a range of situations they might encounter in everyday life; that is, it is not geared specifically to curricula (National Center for Education Statistics 2006, 15). This calls into question the dominant pedagogical obsession with drills, without critical assessments of applications that are not geared to standardized tests.

Another analysis revealed that fourth-graders in the United States made no significant progress in science performance on average between 1995 and 2003, although eighth-graders showed some improvement compared to students in fourteen other countries (National Center for Education Statistics 2006, 19). And while U.S. fourth-graders performed above the international average in the sciences in 2003, the percentage of them performing at this level had *declined* from 1995. Eighth-graders did somewhat better, outscoring their peers in eleven countries in 2003 compared to five in 1995. These were the first significant gains in science since 1995.

Importantly, the gap between White and Black students decreased at both the eighth and fourth grades, but recent studies of differences in educational attainment between White and Black students are not encouraging. While small gains have been made in some grades, African American and Hispanic students in high school can read and do math at only the average level of Whites in junior high. These studies again indicate that the gaps in test scores between Whites versus Blacks and Hispanics become evident in kindergarten and worsen through high school. According to a report issued in 2006 by the Northwest Evaluation Association, minority students grew less than White students at each grade in each subject (Dillon 2006). This situation does not augur well for the NCLB goal of closing the test score gap by 2014.

Looking at science literacy, fifteen-year-olds from the United States scored below the average of the twenty-nine participating countries, with students from fifteen countries scoring higher and students from six countries scoring lower. Overall, the array of tests administered to students from around the world revealed improvements in achievement in some fields for U.S. students in some grades and weak performances in others. While it would be unwise to conclude that the lackluster performance of U.S. students at this time is a reflection of policies implemented since the inception of NCLB, the situation warrants continued monitoring.

From this report and other sources we do know that U.S. adults between sixteen and sixty-five do not compare favorably in literacy and mathematics with their counterparts in other countries. The National Survey of America's College Students, conducted by the American Institutes for Research and funded by the Pew Charitable Trusts found that many U.S. college students who were about to graduate could not handle complex tasks such as understanding credit card offers and comparing the cost per ounce of food. Thirty percent of students in two-year institutions and 20 percent in four-year colleges had basic or below quantitative literacy. More than half of the students at four-year colleges and three-quarters of students at two-year schools could not perform complex literacy tasks such as interpreting tables, understanding newspaper editorials, and comparing interest rates (Baer, Cook & Baldi, 2006).

Such information calls into question the very content of contemporary education. One would assume that the renewed focus on math, science, and reading would improve student achievement in these fields, but the data indicate otherwise. And there is a divergence of opinion between parents and educators about the goals of education in the United States. An AP–AOL Learning Services poll found that parents and teachers disagreed about a wide range of educational topics, from discipline to learning accomplishments. While nearly eight out of ten teachers contended that high schools did a good job in preparing students for college, only two-thirds of parents agreed. Significantly, both parents and teachers agreed that standardized testing has weakened educators' ability to give individual attention to students (Associated Press 2006).

A recent representative national study by the Intercollegiate Studies Institute of more than fourteen thousand students from fifty colleges and universities revealed startling gaps in students' knowledge about American history, our system of government, our place in the world, and our market economy. Only 52 percent of college seniors taking a sixty-item survey demonstrated a grasp of basic civic literacy about the United States, and the prestige of the school was often inversely related to students' scores, with students at some of the most prestigious schools scoring among the lowest. In fact, the researchers noted a mere 1.5 percent gain in civic knowledge from the freshman to senior year (Intercollegiate Studies Institute 2006).

While this report focused on postsecondary education, almost overlooked was the finding that the nation's freshmen entered college with only rudimentary knowledge about these critical areas, scoring only 51.7 percent. One wonders whether the preoccupation with math, science, and reading—as mandated by NCLB—is detracting from the important area of civics. In fact, Orfield (in Lee 2006) notes that the trend to teach to standardized tests is deemphasizing instruction in American history, the humanities, and physical fitness across the nation.

The results of this exaggerated emphasis on test taking are evident in a recent Harris poll that found only 59 percent of adults in Florida could correctly name the three branches of government and only 46 percent understood the separation of powers. The Florida Law Related Education Association found that less than 10 percent of Florida's counties require civics instruction in middle school (Winchester 2006). And while NCLB mandates that teachers be qualified to teach in their subject area by 2007, nationally, only 18 percent of high school history teachers majored or minored in their subject area. At Stanford University, a third of the students who apply to the master's program to become history teachers have never taken a single college course in history (Wineburg 2005).

We should also not overlook the influence social and psychological issues have on learning. Parental involvement, overcrowding in schools, an inordinate preoccupation with discipline, ethnic differences in orientation to standard curricula, and school climates that are not conducive to learning all impact children's educational experience. Our educational system is burdened with the task of providing quality instruction to an increasingly diverse population of students. With limited financial resources, a paucity of qualified teachers, and increasing anxiety over standardized curricula that have narrowed the focus of education, it's a small wonder that graduation rates are flagging while little progress is being made in attenuating the achievement gap between White and minority children.

The theme of this book is that the United States system of public education is facing multiple challenges that imperil its ability to provide quality instruction to all children. While the case can be made for improving resources for schools, increasing the number of qualified teachers, and adjusting the curriculum to make it more culturally and civically relevant, one fact remains—students must feel safe and comfortable in their schools before learning can occur.

The experiences related in this book testify to this fact, yet despite voluminous writing supporting multicultural education, the pendulum has swung in the opposite direction. And while most educators pay lip service to the importance of making schools and classrooms culturally competent, less time is being allocated to such endeavors in the face of pressure to improve standardized test scores.

That our students do not compare favorably in these areas with students in foreign countries despite these efforts, and in view of the significant lack of knowledge in the general population and among students in basic civics, it is time we reconsider the goals and methods of a system that is failing many of our students and depriving them of opportunities to maximize their abilities so they can become productive and well-adjusted citizens.

# Acknowledgments

Writing a book is a formidable challenge that few people can accomplish without help. This endeavor could not have been brought to fruition without the dedicated work of my staff when I served as executive director of the National Conference for Community and Justice (formerly the National Conference of Christians and Jews) for Tampa Bay: Margarita Sarmiento, Mike Trepper, Tarra Woodard, La Shante Keys, Maria Hall, Vianca Burger, Donald Taylor, and Ted Melichar. Their commitment to improving the quality of life of children was an inspiration to me over the years. Linda Gooding and Joanne Willis provided invaluable clerical assistance. Lucy Yeager, Anna Salemi, and Todd Carson were also part of the family and shared in the development of our youth programs. Gerri Gundle-Bradley provided important research assistance in the final writing stage. In the beginning there were also Jill Lyons, Lynn Shuttera, Kathy Zabel, Alice Grider, Kate Kalbas, and Don Woods.

The financial support of the following organizations made my work possible: the Children's Board of Hillsborough County, the Juvenile Welfare Board of Pinellas County, the Conn Memorial Foundation, the Shimberg Foundation, the Saunders Foundation, Allegany Franciscan Ministries, the Banyan Foundation, the Margie Joy Foundation, the Tampa Bay Community Foundation and the Community Foundation of Sun City Center, the Eckerd Family Foundation, Capital One, St. Paul Insurance Company, JPMorgan Chase, and Kanes Furniture.

Julia Dulfer provided invaluable editorial suggestions on earlier drafts of this manuscript. This book would not have evolved into its present form without the scholarly and critical insights of my friend and colleague Lionel Lewis and the support of my colleagues in the Department of Africana Studies at the University of South Florida: Trevor Purcell, Cheryl Rodriguez, Deborah Plant, Edward Kissi, and Eric Duke. I am indebted to all of them for their insights but assume responsibility for the final product.

My wife, Mary, has been my constant companion and listening post. This work and my life have benefited from our lifelong relationship.

# Introduction

The demographics are in place. In fifty years we know what we're going to look like, but we don't know what we're going to be like.

—President Bill Clinton

Many Americans viewed the tragedy of September 11, 2001, as a turning point in their lives and our society—a chance to come together as a people, e pluribus unum—out of many, one. While some people reassessed goals and careers, the lives of 54 million schoolchildren remained virtually unchanged. The pressures and conflicts that punctuate their days and nights actually intensified under the siege mentality that gripped the nation. As they and their teachers struggled with the meaning of the attack, many worried about their safety and security. Stereotypes about minorities proliferated as adults and children searched for scapegoats upon whom to project their anger.

Some teachers took the event as an opportunity to allow students to dialogue and express their fears, and to learn about history, geography, and politics. But others were consumed with the minutiae of testing and paper shuffling, and for hordes of students in overcrowded classrooms, it was business as usual. Many students went about their normal routine, their questions unanswered.

The following pages from my journal provide readers with glimpses of the lives of students, teachers, and administrators. They are not exceptional; they are everyday incidents that shape the reality of school life and make some children successful and leave others behind. Much tension and conflict that occurs in schools and appears here is the result of misunderstanding and miscommunication between Whites and people of color. But schools don't have to be breeding grounds for frustration, anger, and violence, as readers can see from the stories gathered during my fifteen years of work as a consultant in schools.

These insights are derived from workshops conducted with ten thousand primary and secondary school teachers and administrators, two thousand support staff—cafeteria workers, bus drivers, clerical workers, and school resource officers (police)—and fifteen thousand secondary students. The workshops were designed to reduce tension and conflict and increase participants' appreciation of diversity. I also conducted weeklong residential multicultural leadership experiences, called Camp Anytown, for teenagers.

Begun more than sixty years ago by the National Conference of Christians and Jews (now the National Conference for Community and Justice or NCCJ), Anytown is designed to develop awareness of cultural diversity and facilitate interaction among teens from different social and cultural backgrounds. Each camp has a cross-section of fifty students who engage in workshops on racism, sexism, prejudice toward the differently abled, homophobia, the Holocaust and Middle Passage, stereotypes, and community issues. More than sixty thousand teenagers have passed through the Anytown program since its inception. Since Anytown was an integral part of my work, I refer to it often on the following pages. The names of students and schools in this book have been changed to maintain anonymity.

The Anytown experience has its greatest impact when it is reinforced in school. When children receive support and encouragement from administrators and teachers, it provides enormous impetus for improving race and ethnic relations and other social problems. When staff are not supportive, the lessons of Anytown may fade. Indeed, there have been some notable failures, but when a program succeeds it can be triumphant—like on October 15, 1996.

The African American community in south St. Petersburg was torn by riots the night before in reaction to the killing of a Black youth by a White police officer. Dozens of homes and businesses were set ablaze as youth roamed the streets throwing rocks and bottles. The tension and frustration of living in a community that had not appreciably progressed socially or economically for decades, and was under constant scrutiny by some overzealous police, made many African Americans angry.

Three months earlier, we had planned a daylong conference for 110 high school students from around the county. We had no way of knowing how providential the gathering would be. Many participants lived in the area wracked by violence. Those from the exclusively White northern parts of the county were curious and apprehensive.

We met in a teacher-training facility in the middle of the county. As soon as the students arrived we put them into a circle and let them discuss the events of the preceding night. A slim Black youth began: "I'm mad and angry about the rioting. I live there, and I was watching from my front porch as those kids tore up my neighborhood. That's not right! Some of them weren't more than ten or twelve years old. They didn't even know what started the whole thing; they just wanted something to do. I didn't join in, but the media would have you believe we're all nothin' but a bunch of hoodlums and punks. And the police keep hasslin' us just because we live here. I'm tired of it! I don't know what to do, but I'm gonna do somethin'."

"I know what it's like to be angry and alone," said a girl on the other side of the circle. "I live in that area, too. Last year my grandparents were stabbed to death right in their home. I was very mad, but gradually I came to realize that me being violent wouldn't solve any problems. We've got to do that in nonviolent ways."

A tall White student jumped to his feet and began speaking in a slightly clipped accent. "I know what it's like to live in an oppressive country. I come from South Africa. For three years I and my parents stood in front of the government buildings every Sunday demonstrating against apartheid. Do you know what kind of risk we were taking? We did it because we believe in freedom of speech and the justice of our cause, and we lived to see Nelson Mandela set free! I can tell you that nonviolent protest works if you give it a chance."

The students cheered and clapped and set about developing plans for implementing programs in their schools to keep the peace. They conducted two Youth Speak Peace rallies in local parks that each drew two hundred people. They held rallies in their schools and open microphone assemblies so students could discuss the events in St. Petersburg. Weeks later, when a grand jury refused to indict the White police officer who shot the Black youth, another night of rioting occurred. The students held more rallies and a Keep the Peace Week in the city's high schools. Things were tense, but there were no outbreaks of violence in the schools.

For decades, education in the United States has been roundly criticized, even before the landmark Carnegie Commission on Education report *A Nation at Risk* was published in 1983. Every recent federal administration has declared education to be a top priority, and yet there remain deep-seated negative feelings about the state of public education in our society and serious shortcomings in student achievement and behavior.

On January 8, 2002, President George W. Bush signed HR 1, a sweeping education reform bill passed with overwhelming bipartisan support. He declared that "[n]o child should be left behind," which became the name for the legislation. The law mandates testing in math and reading for children in grades 3 and 8, and provides penalties and incentives for schools and teachers based on their test performance. Accountability has become the watchword in public education, as politicians seek to capitalize on the public's frustration with an educational system that leaves millions of children unprepared for competition in a technologically advanced society.

Title V, an integral section of the omnibus education bill, provides for grants to school districts for developing human relations and character education programs. Secretary of Education Rod Paige and the architects of the bill recognized the value of changing school climate by developing responsibility and self-esteem in students and empowering them to become involved in decision making in their schools and communities through Bush's public service program for youth.

Unfortunately, many states have become obsessed with the testing mandates in the law because of the penalties that can be levied for poor academic progress. The assumption that testing alone can improve educational attainment is specious. Students must feel welcome, safe, and respected before they are ready to learn. Many teachers and administrators have not yet made the connection between school climate and academic achievement. They have had little experience in multicultural education and power sharing with students, especially children from social and cultural groups different from their own. This, coupled with reductions in school budgets and diminishing resources, has precipitated reductions in humanities, such as music and art, and human relations programs—even as schools are becoming increasingly diverse, making such programs indispensable. First Lady Laura Bush recognized this when she spoke at the White House Conference on Character and Community in June 2002: "Some people think of education in terms of the 'Three R's'—reading, writing, and 'rithmetic—but another 'R' is essential: responsibility."

The drive to infuse business principles into archaic educational curricula and structures has captivated many politicians and educators, but may be doomed to failure. Our educational system is more suitable to the eighteenth and nineteenth centuries, when large numbers of children were being groomed for manufacturing jobs. Just as anachronistic is the belief that focusing on reading and math is the panacea for the problem, because it ignores monumental interpersonal conflicts emanating from class and cultural differences many students, teachers, and administrators may be ill equipped to resolve.

Any solution to the crisis in American education must acknowledge the fundamental role human relationships play in school life and achievement. The dynamics of interpersonal interaction among and between students and staff must be mastered before children are ready to learn standardized curricula. If children do not feel good about themselves, one another, their teachers and administrators, and the schools they attend, no amount of testing will suffice. Teachers and schools should be held accountable for teaching students the basics, but it is also necessary to include helping them become better people. And this is precisely what is often being overlooked.

"No Child Left Behind," the catchy phrase that has become synonymous with the push to remedy our education system, is an oxymoron known to the countless children and teachers who dread each new school day because of the emotional and physical insults they must bear. The lives of our children are replete with challenges and obstacles that inhibit their learning. A quarter of our children under eighteen (including 1 million African American children) live below the poverty level—the minimum amount of money necessary to purchase a nutritionally sound diet. In the United States today, seven out of ten children live in nontraditional families. One in three children is born to unmarried parents, and one in eight is born to a teenage mother. Half our children will live in a single-parent home at some point in their childhood. A majority of these families are headed by women, and a majority of them live in poverty. One in twenty-five children lives with neither parent, 1 percent live with foster parents, 3.7 percent live with nonrelatives, and 6.3 percent live with grandparents. (For more information on the lives of children living in the United States, see "America's Children in Brief: Key National Indicators of Well-Being, 2006" at www.childstats.gov/americaschildren/pop.asp and the Children's Defense Fund at http://childrensdefense.org.)

The U.S. Census Bureau estimates that one-third of all school age children are, for some part of the week, latchkey children—there is no one to greet them when they return home from school. Five to 7 million of these children are between the ages of five and thirteen. Marian Wright Edelman, director of the Children's Defense Fund, estimates there may be as many as 16 million latchkey children in the United States.

Millions of children have some physical or psychological impairment. Nearly 5 million children have learning disabilities. Nine million have been diagnosed with asthma. Almost 7 million children have no health insurance (Bloom & Dey 2006).

There are 2 million reported cases of child abuse and neglect in the United States annually, with 1,500 deaths and more than 140,000 injuries. Between 150,000 and 200,000 new cases of child sexual abuse occur each year. It is estimated that one in four women and one in seven men were sexually abused before age eighteen. The number of children reported as victims of abuse and neglect has increased 40 percent since 1988.

How do these factors affect education and learning? They are reflected not only in low test scores but in disciplinary referrals, suspensions, expulsions, absenteeism, tardiness, and dropouts. They find expression in arguments, fights, homicides, and suicides. A study by Starfield, Robertson, and Riley (2002) demonstrated the association between poverty, poor health, and behavior problems in children. Children in the poorest social classes were found to have less family involvement and a history of disruptive behaviors leading to injury, illness, and impaired social development.

The 1999 shooting at Columbine High School demonstrated the lengths to which alienated students will go to seek revenge for being mistreated and ostracized. After fifteen-year-old Charles Bishop flew a single engine plane into the Bank of America building in Tampa, Florida, on January 5, 2002, a student at his school recalled, "The problem is no one knew him. He was anonymous. It's like he didn't even exist." How many would-be kamikazes are lurking in the hallways or sitting alone in the cafeterias of our nation's ninety-two thousand public schools?

While the U.S. Department of Education has recorded a decline in school violence in recent years, and children are more at risk of being harmed away from schools than in them, the incidence of assaults and the prevalence of threats is staggering. A report by the National Center for Education Statistics and the Bureau of Justice Statistics (2005) revealed that in the 2003 school year, children aged twelve to eighteen experienced approximately 1.9 million nonfatal crimes at school, including 1.2 million thefts and 740,000 violent crimes (simple assault and serious violent crimes). Of the serious violent crimes, 150,000 were rapes, sexual assaults, robberies, or aggravated assaults. Few significant differences were found among the victims based on ethnicity.

Nine percent of students in this age group reported being threatened by a weapon, and 6 percent of students (9 percent of males) reported carrying a weapon to school. Although this was half the number reported ten years earlier, there is little reason to be complacent. According to the report, in 1999–2000, 71 percent of public schools experienced one or more violent incidents and 36 percent of public schools reported violent incidents to the police.

Bullying in schools is rampant. In 1999–2000, 29 percent of public schools reported that bullying took place on a daily or weekly basis. Forty-three percent of middle schools reported daily or weekly student bullying. In 2003, 7 percent of students between the ages of twelve and eighteen reported that they had been bullied at school during the last six months, and 13 percent reported that they had been in a fight during this time.

Understandably, 6 percent of students reported that they had been afraid of attack at school or on the way to or from school (10 percent of urban students and 5 percent of suburban and rural students), and 5 percent of students either skipped school activities or avoided specific places in school because they feared for their safety. Because of these incidents, 54 percent of public schools took serious disciplinary actions against students in the 1999–2000 school year. This amounted to 1,163,000 disciplinary actions, of which 83 percent were suspensions for five or more days.

In June 1997 I attended a briefing on school violence hosted by then U.S. Secretary of Education Richard Riley in Washington, DC. Seated around the table were twenty representatives from public schools and faith communities around the country, including administrators from Springfield, Oregon, and Littleton, Colorado, where school shootings had occurred. As the discussion turned to ways of involving the community in reducing school violence, a pastor who advises the Chicago school system on ways to create partnerships with the faith community circulated a list. On it were the names of more than fifty African American youth who had been killed between January and June that year in and around their schools in that city. This ongoing tragedy did not attract the attention of Whites until a series of school shootings thrust the issue into their consciousness.

Despite a decline in the number of physical attacks on students, verbal abuse among students expressed as threats, intimidation, sexual harassment, ridicule, gossip, and prejudice are incessant and constitute a serious obstacle to successful educational experiences.[1] In 2003, 12 percent of students aged twelve to eighteen reported that someone used hate-related words directed at them in school, and 36 percent of students had observed hate-related graffiti at school.

Racism and segregation by social class, color, ethnicity, religion, body shape, sexual orientation, and myriad other attributes children use to marginalize one another is rampant, even though our schools are becoming more diverse, with half of all entering students being children of color.

The emotional harm emanating from this psychological pain puts millions of children at risk for educational failure. When we do not prepare students and teachers to feel comfortable with people from diverse backgrounds and physical appearances, we leave a void in their education. They will be less able to interact with people in our society and in the global economy.

Consider the rates for ethnic minority teenagers in the United States who are not in school or working: Native Americans, 16 percent, and African Americans and Hispanics, 12 percent, compared to Whites, 6 percent, and Asians, 5 percent (Annie E. Casey Foundation 2005). Even these underestimate the situation. Nationwide, only 69 percent of entering freshmen graduate high school in four years. Florida, with a graduation rate of 55 percent, has the lowest graduation rate in the nation (Hegarty 2002; Greene & Winters 2002). The consequence of our failure to create safe and welcoming learning environments now becomes clear.

Furthermore, a large number of minority students, especially African American males, are placed in special education programs. Nationwide, a disproportionate number of children in special or exceptional education classes for slow or disabled learners labeled with learning disabilities or behavior problems are African Americans. Losen and Orfield (2002) have documented the disproportional representation of African Americans and other children of color in special education programs. Blacks are three times more likely than Whites to be in special education programs and are more often labeled "mentally retarded." After conducting a comprehensive study of special education referrals and outcomes in twelve schools in a southern city, Harry and Klingner (2006) described the situation as a "travesty" and "unconscionable."

Suspension rates for Black middle and high school students are often twice those of Whites (the principal reason being insubordination or defiance), often because teachers are afraid of children of color, do not feel comfortable teaching them, and cannot relate to them. In essence, we are leaving generations of children behind.

We shouldn't have to wait for more Columbines before initiating comprehensive human relations programs in school. Unfortunately, too many schools receive failing grades in handling interpersonal problems, as can be seen from the snapshots that follow. But it is also gratifying to see students struggle to rid their campuses of violence and prejudice when given opportunities to engage one another in constructive dialogue.

As long as we emphasize one side of the learning equation—the basics of reading, writing, and arithmetic—to the exclusion of interpersonal skills and compassion for humanity, we perpetuate conditions that may lead to academic failure and conflict. Even when we seemingly create better students, are they able to think critically and make ethically sound choices?

In May 1997 David Cash was in a Nevada casino with his friend Jeremy Strohmeyer, who followed Sherrice Iverson, a seven-year-old Black girl, into the ladies room. When their playing got rough, Cash left and waited outside while Strohmeyer beat, raped, and strangled Sherrice. "He told me he killed her," said Cash matter-of-factly in an interview with Ed Bradley on the television program *60 Minutes*. The pair then left the casino, played video games, and went on thrill rides before driving back to their homes in California.

"Why didn't you stop it?" asked an incredulous Bradley. "It was time for me to get out of there. It wasn't something I wanted to stick around and see what materialized," replied Cash. The authorities hunted for the perpetrator while Cash did nothing. "I knew his day of reckoning was coming. I didn't want to be the one to turn him in."

Caught on the casino's security video camera, Strohmeyer was quickly apprehended. To avoid trial and a possible death sentence, he pleaded guilty and was sentenced to life in prison without parole. Cash, an honor student, entered the University of California at Berkeley to study engineering. Students at the university were appalled by his lack of remorse ("How much am I supposed to sit down and cry about this?" he had said.) and demonstrated against his remaining on campus—obviously some of them knew the difference between academic achievement and ethics.

We must address the challenges confronting our educational system by encouraging youth and adult decision makers to take risks and break the stultifying mold that makes many schools soulless anachronisms. We must incorporate comprehensive human relations skills and increase opportunities for dialogue and interaction among students from different backgrounds if we want to make schools safe, fertile grounds where all students can be successful. As Yale University child psychiatrist Valerie Maholmes has stated, "School success and social-emotional development are linked in such a way that it is virtually impossible to isolate the effects of either on children's educational outcomes" (2002, 32).

Many adults, including some teachers and administrators, have a distorted view of what goes on in school—a perception created by sensationalist journalism and pressure from vested interest groups with narrow, self-serving agendas. In fact, most people haven't been inside a school since they graduated. For many students, the "Three Rs" often take a back seat to life-and-death issues, at times making traditional teaching methods and subjects irrelevant. How and when we address the reality of students' lives, and the methods we use to instill in them the desire to be responsible human beings, will determine the ultimate fate of our society.

We must support the valiant efforts of teachers and administrators who are trying, in the face of scarce resources and interpersonal challenges, to improve our children's future. While demanding accountability and higher academic standards, we must also insist that our schools create better people as well as better students.

# NOTE

1. Teachers, too, have been targets of threats and attacks: In 1999–2000, 19 percent of public schools reported acts of disrespect toward teachers and 13 percent reported verbal abuse; and from 1999 to 2003, teachers reported being victims of nonfatal crimes at a rate of thirty-nine crimes per thousand teachers annually (National Center for Education Statistics 2005).

# 1

## Why Kids Are Angry

Can't we all just get along?

—Rodney King

According to the National Center for Education Statistics (2005) there were twenty-two violent deaths at school—seventeen homicides and five suicides—among students ages five through nineteen between July 1, 2001, and June 30, 2002. In 2003, students aged twelve to eighteen were victims of nearly 2 million crimes at school, committed at a rate of forty-five thefts and twenty-eight violent crimes (including six serious violent crimes) per one thousand students.

Despite these alarming statistics, for most kids schools are safer than their homes. Students are twice as likely to be victims of serious violent crimes away from school as in school. Although the rate of victimization in schools has been dropping, the sheer number of crimes, especially those labeled violent (simple assault, rape, sexual assault, robbery, aggravated assault) is staggering and demands attention and action.

For many students, a culture of fear characterizes their life in school, filled with threats, intimidation, bullying, harassment, hate, and alienation. In 2003, 6 percent of students aged twelve to eighteen reported feeling fearful of being attacked at school or on the way to school in the previous six months. Urban students were twice as likely to be fearful as rural students, and female students were more likely than male students. Black

(11 percent) and Hispanic students (10 percent) were more than twice as likely as White students (4 percent) to fear being attacked at school.

Facing the possibility of harm, many students avoid certain areas of their school or not attend at all. Five percent of students (3 percent of White students, 5 percent of Blacks, and 6 percent of Hispanics) in 2003 reported that they had avoided school activities or places in their school in the previous six months (National Center for Education Statistics 2005, 54).

Sometimes kids fight back. They may bring problems from home or the neighborhood onto campus. Rumors often fan the flames. Some children need to be the center of attraction; others feel they have to defend their turf, manhood, or reputation. In recent years there have been an increasing number of fights among girls, rivaling boys in ferocity. Boy/girl problems rank near the top as causes of conflict. Many altercations are the result of miscommunication—most kids don't know one another and may misinterpret words and actions because of cultural differences. Manners and customs affect perceptions about many things, including humor and conflict, and so does sensitivity about prejudice and racism. What may seem like an innocuous comment can cause pain and lead to aggression. It may be kids' (and adults') insensitivity to other people's lives, cultures, and traditions that leads to misunderstanding. Some minority youth seem to walk around waiting for a chance to accuse people of being racist or yearning to jump a naive White kid. Sometimes it's a matter of exercising power—the power they're denied at home, in their community, or by the larger society.

Parents hear stories about Black kids ganging up on "innocent" White students: money being extorted for protection; white girls being sexually harassed; angry Black girls intimidating their daughters, verbally and physically assaulting them, and even cutting their hair as a sign of contempt for Whiteness or perhaps jealousy from being brainwashed into self-loathing.

Bigotry and hatred take their toll on us and on our children, even more than crimes like the dragging murder of James Byrd in Texas or drive-by shootings and desecration of holy places. Hate and prejudice are expressed in many ways: some overt, others covert. They leave their mark on children as surely as if they'd been exposed to corporal punishment. It's in their faces, body language, and words. You can sense it in their anger, which may be expressed in random acts of violence against members of other racial, religious, or ethnic groups, or, more often, against members of their own group. Such is the case with Black-on-Black crimes and gang conflict among ethnic groups.

That many school incidents are exaggerated in the media doesn't placate White parents, who continue taking their children out of urban public schools. More than two-thirds of Black children attend public schools that are predominantly Black. Regardless of ethnicity, significant numbers of children and teachers have experienced or know of violent incidents. The conflict at a rural high school illustrates how blind hate can disrupt an entire campus.

High Pines is a huge complex set in the woods. It includes a large middle school and an adjoining high school. There are about thirty-two hundred students, mostly White. Our first trip there was to conduct a conference for a hundred high school students. It was covered by the media, who videotaped the charts we hung with students' background information and preferences. Some kids scrawled KKK slogans on them, and of course that made the nightly news. As it turned out, one of the culprits was a student assistant of the school resource officer. He was promptly fired, but that didn't deter other like-minded kids from harassing the few Black students on campus. Matthew, a Black student who wouldn't stand for it, had been repeatedly suspended for striking back.

We met with twenty students, the principal, and an assistant principal in a conference room. There were three Black boys, two Latinos, a biracial girl, and an Asian boy; the rest were White. Three of the White boys labeled themselves as "Southern culture."

"You better get Johnny in here," said one of the Southern culture kids.

"Yeah, that's right," said another. "You need to hear him out. He lives in Deer Acres, and folks in that area, they believe different things about mixin' the races."

Deer Acres. An Adopt-a-Highway sign on a main road there signified it was maintained by the Ku Klux Klan. There was an active klavern in the area, and though only a minority of the people were sympathetic to their views, they recruited kids to spread their propaganda on campus. The Klan also broadcast the news on local public-access television.

We sent for Johnny because it was clear he was a leader. The administration knew he was the source of much interracial conflict. If he wasn't wearing a Confederate flag, he had one flying from the antenna of his car. One never knew what kind of racist or insensitive remark he would make.

Johnny strolled in beside the assistant principal and took a seat. He didn't look happy.

"Glad you could join us. We were just beginning to talk about why there's a racial problem here."

"We ain't got no problem. It's their problem," he said, glaring across at the Black students.

"You see what I'm talking about?" said Matthew, who was slumped in his chair. "It's crackers like that who give us a hard time. There ain't but fifteen of us in this whole damn place. Fifteen outta two thousand, and they won't leave us alone."

"I'll leave you alone if you and your friends get outta here," snapped Johnny.

"I ain't gonna leave for you or no other White boy," grumbled Matthew.

"What you got against us, anyhow?" asked Rashon, who was sitting beside Matthew. "We never did anything to you."

"I hate you!" shouted Johnny. "I hate your guts! You don't belong here because I'm White and you're Black and you'll never be as good as me!"

The biracial girl burst into tears and ran out of the room with the principal hastily following. Matthew's friends sensed he was ready for a fight.

"Cool it, man. Don't let him get to you."

"Don't play his game. He's just ignorant. We can all see that."

Johnny stared at them, a smile creasing his lips when he saw how he had hurt them.

"It's true," he said defiantly. "Black people will never be equal to Whites no matter what they do."

"Where'd you learn stuff like that?" asked Rashon.

"I hear a lot about you boys. I got some powerful friends hereabouts. Klan friends. I go to meetings with them, and they're not bad guys. We have lots of talks 'bout crime and family values and stuff. They're really concerned about all that."

"What kind of family values teaches people to hate?" asked a White student.

"Ain't nobody teachin' people to hate. All we're saying is that people should stay with their own kind. Ain't no need to mix the races. What's wrong with this county is that there's too many of them immigrants here. There's even Spanish written on my car underneath the hood."

"What kind of car do you have?" I asked.

"A new Ford pickup."

"Do you know why there's Spanish on it? Because the company built a plant in Mexico where they can hire cheap labor. They put American workers out of jobs. If you've got a problem, it's with Ford."

"That ain't half of it. All them Spanish people comin' here, changing everything. Look what they did to the East Coast."

"Now wait a minute!" shouted Julio rising in anger. "Those are my people you're talkin' about!" Jennifer reached over and made him sit down.

"You don't like Spanish-speaking people?" asked Margarita.

"I don't have any use for them either. It's my country—a White man's country. We made it what it is, and all those people are tearing it apart," he said as he waved a hand at the diverse group in front of him.

"Can't we learn to live together?" asked Rashon.

"I don't think so. Why should I share what's mine with you? Your people didn't work for none of this."

"Man, I don't know where you been hidin'," said Matthew. "Our people were brought here against their will and forced to work for crackers like you. If it hadn't been for my ancestors' work, you people wouldn't have survived."

"That's right," said Lian, an Asian American. "My ancestors built the railroads and worked in sweatshops to make your clothes."

"I don't owe any of you nothin'," snapped Johnny.

When we broke for lunch we tried to engage him in conversation.

"How did you feel when that girl left the room?"

"I didn't feel anything."

"Didn't you see how you hurt her feelings?"

"It ain't none of my business. I only said what's true."

"Have you ever thought about moving away from here? Going to college?"

"I thought about it, but when I found out how much it cost and havin' to go to school with some of those kinda people, I just forgot about it."

The crisis subsided, but the underlying causes didn't disappear. A year later they were still having trouble at the school.

"Your 'friend' Johnny is at the bottom of it. He's a constant source of conflict on that campus," my informant said.

"Can't you do anything with his parents?"

"You haven't met his mom. What a piece of work. If you think the kid has problems, you should talk to her. It's not hard to see where he gets his attitude from. They have to make sure he graduates this year—get him out of there no matter what. I don't care if it's a social promotion or whatever. That kid's got to go. I can't take another year of that family."

Johnny did graduate, but not without trying to make a statement. The principal, a middle-aged White woman, related how she outmaneuvered him: "He really hated me because I wouldn't let him get away with anything. When it was time for him to receive his diploma, I suspected he would intentionally snub me by not shaking my hand. As he came close to me I sort of leaned into him and shoved the diploma into his hand. It wrecked his plan. 'You nigger!' he said as he walked on."

One of the most vexing problems I have encountered has been conflict among students over wearing and displaying the Confederate battle flag. Attitudes surrounding this symbol are highly charged and resistant to change. But sometimes students, with minimal adult intervention, manage to defuse a potentially explosive confrontation.

Twin Lakes High School in central Florida has nearly two thousand students; more than 90 percent of them are white. The school is not far from a well-known area where a group of Eastern Europeans settled and sold their wares for generations. While the ethnic diversity found in many of our nation's schools was not reflected in this student body, it seemed that Blacks and Whites were getting along—at least on the surface—until a six-teen-year-old biracial student from the north enrolled and became outraged when she saw White students wearing Confederate flag shirts in school.

She circulated a petition that called for banning the shirts, but she didn't follow proper procedures and was suspended for three days. The incident brought out underlying tensions between Black and White students that threatened to explode into violence.

I and two of my staff—a White male and an African American female, both around thirty—met with twenty-five students representing the various factions. We arranged our chairs in a circle so everyone could be part of the dialogue. Joining us were a guidance counselor, the school psychologist, two assistant principals, and the teacher who advises the school's multicultural club.

The students segregated themselves: One side of the circle was occupied by ten African Americans, opposite them were an equal number of self-described White "Southern culture" kids. A few other White students, a couple of biracial kids, and the president of the school's multicultural club were also there.

The students set ground rules after we clarified the difference between dialogue and debate: "Show respect." "One person talks at a time." "No put-downs." "Listen and try to understand." "No cursing." "No side conversations." My staff added, "No adults can talk until later," because we wanted the students to resolve the conflict on their own, and teachers and staff frequently intervene and monopolize the conversation.

Tension was high. The Black students glared across at the Southern culture group, with their hunting jackets draped over Confederate flag shirts. Everyone introduced themselves and then stated why they were there.

"Because they're wearing those racist shirts!" exclaimed LeRoy, a large Black male.

"These shirts aren't racist!" shot back Jerome. "They just show that we're proud of our Southern heritage."

"Yeah," said Stacey, a blonde girl sitting alongside him. "Heritage, not hate. That's what we're about."

"You can't tell me that!" screamed Sholana from across the circle. "We know where you all are comin' from. What are we supposed to think when we see shirts with those flags on them and Black folks pickin' cotton?"

"That's right," said Kenesha. "Last week I saw one of you with a shirt that had three boxes on it: the top one had White alongside it, beneath it was a box with brown alongside it and below it was a box with Black alongside it. There was a check in the box that said White and it said, 'The only one that counts.' Is that what Southern culture and heritage means?"

"Hold on!" countered Donald. "You don't see none of us wearing stuff like that."

"Your friends do," affirmed Tyronne. "You hang around with them. Ain't no secret how you feel. Why last week I was walkin' down the sidewalk outside and a bunch of you spit all over in front of me."

"I didn't do that!" said Donald indignantly. "All we want to do is show how proud we are of our heritage. What about those shirts you guys wear with the X? That stands for the Black Panthers."

"Wait a minute," I interrupted. "The flag you have on your shirts is only one of a number of flags used by the Confederacy. You're wearing the battle flag. It was put into state seals and flags in the '60s to protest the civil rights movement."

"And the X shirts don't mean Black Panthers," said Myra, my staff member. "That comes from Malcolm X."

"But he advocated violence. He was a racist!" said Theresa.

"Now that's not exactly true. If you read his autobiography you would see that he changed a lot after he went to Mecca and found all kinds of people getting along," said Myra.

"Yeah, and it was Black people who killed him," said LeRoy. "We don't want you wearin' those shirts because it stands for slavery."

"Slavery? The Civil War wasn't fought over slavery," said Theresa. "There were slaves in the North. It was over taxes. The Southern states didn't want the North to tax them so heavily."

"But it was fought over slavery," I interjected. "The North had abolished slavery and the South wanted to keep slaves because they were free labor. The South's agricultural economy was based on slave labor. The plantation system was dependent on it and if slavery was abolished it would cause a depression."

"It was over states' rights," said Jack.

"That's partly true," said Tom, a member of my staff. "They wanted the states to have the right to keep slavery."

"You know that flag means many things to people," said Larry, a tall White boy sitting a few chairs away from me. "I didn't know very much about that flag that you wear, so I went online last night and I didn't like what I saw. I learned that it's been used by the KKK and other groups to threaten people. You know, I'm Armenian. My grandfather settled here a while ago and opened up his shop. He told me how those KKK boys would come into town with their flags and throw paint on his store and mess it up to try to run him and all the Armenians outta here. If that's what you guys stand for then I don't want any part of it."

"That's what we been tryin' to tell you," said LeRoy. "That kinda stuff is still goin' on around here. I can't go into a store without someone followin' me around like I'm a criminal. I get pulled over by the police when I'm drivin' for doin' nothin'. Just the other day I was in the mall and a White man had a bunch of bills in his hand. He must have just gotten some change. When he saw me comin' toward him he stuffed them in his pocket like I was gonna steal them."

"You people think you are so much—I can't go into the cafeteria without getting harassed because I'm outta my place," said Jamaya.

"Oh yeah. We get it too. I got pushed when I went down F wing—for no reason," said Stacey.

"It's not the same," said LeRoy. "You get it once in a while, but for us it's every day. That's racism."

"Who you callin' racist?" demanded Stacey. "I ain't no racist!" she screamed and she covered her face with her hands and started sobbing.

"I just don't understand some of you. We grew up together—went to elementary school. What happened between eighth and ninth grade? What changed you?" asked LeRoy.

"Nothin'changed me," said Lewis.

"You know I'm fed up with this. You know that incident that happened a year ago with my little brother. He's only nine years old. My father had to go and get him because you guys were taunting him and callin' him a nigger," said LeRoy.

"It wasn't me," declared Lewis.

"You were there. You were there and you could've stopped it, but you didn't."

"I wish you guys were stronger," said Michael. "You know I'm biracial. I've never felt discriminated against. If you say it's happening to you, well okay, but be stronger. Don't let it get to you like that."

"That's easy for you to say," said LeRoy, "but you either don't have to live with it or you don't even recognize it when you see it. You can't tell us what our lives are like."

Shamica, a pudgy little Black girl, began to cry and Audrey, a White girl sitting next to her hugged her as she spoke to the Southern culture group across the circle.

"I really don't know how you can go on hurting people this way. Can't you see what you're doing? Don't you care about anyone but yourselves?"

Jack looked across the room and spoke in a measured tone: "I believe you when you say this hurts. I never wanted to hurt anybody. Believe me, I'm sorry for what I did. [A year before, a noose was found hanging on the school grounds. Jack was the perpetrator and every African American kid in the room knew it.] You won't see any of those shirts again. And you won't hear any of those words again, not from me or any of us. I'll see to that."

After two and a half hours and four boxes of doughnuts, the group had reached some common ground. They committed to changing themselves— to model the behavior that would make their school a safer community.

Three weeks later the group reconvened to assess the school's climate. In contrast to the first meeting, the students were interacting when our team entered the room. No one was wearing a Confederate flag, although three of the young men were dressed in green fatigues. When someone observed that the seating was still segregated, they swapped seats around the circle.

Several decided to work on creating a banner containing a nondiscrimination pledge. A few others volunteered to write a letter to the editor of a local paper that had, they believed, overdramatized the events at the school, accompanied by a picture of the group working together. Other students committed to making presentations on the school's closed-circuit television station and placed a picture of the group in their school yearbook. When they broke for lunch, two African American kids left for McDonalds in a pickup truck driven by a Southern culture kid. Hanging from the tailgate was a Confederate flag.

Columbine High School showed how far animosity among students could go and left a legacy of fear and mistrust throughout America's schools. In the first few weeks following the shooting, students were being suspended for wearing black trench coats and making remarks that would normally have been ignored. Teachers and administrators, who were already struggling against the generation gap, found their paranoia increased exponentially. Now unconventional students were not looked upon as pariahs—but as potential killers. The principal at Somerset High School asked us to help defuse a conflict over kids wearing black trench coats and gothic makeup.

Somerset High is an established school in a large city. It was built decades ago with a large courtyard and open hallway. Many of its two thousand students are from affluent families and their kids are called "preppies." They dress well, are academic achievers, and, like their parents, are very materialistic. The student parking lot is sprinkled with late-model sports cars and sedans. But there are also large numbers of students of color—African Americans, Latinos, and Asians—at Somerset, many of them working class.

Like kids at most high schools in the country, the ethnic students hang out together in the halls and cafeteria and have little in common with their preppy counterparts. They take different classes, play different sports, wear different clothes, and listen to different music. For the most part, the kids tolerate one another, except for the unconventional students. These kids, with their black nail polish and fishnets, were never part of the in crowd, but

after Columbine their affectation for the macabre became a source of consternation—even dread—among many students at Somerset and elsewhere.

The principal had been on the job for only two weeks. "We've got a
bunch of kids wearing long black trench coats and I'm afraid the situation
might get out of hand. Some of them are being threatened by other kids,
and I don't know what they might do. I've gotten calls from parents who
are threatening me if I don't throw them out. Even some of my teachers
are afraid of them. They say they could be hiding guns in their coats. I
asked them to take them off and put them in my office. They didn't like
that, but I've got to restore order here."

The next day we pulled thirty-five students together to talk about the
black trench coats. The kids were hanging out in little cliques: Black kids
to one side, eight unconventionals or goths in the back, a few of our Anytowners sprinkled in, and preppies to another side.

"Let's move the chairs into a circle so we can talk."

A tall husky blond kid with close-cropped hair who was standing alongside one of the goth kids replied, "I ain't gonna sit near him."

"Come on. Sit down. They won't hurt you. Everybody's got to sit in the
circle."

He grudgingly acquiesced. The principal was sitting behind the circle at
the front of the room. There were two women beside her—concerned parents.

"Before we start I want to know if it's all right for the principal to stay
in here or if you'd rather have her leave."

"It's okay," said a Black youth.

"Yeah, she needs to hear what we have to say," said one of the unconventionals. "And so do the parents."

The group agreed to let them stay.

"There's one more thing. There's a reporter from your school paper
who would like to listen in."

"I won't use any names, I promise," she said. "But the other students
would like to know what happens in here today."

A brief discussion ensued about students' need to know versus confidentiality. Then a young man interrupted, "Look, I'm the editor of the paper. I can assure you that no names will be used. It's important that these
issues be aired for all the students. They'll want to know what happens
here and I don't think it's right to keep a lid on this."

The group consented.

"Now, I'd like to know what is going on here. I mean, what's the problem?" I asked.

"The problem is she made us take off our coats," said a tiny girl dressed in black with long hair, black mascara, fingernails, and lipstick that matched.

"You mean the principal?"

"That's right," chimed in another. "And it was cold. Those were the only coats we had."

"I thought it would be best to ask you to do that because I was getting complaints. Some students were scared. I even heard from teachers. I have to maintain order here and wearing those trench coats was disruptive."

"You could have given us some warning," snapped another girl. "You didn't make other kids take off their coats."

"I didn't make you take off your coats. I asked you if you would please leave them in my office. We tried to find other coats for you to wear."

"Not all of us got them. But it was the idea that we can't wear what we want to."

"You know the county has a dress code . . ."

"Where does it say that you can't wear a black trench coat?" asked a boy.

"You said the school's lawyers said we couldn't," said another.

"That's not right. I conferred with an assistant principal and we decided it would be best to ask you not to wear them until we had a chance to work this out. That's why we're here now."

"That's in the past," I said. "We're here to get to know one another and, hopefully, respect each other."

Everyone in the room introduced themselves. The unconventional students, who were sitting in a row, were asked to explain what they believed in and why they dressed that way.

The little girl jumped right in.

"Because we like this style. We prefer to wear black. There's nothing more to it. Some kids like to wear preppy clothes. We like this. It doesn't mean that we're dangerous or are plotting to kill anybody."

"I really resent that," said an older girl. "Why can't we just wear what we want? We're not threatening anyone."

"Not everybody knows that," I said. "That's why we're here, to educate students so they can see that you don't mean to harm anyone. But you know those kids who did the shooting at Columbine dressed in black coats."

"That's not right!" exclaimed one of the boys. "They weren't true goths. There's a whole lifestyle that we have. We would never hurt anyone. Just the opposite."

"He's right," said a girl. "We believe in peace. We just want to be left alone."

"Why do you always wear black?" asked the big blond boy.

"Because we like it. It doesn't mean that we want to hurt people. It's just our style."

"Have you been threatened?" I asked.

A Black student interjected, "Let me tell you about that. You know how much stuff Black people have to take around here. I decided to find out how bad things were for them, so last week I wore a black trench coat and you wouldn't believe the shit I caught. Students. Teachers. They gave me looks and said things you wouldn't believe."

"We never meant to hurt anyone," said the little girl. "We don't deserve to be treated like that."

Other students joined in sharing their views about everything from clothes to politics. Columbine kept coming up. It was obvious the unconventional students resented being associated with it.

"It has nothing to do with what's going on here," said one.

"But it does," said the editor of the school paper. "You've got to understand that people associate the black trench coats you wear with those shooters. It's only natural."

"Well, we're not going to change our style," said the little girl.

"That's all right," he said. "It's up to us to inform the other students about you—let them know there's nothing to fear, that they need to respect you for who you are."

"I've got some teachers who could stand a little education on that, too," said the principal. "We'll be speaking with them next week."

"In the meantime, would you like to work on projects to educate the other students?" I asked.

One group went to work planning public-service announcements for the closed-circuit television system. Another began developing guidelines for a schoolwide poetry, art, and music contest; a third began planning dialogues to educate students about valuing diversity. After two hours and ten pizzas they agreed to meet again the following week. When the bell rang they rose from their chairs and hugged one another.

Over the next four months we met many times, including meetings with the faculty to discuss our objectives and the demeanor of the students. Things began to cool down. We held a daylong conference for the group to rejuvenate their projects. The kids appeared to get along, although they were still cliquish and made little progress on their projects. They seemed self-absorbed. The preppies acted as if issues of racism and discrimination were ancient history. The unconventional kids were into their own combination of mysticism and music. And the Black students looked at both groups and wondered if respect and integration were possible in a world populated by materialistic White people.

At a later meeting with fifty of them we tried to jumpstart their projects again. Since many had been working with one another for several months, we dispensed with icebreakers and began talking about sexual harassment at the girls' request. We tried to help them understand that despite the reduced tension over clothing and lifestyles, other groups of people at their school were still being mistreated. It worked all too well.

We started by viewing a segment of *The Oprah Winfrey Show* about sexual harassment of teenage girls. Sitting in a circle, the girls exchanged experiences.

"I don't like being grabbed," said one.

"Yeah, it makes you feel like a piece of meat," said another.

"What's wrong with showing a little affection?" broke in a boy.

"You've got to be kidding!" shouted a well-developed girl.

"I mean, we don't mean any harm," he responded.

"You may not think it's anything," said the girl, "but it hurts. It really demeans a girl to be grabbed and mauled."

"You can't walk down the halls without someone touching you or saying something nasty," said another girl.

The boys smiled, and that infuriated the girls.

"What do you know about being harassed?" shouted another girl. "You've never had to put up with some of the things we do. I was raped a month ago. And do you know what happened? Nothing! And do you know who did it? My youth pastor. When I told my parents they said it never happened. I went to the minister and he didn't believe me either. That's the kind of help I got from adults in my life. I'm telling you, if any man ever lays a hand on me again I'm going to kill him."

"You need to do something about it, but killing someone won't solve your problem. There are women on death row in this state who did what you're talking about. Who can you turn to for help?" I asked.

A girl sitting alongside me interjected, "I don't know. It's a real problem, and you can't even talk to your parents. My father was involved with my sister and . . ."

Many of the girls began crying as more disclosures of rape, incest, and abuse were made. A few girls were overcome and headed for the restroom. My assistant followed just as another group of girls left, crying. We sent for the school social worker, who met me in the hall and tried to pull them into an impromptu group.

"You wouldn't believe all the stuff that started coming out."

"Oh, yes, I would," he responded. "It's out there everywhere."

"I've got to get back inside and continue."

"They'll come back in when they're ready," he said.

"You've got to report these incidents."

"That's being taken care of. I already know about some of these things. If you tell me who else was involved we'll follow up on it."

Inside the room the remaining students continued talking about the lack of respect boys and girls show for one another. Gradually the ten girls who left the room began drifting back in and took their places in the circle.

"Some of you have had to overcome some serious problems. I applaud you for being able to survive, and I want you to know that you can call me or anyone on my staff if you need to talk to someone. But even more important than that, we know that the most important thing in a teenager's life is having at least one caring adult you can talk to. How many of you have at least one caring adult you can talk to?"

Two students raised their hands.

"Only two out of fifty?"

"Okay. How many of you know a teacher at this school that you can talk to?"

One student raised her hand.

"C'mon. I know there are teachers here who care for you. And your parents—can't you talk to them?"

"My mother hates me," said a smartly dressed girl.

"No, she doesn't."

"Yes, she does," she said adamantly.

We did some activities to cheer them up and bring them together. Then they worked in groups to develop the much-awaited projects they had pledged to complete. They never managed to pull things together, except for a small talent show, but some students got counseling for their problems, and we helped the staff to understand why they dressed and behaved the way they did.

Student disclosures about personal problems have increased in these workshops. Despite the presence of strangers, feelings run high, and students are not reluctant to discuss incidents like the one involving a prominent member of the community who fled town before authorities could arrest him for incest.

Many girls are resentful of boys who "hit and run" leaving them to raise babies they were never prepared for. "I'm the mother of two little babies," said a student in a dropout prevention program. You better believe me when I tell you, if any of you come around and leave me with another, I will hunt you down and make you pay!"

"I feel the same way," said another young woman. "I love my son. He's a year old now and I don't want to say I made a mistake, but if I knew then what I know now, I never would have done it. I'm trying to raise him and go to school. He stays with my mother during the day. At night I'm too tired to play with him, and he's usually asleep when I leave in the morning."

In a discussion group with seventy students at a high school, the girls started disclosing information about abuses they experienced from the boys. There seemed to be an ethic of insincerity that left many feeling manipulated.

"What can we do to get them to understand we have feelings and don't want to be used?" asked one girl plaintively.

"Tommy would never do that," sobbed another almost inaudibly.

The principal was sitting in the circle with us and broke in: "We all know how great Tommy was. He'll be missed. But we have to move on. I know how much he was liked here, but he wouldn't want you to dwell on the past."

That's when we learned that Tommy had committed suicide two weeks before.

The life-and-death tragedies that course through our schools were brought home once again at Chapel High, in a rural, virtually all-White area. Many of its eighteen hundred students worked part-time on local farms. The dozen students who helped plan the upcoming workshop seemed enthusiastic when we left at noon. Two hours later a student was killed in the parking lot by an acquaintance who had a stolen gun. A week later, before our workshop with seventy students, the social worker asked us to avoid discussing the incident unless it was brought up. No one mentioned it. I could not comprehend how something as horrific as this would not surface during daylong discussions about problems at school.

Until recently, many southern districts have had court-ordered busing to desegregate their schools, which only began to be integrated in the early '70s. This often created artificial integration, with little more to show for it than increased numbers of Black students in previously all-White schools. Too little was done to foster interaction among the different ethnic groups, who resegregated upon entering the school and attended classes that were often monochromatic because of tracking and options that channeled students of color into lower-level courses. For children who were taken from their neighborhoods each day and forced to ride buses before dawn into "hostile territory," no welcome mats were waiting—but looks of disgust, contempt, and disdain were not uncommon. Many Black students were angry and rejected these White-dominated institutions, and sometimes the educational process itself.

This phenomenon was evident at suburban Roosevelt High School, where two hundred Black students were bused in to comply with a court-ordered desegregation plan. A week earlier eight students had helped to plan our workshop, but no one followed through. At 7:45 A.M. the students started to arrive. There was no registration table to check them in and send class-cutters back. Two custodians wheeled in television sets with a tangle of wires dangling to the floor.

The previous year they had done the same thing; this year, we had agreed on 50 to 70 students, but they kept coming until the gym was filled with 140 unruly kids. Nearly every Black student in the school was there.

Bobby Jones, the multicultural adviser, was also the football coach. The principal was charming and dedicated. As African Americans, they were challenged in this bastion of conservatism, where Whites moved to escape Blacks, and Blacks were bused in to create artificial integration that did little more than anger both groups and reinforce stereotypes.

Lunch created a special problem—too many kids and too little food. The pizzas arrived late, and the students gulped them down as fast as the boxes were opened. The multicultural club stayed in the back room staring at the pile of empty pizza boxes. But the kids seemed to be having fun as they strung out across the gym, trying to find their place in line according to the day and month of their birth without speaking. Just then Lashonda, a senior and president of the club, came over to me: "There's a note tacked on the bulletin board in the teachers' lounge that says, 'The Youth Conference failed again.' They don't care at all about trying to help us. All they do is complain, and we're not even done yet."

"Is that true?"

"You bet it is," replied Bobby.

"How did the kids find out about it?"

"Oh, they have their ways. What troubles me is that most of the faculty don't have the slightest idea of what we're trying to do or the problems these kids are facing."

"How could they? Only three or four even stopped in, and they left after a minute or two when we started talking about racism."

We split them into two groups and they began listing topics for discussion. The issues were coming out fast. Unfortunately, some of the kids had left—including the big skinhead who had challenged us all morning about our organization's mission.

"You can't get people from different backgrounds livin' together. They're not supposed to. I'm not against Black people, but Whites and Blacks just don't mix."

"What about Jews?"

"Why? Who do you work for?"

"The National Conference of Christians and Jews."

"Ha! That's a joke." He looked at me crossly. "Are you Jewish?"

"Yeah."

"Well, what are you trying to do, teach us some propaganda about Jews and Christians living together like White and Black people?"

"That's right. Don't you think it's possible?"

"No, and I don't think I'm goin' to stay and listen to this nonsense."

Three friends followed him out.

It was difficult to listen to both groups as their voices grew louder with emotion. One group was talking about interracial dating, how Black girls are labeled as sluts for going out with White boys.

"They should stick with their own kind," shouted one as others nodded in agreement.

"What's wrong with dating someone you love? It shouldn't matter what color he is," responded another Black girl.

The White kids sat and watched as cliques of Black girls became increasingly agitated with one another, vying for the right to speak. We enforced the marker rule—only the person with the marker could talk—but they found other markers and kept talking over one another. It was difficult to keep them apart. Obviously, some had lost boyfriends to White girls. Yet, no one tackled the issue of why some Black boys want to date White girls—the concepts of status, and power, and the role of dominant White standards of beauty. Instead they assailed one another for violating an unwritten code.

"I ain't got no use for no one who goes out with a White boy," shouted a small, pudgy girl as she rose from the floor.

"Who are you to say somethin'?" shouted back another. "You ain't nothin' but a hoochie mama!" Fighting words. The smaller girl headed for the center of the circle.

"Who you callin' a hoochie mama?"

"You heard it. If the shoe fits, wear it!" Several girls jumped up and restrained her antagonist. I grabbed the microphone to restore order.

"What other things do you want to talk about?" I asked loudly. Bobby saw I could use some help, and we merged the two groups.

The principal joined us, and the meeting turned into a gripe session about school rules and policies. The questions became more biting as some of the Black students began to vent their anger and frustration against the two administrators.

"Why do you never cut any of us any slack?" shouted the small girl who had cooled down and was now ready to reenter the fray. "You let White kids get away with everything."

Bobby looked disgusted as he handed the mike to the principal. She waited calmly for quiet.

"You know that's not so. I and the other administrators try to be fair to everyone."

"That ain't true!" shouted the girl, again becoming agitated.

"I'm not getting into a shouting match with you."

"You know Black students are treated differently here," chimed in someone else. "We get more suspensions and referrals than all the Whites together."

A chorus of "You tell her, girl!" echoed in the gym.

Bobby took the mike back. "You know we don't show favorites." He began to get angry. "Stay right where you are and sit down! Why is it that some Black students have a tough time dealing with the facts? You know what I'm talking about," he snapped.

"Yeah, dat's right!" came a mocking reply.

"Why is it some of you have to live down to the stereotypes?" Silence. He continued. "If you'd abide by the rules, you wouldn't get into trouble." He pointed to three Blacks males. "If you had done your schoolwork, you would have been able to stay on the football team. What a waste of talent."

The bell rang as he finished, and the kids scattered. A few hung around to confront the principal, but she would have none of it.

"You can take that up with me at any time. There are avenues for appealing my decisions. You know the procedures; you've used them before. This is not the place to push personal grievances."

I turned to Bobby and asked, "What do you think?"

He was crestfallen. "It hurts to see some of them act like that, especially in front of White students, but we have to deal with it. So many of them are angry about having to come here."

"But you're trying so hard to help them, why don't they realize it?"

"I think they do know. It's just that some of them have too many problems they can't deal with, so they try to get back at the system through us."

"Sometimes I wonder if we leave kids worse off than when we started."

Bobby smiled. "Don't worry. It's been good. They carry these feelings around and need a chance to get them out. They have to learn how to deal with them."

Outside, Maurice, a 6-foot-2 African American kid who had been in the workshop, gave me a bear hug. "Thanks for coming."

Two Arab sisters who had also been there walked over.

"Well, what do you think?" I asked.

"I liked it a lot," said one.

"There's a girl I almost got into a fight with the other day," said the other. "I just went up to her and apologized for the way I acted. She said it was all right. That's what I got out of today."

In the same gym a year later, the large White skinhead came up.

"Remember me?"

"Oh, yes. You were the guy who got mad at what I was trying to do."

"That's right. I thought all of your stuff was wrong—race mixin' and tryin' to get along with different groups—but I've changed a lot since then."

"How do you mean?"

"I've learned about other people, a lot more than I knew before. I'd been hearing only one thing from my friends."

"Other skinheads."

"You know some of them. I heard they gave you a hard time at the Jewish place."

"You mean at the Jewish Community Center last spring? How did you hear about it?"

"I've got my sources."

"They weren't skinheads."

"National Alliance. They come around here."

"Why are you here now?"

"I want to tell the rest of them what I've learned. I met this girl . . . she's Jewish. She really changed me. Her parents were nice, too. They had me over for dinner and let me go out with her. They treated me like I was important. I've learned to respect all kinds of people since then, even though I don't go with her anymore."

"Why not?"

"She cheated on me. Slept with my best friend. It was like cutting my heart out."

The day went on uneventfully. We had less than half as many kids as the previous year, and Bobby stayed with me most of the time. Still, no teachers even peeked in to see what we were doing. Having only fifty students made for a more intimate group. When it was time to dialogue, my ex-skinhead friend was the first to speak.

"You all know me, but you don't know how much I've changed since last year. I've learned how important it is for us to live together and to get along. I was as racist as you can get, but I don't believe in that anymore."

Tension remained high at the school, so the PTA invited us to participate on a panel on school violence. For a while it looked like we'd have more panelists than audience. The president of the PTA apologized.

"I'm sorry we didn't have a good turnout. I publicized this for three months. I put ads in newspapers, sent letters home. I just don't know what to do."

Bobby and the principal remained committed to the students. Classes were suspended for three days so a team of specialists could help students improve skills in math, reading, and science. It's comforting to know people care, and despite their anger, most kids know when someone is for real, and appreciate it.

That former skinhead indicated that a White supremacist network existed among disaffected youth in the region. Our experience at Pace Junior High in a city forty miles away from his high school confirmed this. A student's mother called me about her son.

"He's really a good kid, but I'm scared. He's fallen in with a bunch that I don't trust. I found some literature in his room. It's awful—racist, hate stuff, cartoons of Black people and Jews. I don't know where he got it. My husband and I never taught him that. I'm afraid he'll get hurt. He's wearing strange clothes and carrying this stuff around. He's making himself a target. The school's doing very little. There's lots of fights every day. All they do is suspend kids. That's no real solution."

Latrika Jones, a fifteen-year-old who had attended Camp Anytown a year before, went to school there.

"There's plenty of fights in our school. Not all of them are racial though," she averred. "There are some skinheads that hang out together and say nasty things to people. There's far too much violence on campus."

The principal was about fifty, with curly gray hair and a moustache. He seemed amiable and concerned about the violence, and very tense, as if he was anticipating something as we talked. Suddenly, he leaped to his feet and darted out of the office. He was back seconds later.

"No problem. Just checking," he said with relief.

With his help a meeting with the so-called skinheads was organized. We met in the back of the library, which was put off-limits to others. There were fifteen White males of varying ethnic backgrounds. Most had their heads shaved or partially shaved on the sides. Some wore long, thick chains that dangled from their belts with the ends tucked in their pockets. A few had bandannas signifying gang membership—Bloods, Crips, Folk Nation. But it wasn't a gang problem. It took just five minutes to figure out why these teenagers had gravitated to one another and espoused White supremacist slogans: They were afraid of the Black students.

The school is located in an area with an overwhelmingly White, poorly educated, working-class population. The more affluent Whites put their children in private schools or home school them. Some, like a friend of mine who is a member of the Baha'i Faith and a staunch advocate of racial equality, kept his children there for a while but eventually pulled them out.

"I tried," he said apologetically. "But there's not much learning going on. There are a lot of angry kids and overwhelmed teachers." His thirteen-year-old daughter was taunted by belligerent African American boys at the bus stop, and another girl's ponytail was cut off at school by Black girls.

Much the same sense of fear, apprehension, and rage permeated the room as we sat and stared at one another. They were a fairly unimposing group.

"I know who you are," said one of them.

"Have we met before?"

"No, but I have a friend at Blanton [a high school in another county fifty miles away] who worked with you when they had some trouble there."

"We don't have any problems. It's them niggers who've got the problems," said a chubby kid. Laughter around the room.

"What kind of problems?"

"Those f—in' porch monkeys don't qualify as human bein's," added a tall, slender Latino.

"They don't know how to act, and they can't talk straight. All they do is push people around," said a blond kid.

"They're not gonna push me around," said a heavyset one. "I've got a black belt in karate, and they better stay away from me."

"I won't take any shit from them, either," shouted the Latino. "I've got a gun. I'm not kiddin'. I'm gonna shoot one of those assholes the next time they hassle me!"

"That's right, Ray," chimed in his friend. "Some of my father's family are in the Klan. They won't take any shit from no niggers. My dad drove me here the other day. He had a gun in his car and wanted me to point out the ones who were giving me trouble. He was ready to shoot their ass right there."

"You think that will solve anything?" They nodded. "It won't. It'll only cause more problems."

"We don't need to do anything ourselves; we've got friends," said the blond. "We've been in touch with people from the Klan and the Church of the Avenger downtown [a local White-supremacist organization]. They said anytime we need help to just call and they'll send a carload of guys to clean the niggers outta here."

"Look. There has to be a better way. Suppose I set up a meeting with some of the Black students. Would you be willing to talk with them?"

"Talkin' won't do no good. They can't even understand English," said the heavy kid.

"We're not getting anywhere this way, so what about it?"

They agreed to a meeting the following week.

In talking with the principal and the school resource officer, we learned that more than a hundred Black ninth-grade students had been transferred there that fall. Many didn't want to attend the predominantly White school and resented being bused out of their neighborhoods. There was also an overcrowding problem. Built for eight hundred, the school now had more than twelve hundred students, many in portable class-rooms. The principal attributed the fights to the crowded conditions, but the school resource officer confirmed that outside agitators had been passing out racist literature.

They didn't seem surprised about the threat of guns at the school; they'd heard rumors. We thought it would be helpful to bring the two sides together. The school year was nearing an end, and we hoped to avoid a major confrontation.

"Next year they'll go to other schools and be somebody else's prob-lem," the principal muttered.

Fear for their safety fueled the skinheads' racism. Few of them under-stood the neo-Nazi philosophy that underpins the movement. Most lacked rudimentary knowledge about World War II and fascism. If you asked them about the Holocaust, many would say that it never happened. They were quick to spout slogans but didn't comprehend their meaning. In short, they're the epitome of Eric Hoffer's "True Believers," contempo-rary know-nothings who practice cerebral hygiene. They have a hard time telling you anything about the government of this country and contempo-rary current events, let alone world history.

U.S. and world history are required courses. Teachers cover the mate-rial, but somehow it's lost on many kids—and not just the neo-facists. Most haven't a clue about civics. Once, while we were showing a video on the Holocaust to about forty students at an urban high school, a boy sat there with his hand up. Before we could call on him, the bell rang. After he left, his teacher told us he was going to ask who stopped the Holo-caust—not surprising in view of a 2003 U.S. Department of Education re-port that more than half the twelfth-graders in the United States thought Germany, Japan, or Italy were our allies in World War II.

You could feel the hostility as the skinheads took their places on the right side of the room and the African Americans on the left. We hoped reason would prevail. Many children have difficulty communicating with one another. It's not just a cultural and socioeconomic chasm between them, but also an absence of civility, that leads to confrontation. It's an inability to empathize with another—to refrain from rudeness and to communicate without put-downs, to listen and actually hear, understand, and confirm someone else. Like their parents, kids don't believe or trust one another; that mistrust colors their interaction and complicates communication.

We asked the kids to establish rules and adhere to them. They hit the important ones, like not interrupting, no side conversations, don't get angry, listen, no foul language, and be honest. In this way they assumed responsibility for their behavior.

"Look, we've got problems between the White and African American students, and we all know it," I began.

"Why do they have to call themselves African American?" asked the heavyset skinhead.

"It's what many Black people prefer to be called today."

"Then I want to be called European American." A big smirk came across his face and the other White kids chuckled.

"Fine. I'll call you anything you want."

"Why do they wear shirts with Confederate flags on them and those chains?" Latrika asked.

"It's part of our Southern culture," shouted a boy in the back. "Ain't nobody gonna take it away from us."

"Those shirts are against school policy because they offend some people," I said.

"It shouldn't offend nobody. It's our heritage," said the big one.

"What's your name?"

"Tony."

"Well, Tony, would you like it if someone wore something that offended you?"

"They do! Some of them wear 'Black Power' shirts. And sometimes they got on shirts with a big X that say 'By Any Means Necessary.' With that Black hand holding up a rifle; you know what that means!"

It was obvious where the discussion was going. Once three of us spent a week trying to educate students about the different meanings of the

Confederate battle flag. The funny thing was that the some of the strongest advocates for wearing the flag were transplants from Ohio and Michigan. We tried to teach the kids about Malcolm X, to show them how he moderated his views near the end of his life and disavowed violence as a solution to racial problems, but some of the kids remained intransigent.

Now, we didn't have time for history lessons. The animosity between the two groups was palpable. Were the threats about the guns more than just teenage bravado—the same kind that kills thousands of kids every year?

"We won't get anywhere by yelling at each other. The bottom line is that this place isn't safe for a lot of kids. You want things to go on the way they've been? Do you like having to look over your shoulder all the time?"

"That's why we stick together," said one of the skinheads. "We take care of each other so those guys will stay away."

"Do you like worrying about getting beaten up? Or suspended?"

"That's why some people do what they do," said a Black youth. "Not all this stuff is racial. Some of us don't want to be here and try anything to get out. Like Randy Jones," he said as he turned to the other Black students. "He's a wild one. Last week he stood outside and said he didn't want to be in school and was gonna smack the next kid that came along so he could get suspended, and that's just what he did. He went up behind him and hit him aside the head. It just happened that he was White. He's gone for ten days now, like he wanted." A few of the Black students smiled, but the Whites didn't think it was funny.

"They're always pushin' us around," Tony shouted. "You can't go anywhere without them callin' you names and shovin' you."

"That goes both ways!" said Latrika. "You White boys are always saying things about them and wearing those red scarves and flags in your pockets."

"What's wrong with that?" asked Tony. "There ain't no law against the way we dress. We're just mindin' our own business."

"If that's all you were doing, we wouldn't be here now trying to stop all this fighting," Latrika reminded them. "None of us wants to keep having fights." A grudging murmur of assent came from both sides. "Then if you believe things need to be calmed down, what can be done?"

"Why not send all the Blacks back where they came from?" shot back Tony.

"Why don't you go back where you came from?" replied a Black youth.

"This is where we're from, man. Don't you know your history?"

"Your people stole this land from the Indians. It ain't yours. You White folks."

"This isn't going anywhere," I said. "What can we do as a group to cut down on the violence? You don't have to love one another, but school's over in a few weeks. There must be a way to stop the fighting . . . unless you like it that way."

Looking through the skinheads' haughty veneer, through the ostentatious display of bluster, you could discern the troubled, scared adolescents huddled together. They didn't want violence but couldn't lose face by admitting it. Latrika offered a solution.

"Why don't we have a 'Keep the Peace Week' with everyone pledging not to fight? We could have T-shirts with the motto on it."

"Who's gonna pay for them?" asked someone.

"We'll get donations," replied Connie, a White teenager who had been quiet up to then. "And we'll make a 'Keep the Peace' quilt that everyone can sign as a pledge against violence."

"I ain't gonna make any quilt," said one of the boys.

"You don't have to," replied Latrika. "Only those who want to. We'll get every homeroom to design a square. Then we'll sew them all together and hang it where everyone can see."

"We're not having any part of that," said Tony.

"What about just pledging to stop fighting?" I asked.

Muted words were exchanged among them, and Tony turned back to me.

"We'll stay away from them if they leave us alone."

"Okay, then. It's a deal. No more fights till the end of school."

"What about them?" he said pointing to the Blacks on the other side of the room.

"You don't have to worry," said Latrika. "As long as you stop mouthing off and quit wearing those Confederate flags, things will be calm."

The principal had come in a few minutes earlier.

"Let me remind you it's school policy not to wear gang colors. That goes for these flags, too. I like the idea of a 'Keep the Peace Week.' I'll get some parents to help with the quilt. I think teachers will give you some time in homeroom to work on it if you bring the materials." He left the room. A few skinheads grinned as one pulled a forbidden Confederate flag from his pocket.

Latrika and Connie stayed for a planning session after the other students had gone. Latrika's mom helped. One of the biggest obstacles was convincing teachers to yield homeroom time. We met with the faculty and pitched the idea. They grudgingly acquiesced, but many didn't think the kids could pull it off.

Latrika and Connie found two PTA volunteers who were expert quilt makers. They helped with the logistics and design. Latrika called a fabric store to get materials donated but was told they needed confirmation of the project from the school and clearance from their headquarters in the Midwest.

"Looks like you'll have to put it on hold," said an assistant principal.

"No, ma'am," replied Latrika. "I faxed the request this morning, and they gave me authorization."

Two weeks later three hundred students, wearing distinctive lavender-and-white T-shirts, gathered in a small auditorium to celebrate the kickoff of Keep the Peace Week. A large, colorful quilt hung across the stage front. School district administrators attended, and Latrika's mom gave a rousing speech as the kids cheered. Soon after, Latrika and her mother met President Bill Clinton at the airport, where he autographed the quilt and praised their work. Fighting subsided during that time. The principal was transferred during the summer. When students arrived for the fall term they found several new sidewalks had been added to change the traffic pattern, but nothing further was done to improve interpersonal relations and the fighting resumed.

Bullying is an area of student concern that many teachers and administrators overlook or avoid, to the dismay and danger of students. An ABC television documentary revealed that when teachers actively search for bullying behavior they can miss it *even when it occurs in their presence on the playground.* Yet it is ubiquitous. On any given day, 180,000 students stay home because of bullying, the most common form of violence among students. It can take many forms, including physical or verbal abuse, threats, intimidation, extortion, teasing, sexual harassment, and ostracism.

Despite its omnipresence in our schools, bullying is often shielded by ignorance or indifference of students, teachers, administrators, and parents who are either unaware of the problem, or, through an unwritten code of silence that permeates schools and society, refuse to do anything about it. Squealing, "ratting," or tattling seems to be an un-American value, a rather odd concept in a country that prides itself on pulling for the downtrodden and underdog.

Technological advances have also elevated bullying to a new level. Through the use of cell phones and the Internet, for example, e-mail, MySpace, Facebook, and YouTube, students can anonymously harass their peers and make defamatory comments about them. Wiseman (2007) describes the magnitude and impact of cyberbullying, noting the devastating and chilling effect it is having on today's youth. In 2007 it was estimated that 90 percent of middle school students had their feelings hurt online, 75 percent had visited a website bashing another student, and 40 percent had their password stolen and changed by a bully. (See also www.wiredsafety.org.)

Perhaps kids are bullied because they look or behave differently from other children. We do know that a common characteristic among many of the school shooters was their isolated, alienated personalities that frequently led to their being bullied. This was the case at Columbine, where the shooters were tormented by a 220-pound wrestler and members of the football team (Adams & Russakoff 1999).

As the evidence started accumulating about the profile of shooters and attention focused on the problem of bullying, we introduced an activity in middle and high school workshops that was designed to heighten students' awareness about the scope and implications of bullying and other forms of discrimination. We wanted students to share personal experiences of being marginalized so they could empathize with one another and, hopefully, eschew such behavior.

In the exercise, students line up on one side of the room. They are asked to do the activity in silence—a formidable challenge to some. A series of statements are read, and if the statement applies to them, they walk across the room, get a small round sticker and place it on their name tag. They pause before returning so the rest of the group can observe how many have been discriminated against. If they don't feel comfortable about getting a sticker they can remain with the group, but we ask them to consider whether they would be getting stickers and why.

The statements increase in intensity as the exercise proceeds. Although there is often talking and laughter, the activity elicits the desired response because most students wind up with many stickers and can see the extent of the discrimination that exists in their world. Students then discuss in small groups how they felt during the activity. They record the number of stickers they got, and, most importantly, they share the experiences that led to their getting stickers. Lastly, they discuss what they can do to avoid giving people stickers or labels.

It is not uncommon to find a majority of students with a dozen or more stickers, and though some are reluctant to share their stories, others don't hesitate to recall the indignities and injustices that have marked their lives. Below is a list of the statements. Items about rumor and gossip were added because they are also a source of conflict among students.

Please come forward if you have ever been made fun of, put down or discriminated against because of:

1. The group you hang out with
2. The clothes you wear
3. The music you like
4. Your religion
5. Your skin color
6. Your body shape or size
7. Your physical or mental ability
8. Your gender
9. If you know someone who has been bullied
10. If you think bullying is a problem at your school
11. If you have ever been bullied at school or in your community
12. If you wanted to get help to stop bullying but didn't know what to do
13. If you think gossip or rumors are a problem at your school
14. If you have heard a rumor about someone at your school in the last week
15. If you have ever tried to stop a rumor or gossip from spreading
16. If you have ever been put down or discriminated against by a teacher or administrator in your school
17. If you have ever discriminated against or put someone down

Some statements generate unanimous reactions among students. For example, nearly every one receives a sticker because bullying is a problem in their school, and virtually everyone picks up a sticker because rumors and gossip abound. Most claim to have been discriminated against by teachers and administrators. And all acknowledge that they have discriminated against one another.

The ensuing small-group discussions produce emotions and tears as kids recall racism, abuse, and ostracism. The braver ones share their stories with the whole group, hoping in some small way to end their hell and spare others the indignities they have endured.

Students' desire to discuss these issues are widespread and their ability to rebound after such experiences—what is referred to as resilience—is considerable. Many children ask for help, while others succumb to the hardship and depredations, adding to the statistics on school failure, violence and tragedies. Time and again, even when they leave the dialogues angry, they say they had a great time and ask their advisers for more opportunities for discussion. Before leaving, they are asked to make concrete commitments to improve tolerance and understanding, for example, peace-keeping days, posters promoting equality and understanding, ethnic fairs, community service, tutoring, and mentoring—but without dedicated staff to follow up, these pledges are hollow.

With increasing pressure to perform well on standardized tests, teachers have less time to allow students to engage in activities that appear to fall outside of the narrow test-oriented goals. Harried teachers are less inclined to spend time working with students outside of class to resolve interpersonal problems—they would rather escape at the end of the day. Yet an Indiana University study of eighty-one thousand students in 110 high schools in twenty-six states revealed that two out of three students reported being bored in class every day and 17 percent said they were bored in *every* class. Nearly a third of the students said they were bored because of "no interaction with the teachers" (Indiana University Media Relations 2007).

## Students' Lives

Thirteen million children live below the poverty level in the United States, and 26 million children eat free and reduced-price lunches in school. Every thirty-five seconds a baby is born into poverty. Every nineteen minutes a baby dies before his first birthday. Every second a public school student is suspended. Every nine seconds a high school student drops out. Every twenty seconds a child is arrested. Every twenty-two seconds a baby is born to an unmarried mother. Every thirty-five seconds a child is confirmed abused or neglected. Every eight minutes a child is arrested for a violent crime. Every forty-one minutes a child or teen dies in an accident. Every three hours a child or teen is killed by a firearm. Every five hours a child or teen commits suicide.

—"Moments in America for Children,"
Children's Defense Fund, November 2005

The spate of school shootings during the late 1990s may have been an aberration, but frustration and anger still permeate our schools. Kids are mad about having to attend classes they think are irrelevant. Too few teachers are adept at framing their material in a manner sufficiently interesting to draw students into the irresistible web of mystery and challenge that education can be. For many, school is a waste of time, and teachers are as out of touch with their world as little green men from Mars. The Indiana University High School Survey of Student Engagement found that 75 percent of the eighty-one thousand students surveyed reported being bored in class because "the material wasn't interesting." Forty percent were bored because the material "wasn't relevant to me" (Indiana University Media Relations 2007).

Think for a moment about the historical frame of reference of today's teenagers. They were born in the 1990s. Though they may have heard of it, they have no recollection of the Vietnam War. John F. Kennedy is as remote a figure as Franklin D. Roosevelt. Frank Sinatra, Elvis Presley, the Beatles, and rock and roll are from another time and culture. They know nothing about air raid drills, bomb shelters, polio, measles, and smallpox. For many of them, the Cold War was a fight against nasal congestion.

The anguish of Cambodia, Yugoslavia, and Rwanda do not conjure up painful memories of human suffering, any more perhaps than the distant conflicts in Afghanistan, Iraq, and other parts of the Middle East. And although their teachers may have touched on these topics, they do not register in any meaningful way for a significant number of students who are preoccupied with their daily struggle for sustenance, safety, and survival at home and in school.

The increasing emphasis placed on teaching to state standardized tests to placate Washington bureaucrats, who monitor adequate yearly progress for compliance with the No Child Left Behind legislation, is gutting programs from penmanship to art, music, social studies, and physical education. (See Ave [2006] for observations about students' inability to write in the cursive form because teachers have little time to teach it.)

This may contribute to the feeling of many students that school is irrelevant. But upwardly striving students can be thrust into a supercharged environment, pitting one against another for scholarships and admission into select colleges and universities. In the race for status and recognition there are many losers—or at least that's the way some kids feel. For some, getting a low grade means failure. For others, especially children of color, it may increase status, because school is a White institution, whose books talk about things like manifest destiny and the accomplishments of White explorers, scientists, writers, artists, and inventors. Acting White, that is, studying and earning good grades, can lead to ostracism and even physical duress in some youth subcultures, because academically successful children of color may be perceived as sellouts to the dominant White society that makes the rules deemed exploitative and alienating.

Rules are another source of irritation. There are enough restrictions on dress, behavior, and freedom of speech and assembly to make students feel like prisoners. Even makeup and hair color come under close scrutiny by the school's fashion police in the belief that appearance influences achievement and decorum. In the unending attempt of adults to socialize children into their world, school routinely deadens youthful enthusiasm for experimentation, and with it motivation and creativity.

School newspaper stories are routinely censored by administrators who fear that students can't handle truth or volatile subjects like sex, drugs, and free speech—as if they don't already engage in them. In 1988 the U.S. Supreme Court (*Hazelwood School District et al. v. Kuhlmeier et al.*, 484 U.S. 260) ruled that high school administrators have the right to censor student newspapers, an option that was not lost on a principal in Florida. He pulled a story from his school's newspaper because it gave the standardized test scores of White and Black students in the school. The data were then published in a story about the censorship on the front page of the *St. Petersburg Times*, revealing that only 16 percent of African American students were performing at grade level in math and just 4 percent were reading at grade level (Stein 2006).

Aside from the censorship issue, this story points up the lackluster results of the obsession with standardized testing under NCLB. A Harvard Civil Rights Project report (Lee 2006) revealed that very little progress has been made in improving reading and math scores of children and virtually no lessening of the achievement gap has occurred since the implementation of the legislation. States' reports of successes in making adequate yearly progress under NCLB were largely attributed to their less rigorous standardized tests compared to the representative standard test of the National Assessment of Educational Progress. With federal expenditures of more than $412 million annually to help defray states' testing costs, the report questioned the efficacy and wisdom of the high-stakes thrust of NCLB in light of its meager accomplishments in improving reading and math and lowering the achievement gap.

Adolescents are very status conscious and sometimes cruel. They observe who takes remedial preparatory classes for the tests as well as the disproportionate number of children of color in special education classes. They are also cognizant of the codes of conduct that govern all facets of their life, from cheating and smoking to stealing and lying, yet all of these behaviors are rampant among them and staff as well. That isn't to say rules aren't needed to regulate school populations, but it points out the futility of attempting to mandate behavior in the face of hypocrisy.

The disparity in wealth and resources between White and minority schools is alarming. Jonathan Kozol (1991) documented this more than a decade and a half ago, yet the differences are still glaring. (Stiefel, Rubenstein & Schwartz 2004). Even when you don't see it in the physical plant, it surfaces in the quality of teachers, resources, and parental involvement. And while some inner-city schools are well equipped, they often lack talented teachers, many of whom don't want to work in stigmatized areas or with poor students. Schools needing the best talent in the system must often make do with the inexperienced and the recalcitrant.

Disparities are visible in students' clothing, possessions, and leisure activities. Having dress codes and uniforms may achieve a modicum of standardization, but the desire for uniqueness and status finds expression in myriad ways that cannot be regulated by administrative fiat. There are in groups and out groups, jocks, cheerleaders, nerds, skaters, druggies, preps, metalheads, and a host of other categories that separate students into many layers of social acceptability.

Like the "Trenchcoat Mafia" at Columbine some kids take pride in being different. There are clubs for foreign languages and activities ranging from forensics to band, each having a different status in the teenage pecking order. The ostracized and alienated take refuge in gangs from the depredation of marauders or the insults heaped upon them in school and out.

As if the pressures to achieve, conform, and be accepted are not enough, the home lives of millions of children are pathetic. Fifteen million children have no health insurance. Millions more live below the poverty level and have inadequate food and shelter. There is no doubt that some children are physically safer in school than out, but we cannot ignore the emotional trauma inflicted upon them on campus by their peers and staff, who consciously or unconsciously magnify their pain and suffering.

Think for a moment what your life was like as a teenager. Was it pleasant, or would you rather forget it? Schools are not only designed to educate children about intellectual matters, they are also training grounds for power and privilege—where we learn our place in society and life, and sometimes where we learn we don't fit in.

Hooking up with that special girl or boy, or uncertainty about one's virility, femininity, or sexual orientation, may interfere with learning. This is a part of schooling that's all too often ignored in our preoccupation with tests and grades. When schools start to recognize the importance of educating the whole student, perhaps we will reduce the emotional and physical trauma that plagues our campuses and begin to lay the foundation for learning.

Some of the examples of the kinds of problems children are dealing with may seem trivial and others shocking. As you read, think about how you would react to similar situations and what effect they would have on your interest in academics and your will to succeed.

Police reported that a live newborn baby was found in a trash can by a custodian in the girls' bathroom at Harbor View High School, which has over two thousand students from a wide range of ethnic groups. Authorities scanned videotapes of students entering the bathroom. Later that day the mother was identified from the tape and conversations she'd had with friends—she went on to class as if nothing had happened and told her friends. She was fifteen and had good grades. Charges were filed against her for child abuse and the baby was placed in the care of her grandmother.

A few days before this incident we observed a class at Harbor View. The teacher was having difficulty maintaining order and respect among her fourteen female and two male students. Now, near the end of the term, the class was in total disarray.

The empty room looked like an infirmary, with seven hospital beds and assorted paraphernalia. Signs over each bed warned of STDs and AIDS. On the blackboard were four rules for the day: Show respect for others and yourself. Behave with maturity. Provide a good work environment. Come to class with good study habits.

The class was a preparation for medical techs. The middle-aged White female teacher was a former nurse. She was talking with another guest speaker who was scheduled at the same time, and apologized for the mix-up.

"These students are really rude. There's a young girl who sits in front. She's part African American and part Caribbean, I think. A real problem. She taunts me and the other kids. I called her mother and told her I was giving her daughter a detention. 'You can't do that,' she said. 'I can't leave the office to come and pick her up after school.' That's the kind of help I got from her. That child and others continue to be a problem. Watch and you'll see what I mean.

"They can be cruel. There's a very large Black boy, Maurice, who is a really nice kid, but he's slow. He doesn't bother anyone. You should see the way some of the White girls put him down. I haven't been able to stop it. It's as if everyone hates everyone else. I've never seen anything like it."

The students began to trickle in and take their seats. Most sat in pairs—Whites with Whites in the middle and the rest scattered, with the problem kid in front on the far right. The guest was a middle-aged White woman, herself once a battered spouse. She began by telling them how widespread that kind of abuse is: "You've got to get out of a dangerous relationship! Fortunately, there have been some changes in the law that are helping. If the police are called to a home on a domestic violence complaint, they have to make an arrest."

"Oh yeah?" shouted a girl as her hand shot up. "They came to my house Saturday and didn't arrest anybody."

"Sometimes the police don't want to get involved, even though they're supposed to. That's why you need to know the law and keep filing complaints. And you should write down their names and badge numbers. You have to press them on that."

They were transfixed, watching her as she described the cycle of abuse and the warning signs that lead to dangerous relationships.

"There's more than just physical abuse, isn't there?" asked one girl near the front of the room.

"It can take many forms, like words that belittle you. It is certainly hurtful to be told you're worthless." Still no movement, their trancelike state interrupted only by sporadic hands raised to ask questions. They were often framed as experiences "of a friend" and requests for more information on certain issues.

"It's not only women who get abused, is it?" asked one of the young men. There was some snickering.

"As a matter of fact, that's true. It's often difficult for men to admit, but it's going on more and more. Maybe not physical abuse, but verbal. Let me tell you about something that happened recently when I was in a class.

"After I finished my presentation a big, good-looking boy came up and asked if he could talk with me about a problem. He didn't look like someone who would be afraid of anybody, but he was almost in tears.

"'I'm sixteen, and all of my life my father has been horrible to my mother. He beats her and calls her names and stuff. I want to stop it, but then he beats me, too. I can't stand seeing it and I don't date anyone because I'm afraid I might do the same thing. So the other kids say I'm gay—I must be or else I'd be screwin' around.

"'Finally, I had enough and got a girlfriend to keep them quiet. The rumors stopped. But I didn't love her and never slept with her. She got angry after a while. I told her that I just didn't want to do it because I respected her. She said that if I didn't she was gonna tell everybody that the rumors about me were true. She was even gonna tell my parents. And if she does my father will blame my mother and beat her again. I don't think she can take any more. She just got outta the hospital last week. I don't know what to do.'

"So you see, you don't have to hit people to hurt them." The room was hushed, as a few students squirmed in their seats.

She answered several more questions and the bell sounded. Many wrote down the number of the spouse abuse hotline after being assured that calls were confidential. The teacher came up to me while a student was tearfully relating her problem to the guest in front.

"Well, you picked a day that was certainly atypical! I've never seen them behave this well before. It's not at all like them."

"I guess you found out why they're so disrespectful and angry and unruly."

A week later the "problem" kid and a friend were sitting together in the front row. They paid no attention to our workshop and conducted their own conversation until Maurice began to speak.

"Hold it!" I said. "When someone's talking you keep quiet! Get that? And when you talk we'll be quiet. Maurice is trying to say something and you're not showing him any respect!"

They looked surprised and didn't interrupt again. Others discussed stereotypes they had of one another. The teacher, who had been writing at her desk, walked over to the "problem" kid and handed her a paper. The girl got up and left with a sneer. We turned on a video and sat down next to the teacher in the back of the room.

"You wrote her up?"

"Yes, and it was long overdue. I should have thrown her out of here ages ago. Those two have disrupted this class for months. I've taken enough from them. I almost quit because of them."

The chance to draw them into the discussion was gone. The teacher didn't realize what she had done, nor do others who routinely throw kids out of their classrooms because they lack the skill to control them. That doesn't solve problems. It only makes the kids more sullen and contemptuous when they return.

Lane High School is a fairly diverse school since the court ordered it integrated thirty years ago. Now more than two thousand Black, White, Asian, and Latino students course through the crowded halls of the building. Like many high schools, most ethnic groups hung out in certain hallways, and the students sitting on the floor of our room were discussing this.

"Why do all the Black kids stick together?" asked an indignant White girl during our workshop.

"What are you gettin' so upset about?" a Black teenager shouted back. "No one complains about all of you hangin' out together?"

"You know what I mean," the girl responded. "They always sit together in the cafeteria."

"Maybe they're more comfortable that way, and they don't feel wanted at the other tables," said another.

"Well, that's the way they make me and other Whites feel when we go into D wing," said the first girl. "You can't even walk by without them gangin' up on you, pushin' and shovin' like they own the place."

"And what's all this stuff about Black History Month, anyway? We don't have White History Month?" said a White teenager as he glared at the Black students.

"Are you kiddin'? Every month is White History Month. That's all we get in those textbooks. There's almost nothin' about Black folks except slavery and how we planted peanuts."

"Yeah, and you gave us the shortest month of the year, February!" said another.

"Do we have to celebrate every minority group?" a White boy asked plaintively. "I mean, aren't we all Americans? Why do you people have to call yourselves African Americans? Can't we just learn together?"

"We can't learn much about our heritage from the books we have. They're full of stuff about you all, but there's precious little about what we did for this country," a Black youth responded. "You know what they say about history—it's just some White guy's recollection of what happened. Anything they didn't like they left out. And we're the ones who are always left out."

"Yeah! That's right. We need more courses on Black history and more Black teachers here. You hear what I'm sayin'?" said another youth. "And I'm proud to be African American. You can't take that away from me.

White folks have robbed us of just about everything else. And now you don't want to let us define who we are," he snapped. "We can live together if some of your people would just leave us alone and let us do our thing. Why does it matter to you what we call ourselves?"

"It looks like you're separating yourselves from the rest of us. We need to work together," said the White boy.

"Brother, I don't know where you been livin', but from where I see it, we're already pretty far apart. Don't no one gonna tell me what I can and can't call myself, especially no White man. They been tellin' us what to do for too long, and now it's time for us to git on with our lives."

"What's it like to be a student here?" I asked.

"It'd be a lot better if some of his friends weren't here," exclaimed a Black male as he glared across at a boy's marine-style brush cut that left only blond stubble on his head.

"What ya mean?" shot back the boy, who had been silent until now. "What's the matter with my friends?"

"You know what I mean," replied his accuser.

"I have lots of friends."

"Those skinheads you hang around with."

"They're not skinheads, they're just racially conscious White men."

"What is that supposed to mean?" snapped another.

"Oh, it's okay for you Blacks to celebrate your heritage, but not for us?"

"Ain't nobody sayin' you can't feel good about who you are, but it ain't right for you and your friends to come to school wearing 'White Power' shirts and flyin' Confederate flags from your cars and all," complained a girl.

"What about those 'Black Power' shirts some of you wear, and the X shirts that say 'By Any Means Necessary'? I suppose that's okay?"

"Nobody wore them until your friends came in here with those flags," said the girl.

"All we're doin' is showin' our concern and interest in our Southern heritage."

"And I guess you don't know anything about the wall painting either? The one our multicultural club sponsored on the back wall near the parking lot. Somebody wrote some racist stuff across it," said a White girl.

"Yeah, and it was really nice. Juan did a great job," said someone.

"We're making sure it's restored," replied Ms. Jamson, a Spanish teacher who was sitting behind the circle. She was the multicultural club's faculty sponsor. "We're not going to let a few people ruin the spirit of what we're trying to accomplish."

"We need to continue this dialogue, but it's time for lunch. Where are the pizzas and sodas?"

"The bell was supposed to ring ten minutes ago," said Ms. Jamson. "I'll go see what's going on." She returned in a minute with a look of dismay. "There's no one in the halls. I don't—"

"May I have your attention, please," came the voice of the principal over the intercom. "There's a problem, so please remain in your rooms for about ten minutes. We should have this taken care of by then. Thanks for your patience." The kids were already milling around. "We better sit tight and keep the kids busy," said Ms. Jamson, and she asked the students to start getting the place ready for lunch. Three young women standing near the door with their backpacks said they had to go to math class.

"Well, no one can go anywhere right now," said Ms. Jamson. "Sit down and take it easy."

"May I have your attention. I'd like to ask teachers to bear with us and then have students proceed to their next period. All classes will be shortened by ten minutes for the rest of the day. Please wait for the all clear. Thank you."

Ms. Jamson, looked around nervously. The kids were sitting in little groups, some even integrated. Time dragged on.

"May I have your attention. You may proceed to your fourth period classes now. Thank you for your patience."

"What was that all about?"

"I don't have a clue," replied Ms. Jamson. At last two students entered carrying stacks of pizzas followed by two others with a cooler full of sodas. The students, unfazed by the disruption, were eating when Ron Farley, the school social worker came in.

"What's the matter?" I asked. "You look like you've been through the wringer."

"These kids never cease to amaze me. You know what that was all about? A girl had a problem with her boyfriend. She felt she couldn't live any longer without him, so she climbed up on the top of the main building and threatened to jump. Between us and the police, it took about an hour to get her back in. Some say she's pregnant. I don't know. Never a dull day around here."

After lunch they shared what they learned that day.

"We have to respect each other."

"Some people like to be together because they feel isolated here."

"It's all right to feel different as long as you feel good about yourself."

"Today has been awesome."

Being a high school social worker is one of the most difficult jobs on campus. It's certainly one of the most demanding because there are two thousand potential problems walking the halls. At any moment life-and-death dilemmas can surface—and often do. They run the gamut from sexual abuse to aggravated assault and conflict between students, parents, and faculty. There are physical and mental health problems, pregnancy counseling, interpersonal relations, substance abuse, and police encounters.

Social workers may be surrogate parents for the abandoned and dispossessed, friends to the isolated and alienated, confidants and advisers for the searchers. It's hard to imagine the workload they bear and the grief and pain that are laid on them each day. Some districts have few trained social workers and they are severely taxed. Many are beyond burnout, trying to help kids cope with a world that doesn't seem to care very much about them.

Two years after the attempted suicide at Lane High School, we were conducting another workshop. Ms. Jamson had taken a leave of absence, and Mr. Farley, the social worker, became the multicultural club sponsor. A Vietnam vet, he has a long ponytail and tattoos on his arms. He loves his job despite the workload, but he's frustrated with the lack of follow-through by the kids.

"They're apathetic, and every time we have a club meeting a different bunch shows up. I don't know what to expect today," he said as the late bell rang at 7:30 A.M. "It looks like you've got a good group here. About thirty? That should make for some lively discussion."

Mr. Farley grabbed the pager at his side. "Sorry. I've got to go."

The day went smoothly, including an excellent discussion on overcoming student apathy. The students divided into teams and planned a series of multicultural events designed to involve the entire school, beginning with a fair. Before they left at 2:00 P.M. they signed up to help rebuild the club and created assignments for nearly everyone present. Finally, they reflected about the day. As the bell rang Mr. Farley returned.

"I'm sorry I wasn't able to help out," he apologized. "Sometimes I really wonder about this place and the system. Today I worked with a sixteen-year-old boy who had a gun. He said he wanted to come to school and kill some teachers. They got the weapon away from him. It was a pellet gun, but his father had a bunch of real ones he hid somewhere.

"His family came here about six months ago. The kid's got Tourette syndrome and is supposed to be on medication, but they lost their Medicaid coverage when they moved. In the meantime, they needed me to have him Baker Acted [temporarily institutionalized]. He'll go into a hospital for evaluation, and then they'll probably let him come back here."

Some encounters with students don't always turn out well. At an urban high school, the White, middle-aged biology teacher was having problems with some African American boys.

"I don't know what to do with these Black boys. They mistreat the others and show no respect for me. I feel sorry for those who want to work. It's not very high-level stuff, but most of them could do the work if the climate were better."

Her classroom was brightly lit, with desks arranged in neat rows. Four African American young men were joking loudly off to my right. We moved the desks into a circle so we could see each other as we talked.

"Okay, what's the problem?"

"Ain't no problem," said Jerome, a thin boy to my left. The others laughed loudly.

"I was told you guys were causing some trouble, and I came to see if I could help out."

"What you mean 'you guys'?" said Lamar.

"The four of you. You've been sitting there laughing and carrying on. I watched from the hall before I came in."

"You been spyin' on us?" said Tyrone.

"I saw how you disrupted the class."

"That ain't the truth!" shouted Jerome. "That White boy Andy over there," he said pointing a finger at a redheaded youth sitting across from him. "He's the problem. He's a fag." The others broke out laughing.

"Yeah, he's gay," added Lamar.

"I am not gay!" said Andy.

"Yeah, you're gay all right," said Lamar. "I don't like goin' to class with gay boys."

"I told you, I'm not gay!" said Andy emphatically.

"You is gay, you is gay, you is gay!" shouted Jerome.

Andy's pale freckled face turned beet red as he jumped to his feet and ran out the door.

"See what you guys did? You chased him away, and that wasn't right."

"Oh, he'll be back. He don't mind," said Jerome.

The teacher, who had been standing in the front of the room, was despondent. The eight other students, all but one of them White girls, acted as if nothing unusual had happened. No one said a word.

"That's the way it's been going all semester," said the teacher after class. "They're not bad kids, but they just want to clown around. I don't know what to do. I guess I better send them to the office. They're all on the football team. You'd think they'd behave better so they wouldn't get into trouble."

Andy dropped the course and enrolled in another biology class with a different teacher. A few months later we saw him at another workshop along with Leonardo and Antonio, two African Americans who had attended our multicultural leadership Camp Anytown. They were both stars on the football team. We had missed a golden opportunity by not asking them to help with Andy's class.

Elementary school children seem to be fairly well adjusted until they get into the sixth and seventh grade; then you have eight hundred to a thousand or more prepubescent children running around. Many middle school halls, cafeterias, and playgrounds look like sharks attacking bait-fish. There is a high incidence of fighting. It's unfortunate that these children can't visualize alternative ways of resolving conflict than by force. On many campuses, might makes right. Some kids are big, so it can lead to serious injuries.

Numerous middle and high schools have introduced programs aimed at reducing disputes, such as peer mediation, conflict resolution training for staff and students, peer counseling, student mentoring, and teen courts. Anything that helps bring kids closer together so they can talk to one another is positive. That's the premise of our youth workshops: help kids get to know one another, respect each other, and learn ways of avoiding and defusing conflict. It's disconcerting to see how volatile some kids are, how little control they have over their impulses, and how rarely they consider peaceful ways of resolving their problems.

Hanover Middle School opened four years ago in an all-White, upper-middle-class area. James Hilton, the principal, is a very creative administrator. At his former school he had authorized the creation of a multicultural leadership course that met every day. With the help of an outstanding teacher, hundreds of students learned about each other's culture and the value of diversity.

The kids played a vital role in maintaining calm one day after a bus carrying Black children was followed by a carload of White men brandishing guns. When the bus arrived at school, the students were panic stricken. The multicultural class went among the students to counsel and console and prevented the spread of rumors that could have led to serious conflict. Jim started a similar class at Hanover and invited us to conduct a youth conference there every year.

The facility was impressive. It had a huge open courtyard with steps forming an outdoor amphitheater. The faculty had been hand picked, and they had introduced some novel programs. Yet there were problems. Kids had been busted for drugs, and the campus was plagued by fights, some with racial overtones.

When we arrived several students were shouting and fists were flying. Two boys ran away and a third was collared by an assistant principal. At the media center sixty students and a few teachers were waiting. Each youth workshop has a theme selected by the student planners. That day's theme was "Let's Keep the Peace."

The media center at Hanover was a rectangular room about thirty yards long and fifteen yards wide that doubled as a library with a few computers, televisions, and VCRs. About thirty circular tables each with four small chairs were spread around the open spaces. The walls and central aisles were filled with bookcases, but the holdings were neither current or extensive. Media centers usually have picture displays of animals and posters of celebrities reminding kids how important it is for them to read.

Media specialists (they don't call them librarians any longer) can be very helpful and friendly, or dour and downright rude, like the one who used to work at Brightwater High School. When we toured that facility, the elderly Mrs. Grimes was aghast to hear we would have fifty students there for a day.

"You can't do that in my center," she said.

"I think you ought to tell that to the principal; he authorized it."

We held the conference a week later, but she never set foot inside until the kids left. Then she told us how to rearrange the tables so that every one was in the exact spot it had been in. She never smiled, not once. She retired at the end of the year. Unfortunately, some of her colleagues are still around, harassing kids with their inflexible fastidiousness.

It's not unusual to find a school's media center virtually empty. At Jackson High School, with over two thousand students, you can count the students there on one hand. The bathrooms are locked, and students have to request a key if they want to use them. At Martin Middle School, the media specialist refuses to allow any food inside. When the cafeteria staff prepared special hot buns for the kids at my workshop, he sat behind the counter and pouted. You could almost see steam coming out of his ears. We didn't know a promise had been made to keep food out, and offered him a bun. Bad move.

But the media specialists at Hanover were very accommodating. They hung mobiles from the ceiling and posters on the walls, and arranged to have the entire workshop videotaped for future use. They worked well with the kids, smiling, eager to please, and flexible about rearranging the furniture.

Jim Hilton greeted everyone and popped in and out as we went through a series of get-acquainted activities. The first hour and a half of our workshop is spent establishing rapport among the kids. That's vital if the ensuing discussions about social issues are to be candid. It's a bit trickier with middle school kids, because they're not as articulate and need to let off energy, so we try to keep them moving as much as possible. The year before at Hanover, four boys were intent on clowning and disrupting the event and were sent back to class. One of the kids, Harold, said he didn't want "to get to know any wild colored kids. They're better off stayin' with themselves and left alone."

Several teachers helped guide the small-group discussions this day. After lunch we got into a circle and began a dialogue. Jim returned and sat down on the floor with us. Two of the girls from the school's multicultural committee began: Rachel wrote down the main points on a flip chart and Konika led the discussion. She asked what main issues concerned them. The kids sat in silence.

"Come on. You gotta help me out," she pleaded. "What's buggin' you about this place?"

"Too much homework," said one boy. He laughed.

"What about our theme for the day?" said Konika. "Keep the peace."

"I saw some kids fighting on my way here this morning. Do you have a problem with fights here?"

"Lots of them," said a boy across the circle.

"Every day," said another.

"Why do people fight?" Konika asked, taking my cue.

"People call each other names."

"Someone pushed somebody."

"Rumors."

"To prove something."

"To get attention."

"'Cause something started at home and they brought it here."

"Somebody stole something of someone else's."

"Racism."

"Bullies pushin' kids around."

"Stickin' up for your friend."

"Gangs."

"Do we have gangs at Hanover?" Konika asked. Jim looked perplexed.

"Not really," said Arthur, "but there are kids who hang out together, and they watch each other's back. Ya know what I mean. If one of 'em gets in trouble, the others come help him out."

"Our theme is keeping the peace," I said. "How can we stop fights?"

Silence. Blank looks. Fifty kids sat there and couldn't come up with one way of decreasing the violence on campus.

"What can you do if someone calls you a name?"

"You gotta say somethin'," replied a boy.

"If you don't, everybody else will think you're a fool," said another.

"So you call him one back and then what?"

"You get to it," said the first boy with a big smile on his face. The other kids laughed.

"It's not funny. Someone could get hurt. And you know it's school policy: fighting gets you a suspension, even if you aren't the aggressor," said Jim.

"If you walk away," said the first boy, "everyone knows you're chicken. They'll keep pickin' on you. Never leave you alone."

"You mean to tell me you've got to fight? Even if you're sure of getting beaten up?" asked Jim.

He smiled and nodded.

"That's right. Just stay there and take it."

"Suppose you were walking home and a bunch of kids were down the block waiting for you. What would you do then?"

"Just keep on walkin'."

"Why wouldn't you turn around and go a different way?"

"They'll get you another time. If they want you, they're gonna get you. You might as well get it over with."

"But that won't be the end, will it?" I asked. "You know things don't always stop there. A kid gets beat up, and he comes back for more another time. And he gets beat up again and maybe again. Then what does he do?"

"He gets his friends to help him," a chorus replied.

"Or his brother; maybe even his father or an uncle. And still it doesn't stop. If you beat someone up today, he may come at you with a weapon. Do you know the three leading causes of death for people your age are suicide, homicide, and accidents? All three can be prevented if you stop and think before you get involved in something. What could you do to avoid that situation?"

Either they were too shy or the message just wasn't getting through. Didn't anyone know ways of avoiding or de-escalating conflict?

"If someone was bothering you—hassling you at school—who could you go to for help?"

"Maybe a teacher," replied a girl.

"Now you're thinking. Who else could you talk to? How about Mr. Hilton?" The kids smiled and looked at him. Everyone knew he was accessible.

"Mr. Hilton is a good guy, but he's busy a lot," said the girl.

"Well, what about one of the assistant principals?"

"I guess you could, if you were really hard up."

"We're always ready to talk with you about such things. You know you can trust us," said Jim.

"Well, you've got to go to someone. How about your parents?"

"Why would you want to go to them?" said a tall girl.

"Because they care about you and just might be able to help." Obviously, she didn't agree.

"What about the SRO [school resource officer/policeman on campus]?"

"Cheryl and I went to see him last year about a kid who was harassing us, and he didn't do nothin'," a thin Black girl exclaimed.

"What was the problem?"

"There was a kid who kept calling us names—racial stuff. He even spit on me and threatened to beat us up. We went to Mr. Hale [the SRO], and told him but nothin' happened."

"That's not exactly right," Jim jumped in. "Our system has rules and a process for such things. Unless it's something life-threatening that's got to be taken care of immediately, everyone has to have what we call 'due process.' I know the situation you're talking about because Mr. Hale and I discussed it. We documented all the complaints about the boy you're talking about, and when we built up a case we took action. Harold isn't in school anymore, is he?" The girls nodded. "So you see, we do care about you, so please come to us for help."

Giving the kids the chance to interact with faculty and staff in situations like this helps break down barriers and decreases stereotypes about adults. It also helps kids articulate issues and find ways of resolving disputes. We can't afford to let schools be perceived as hostile, bureaucratic institutions with uncaring staff. Yet relatively few teachers or administrators set aside time for discussions with students.

It's not often that teachers join our workshops, even though they're invited. When they do, they frequently try to control the discussions, assuming kids are incapable of having opinions and conducting meaningful conversations without adult supervision. This isn't surprising because many didn't have such opportunities themselves. Others lack rudimentary facilitation and conversational skills, while even more are preoccupied with rigid curriculum deadlines, complaining about being compelled to focus on the standardized testing mandated by NCLB. Worse still, some teachers don't trust or even fear the dialogic process—afraid that emotions may show or get out of hand, as if they aren't already seething beneath the surface.

At a daylong workshop for twenty teachers at Clements High School, two hours into a discussion about issues of concern to students, a forty-year-old man blurted, "What does any of this have to do with me or my students? I teach advance placement physics. All my kids are going to college."

"I suppose none of your students have other courses or lives outside of your class? Or sex lives? Or issues with drugs or alcohol? Or problems with their parents or boys and girls?"

He was speechless. Six months later, after we initiated a schoolwide system of student-led dialogues, he asked me for a job.

We had been planning a workshop for seventy students from six middle schools for six months. Working with that many kids of this age can be exasperating. Getting them to sit still for a few minutes is like trying to put a glove on a jellyfish: raging hormones and constant motion. But these kids had been selected as leaders from their schools' multicultural committees.

The conference was postponed twice, but it looked as if it was finally going to happen. The kids were to arrive at the training facility by 8:30 A.M. We'd put them through some icebreakers, see a video, settle them in small groups, and let them discuss prejudice and discrimination they had experienced.

It was 8:30 and only one school had arrived. We were posting signs about diversity around the room and putting supplies on the tables. Usually the kids sit on the floor in a circle, but there was no place to stack the tables so we were stuck with a more impersonal layout. After a few more schools arrived the kids filled in "culturegrams"—charts that ask students their names, place of birth, ethnicity, favorite food and music, heroes, and career plans—laid out on the floor.

The group was very diverse. Three kids came from Albania and one was a Muslim. There were Asians, a Bosnian, Latinos, and African Americans. It was a great group to work with. They were calm and attentive. We waited another fifteen minutes for students from the sixth school to arrive—they never did, nor did they call to tell us they wouldn't be coming.

The first game was Hello Bingo. Every child got a sheet of paper with twenty-five boxes, each containing a statement about some characteristic or ability possessed by students in the room, for example, likes Vietnamese food, has lived in another country, is ambidextrous, can count to ten in three languages. They must circulate and find someone who can sign a box that pertains to him- or herself. Some of the boxes are harder to complete, for instance, celebrates Passover, Kwanzaa, Ramadan. It's a great mixer after the kids figure out they can't complete it by asking only their friends.

After we have a few winners we go over the answers to see if everyone knows what the holidays are. We usually have to explain Kwanzaa—few Black kids celebrate it or know that it represents an attempt to reestablish roots and develop traditions that extol the values and virtues of an African culture denied their ancestors.

Students often know what Passover is. Some proudly claim it as a Christian holiday. We explain it originated 1,250 years before Jesus was born, but acknowledge that the "Last Supper" may have been a Seder commemorating the exodus of Jews from Egypt. We refresh their memory by referring to Charlton Heston in *The Ten Commandments* and the cartoon feature *The Prince of Egypt.*

Even fewer know that Ramadan is an Islamic holiday of rededication to the faith, observed by over a billion people around the world. It involves fasting for thirty days during daylight hours. The kids that day couldn't comprehend how anyone could do it. We asked if anyone observed Ramadan. Silence.

"I thought we have a student who does. Didn't someone put down Muslim as his religion?"

"That's me," a boy acknowledged.

"Where are you from?"

"Albania."

"Would you tell us about Ramadan?"

"That's the time we sacrifice a small animal and use the blood . . ."

"Sorry I asked," I said.

"He takes it very seriously," admonished his teacher.

"Don't you fast during Ramadan?"

"Yes, for thirty days, and so does the whole country."

"It takes a lot of dedication and commitment, and that's what the holiday's all about. Muslims can't even drink water during the day. Name a famous basketball player who is Muslim."

A young Black student raises his hand and smiles. "Kareem Abdul-Jabbar."

"No! He ain't in there anymore," says another youth. "Hakim Olajuwon."

"You're both right. When the Rockets were playing the Bulls, Olajuwon got a triple double—more than ten points, ten assists, and ten rebounds—against Michael Jordan, and he didn't even have a drink of water during the game."

We moved on to other things: a snack, a video, and a discussion of stereotypes. After lunch came another video about prejudice, Jane Elliot's

*Eye of the Storm*, in which third-graders are segregated based on eye color. It never fails to enthrall young and old alike because they see how easy it is to be cruel, and how we inflict pain when we don't think about the consequences of our actions.

The kids were great, and the place was reasonably clean. It was a good session. Heading for home fifty miles to the north, I drove toward one of the worst human tragedies in the history of our region that had been unfolding all day. While helping seventy children learn how to get along with one another, teaching them to value their differences and reach out to share in peace and understanding, a four-year-old boy had been shot by his mother's boyfriend. The man took him to a fire station in search of emergency help, alleging it had been an accident. The child died. Some of the paramedics were so upset by what they saw they needed counseling.

Two detectives questioned the man. Doubting his story, they took him to the police station. They didn't know his true identity or that he had a history of violence. Nor did they know that he had a key to the handcuffs, which he unlocked. He grabbed one of the detective's guns, murdered them both, and fled in a hijacked truck. On the way he murdered a young highway patrolman who had been on the force less than a year. When the tires on his truck were shot out, he took refuge in a gas station and held a woman hostage. Later that evening he took his own life. As the story unfolded we wondered what those children would think when they got home and heard the news.

For some children, schoolwork is not a priority, food and shelter are. That point was brought home to me at J.T. Hartwell, a special education school for middle and high school students. Most of the three hundred students there were suspended or expelled from regular schools because of behavior problems. They couldn't get along with other students or their teachers. Many of them have anger management problems and may strike out at students or staff.

The school resource officer at Hartwell is always busy breaking up fights, escorting kids home, surveying the campus, and making court appearances. A number of kids have committed felonies, ranging from theft to aggravated assault. Tension runs high at such schools because things can get rough. Yet Denise Fagan, Hartwell's affable middle-aged principal, and most of her staff try to make a positive difference in the children's lives. They buy supplies and snacks and bend the rules if necessary to keep them from being sent to jail or juvenile detention centers.

But some rules can't be compromised without jeopardizing the safety of the other students and staff. For example, when teachers complained that students refused to enter their classrooms, Denise established zones on campus to regulate movement to and from class and avoid loitering. A couple of areas were declared off-limits. One morning Denise found a fifteen-year-old boy in a forbidden area.

"What's the matter with you?" she asked. "You know you can't hang around here. I could suspend you for it."

"Please don't," pleaded the boy. "I promise I won't come back."

"I've heard that before, but I guess I can overlook it this once. Just don't let me catch you here again."

"Sure. You have my word."

"About two hours later I saw him there as if nothing had happened," she told me. "That's it," I said to him. "You're suspended for three days! I'm going to have the SRO take you home. Come along to my office."

"He's a big kid, but he started to cry and begged me not to suspend him; he didn't have any place to go. He'd been living with friends or under bridges."

One of our weeklong residential multicultural Anytown camps had a particularly difficult group of kids. Some were unruly and restless; others were withdrawn, bordering on depression. The teenagers came from different schools and represented a wide range of social and economic backgrounds.

Kids often arrive at Anytown without knowing any of the other fifty students. After a couple of days most overcome their shyness, come out of their self-imposed isolation, and immerse themselves in workshops on stereotypes, racism, community affairs, school, family, and friends. But many of these kids would not participate.

One of the most significant workshops at Anytown is conducted on the evening of the third day and involves gender issues and dating abuse. Our staff had discussed the detached behavior of some of the delegates on several occasions and we were prepared for problems — at least we thought we were. Emotions began to surface as soon as we started. A representative from a local spouse abuse shelter helped with the discussion. Hands shot up as kids around the meeting hall wanted to share their experiences and pain. Even some of the withdrawn kids became animated.

"What can you do when your best friend's boyfriend hits her?" asked a girl.

"I've got a friend whose dad beats her mom and I don't know what to do about it," said another.

"I thought about running away from my boyfriend after he hit me, but I was afraid he'd hurt me more. What should I do?" asked a teenager plaintively.

The workshop usually lasts for two hours, but it was more like three before our guest left. Many kids were visibly disturbed, so two school social workers and a school psychologist invited anyone who wanted to discuss the issues further to join them in the chapel. About half an hour later I walked across the campus to see how they were doing. Stretched across the front row of the tiny chapel were eleven kids from diverse backgrounds. The leaders were allowing each teenager to discuss personal problems. I sat at the rear and listened as one after another disclosed tragedies stemming from the death of loved ones to abuse and neglect from parents and friends.

"My momma works and doesn't have any time for me or my two little sisters," said a beautiful Black girl. "I have to cook and do all the cleaning. When she comes home she expects me to have dinner ready for her, even if it's two in the morning. And if she doesn't like the way I clean the house she beats me. She came home the other night and screamed at me for not cleaning the kitchen. Then she grabbed my hair and dragged me across the floor. She beat me all over and said I was good for nothin'."

"My father has a drinking problem," said a White girl. "He's got a good job, and nobody there knows it, but when he comes home sometimes he's awful to my mother. You should hear them yelling at each other. And he hits her, too. I want to help, but I don't know how."

Everyone had spoken but Victor, a White, middle-class youth. His behavior during the week had been somewhat erratic, as if he was tuning us in and out. Something was bothering him. Maybe it was good for him to know what other less fortunate kids had to cope with.

"Would you like to share anything with us, Victor?" asked one of the social workers.

"Uh, I'm not sure." He squirmed.

"That's all right. You don't have to say anything if you don't want to."

"Well, about two weeks ago I had a fight with my best friend. We went at it all day. He cussed me out. I called him everything I could think of. I said I didn't want to be his friend anymore, that I never wanted to talk to him again.

"I went to school the next day still mad, but I didn't see him. When I came home my father showed me the paper—he had hanged himself." Victor began to sob as a counselor ran over and hugged him.

"The day before I came here," he continued, "I was out walking and his brother rode up on his bike. 'You killed my brother!'"

"It's all right. You're with friends here," she comforted him. "You're not responsible for his death. It's okay if you cry, for all of us to cry. This is a safe place. You need to talk about these things so we can help heal and move on."

It was a very long night. Disclosures about personal lives and problems are common at Anytown and during school workshops. Each year the number of heartrending and hair-raising stories increases. During an activity on sexual harassment it's not unusual for many girls to weep openly and disclose that they're in abusive relationships with boys or having similar problems at home. Incidents of rape and abuse are frequently divulged, many having occurred when the girls were under ten years old.

"My stepfather beats my mother," a young African American boy once confessed. "I asked him to stop but he wouldn't, so I punched him. He threw me to the floor and held a gun to my head and said if I ever touched him again he'd kill me."

"I had an abortion just weeks before I came here," a sixteen-year-old cried. "My mother always tells me that I'll never amount to anything. Now she says that I've proved she's right." A thirteen-year-old sat down and gave her a big hug as they cried together. She'd had an abortion three months earlier.

Whatever happened to fun and games? To childhood? It's amazing how much baggage some kids carry around. Most teenagers are egocentric and think the world revolves around them—that their problems are unique and monumental. After all, they are only kids and have not developed a long-range perspective or the wisdom to cope with their problems. When they share experiences, they realize that they are not alone. And when caring adults are present they can be referred for professional help. Unfortunately, too few parents and teachers are consulted or allow kids to discuss such issues. When they do, the results can be gratifying.

At a high school dialogue with sixty-five students, several girls tearfully related negative experiences they had with boys.

"You don't understand!" sobbed one of the girls. "No one understands. And there's no one I can talk to—not even my friends." Yet they shared and learned from one another. And the principal, who had been sitting in, demonstrated that he cared, too. Three weeks later they had developed programs for reducing the conflict in their school and community.

There is far too little dialogue about race relations in the United States. Despite the recommendation of Clinton's commission on race relations, One America, that we need to have candid conversations about racism and its effects on our society, and the gallant efforts of groups like the Study Circles Resources Center to foster discussions on this topic, most adults have never engaged people from different ethnic backgrounds in such discussions. The paucity of experience, combined with the fear that one might be labeled (or attacked) for being insensitive or racist for comments made during such discussions, has prevented many Whites from participating in race relations dialogues.

The reluctance to engage the other in reasoned discourse is also widespread among high school students, even in integrated schools. Given the self-segregated nature of social relationships within our schools; the focus on teaching to standardized tests that has reduced time for classroom dialogue; the tracking of students by ethnicity into separate educational programs, for example, gifted, honors, and advanced placement, where few Blacks and Latinos are found; and the fear of being misinterpreted by saying something that is politically incorrect, small wonder that students feel uneasy about discussing racially charged issues. This condition nearly caused a catastrophe at Hollyhills High School.

It was spring, a time of growth and change. The blossoms on the shrubs and flowers around Hollyhills High School were vibrant yellow, red, and orange. The school, built twenty years ago, is located on the fringe of the downtown area of a large city in central Florida. Its two thousand students are a mix of Whites, Blacks, Latinos, and Asians. The community is naturally integrated and the student body reflects this.

While race relations at the school over the years had been rocky at times, in recent years Hollyhills had been calm, with a dedicated faculty assisting students in a variety of multicultural activities. But spring in schools across the nation can be a time of anxiety over final exams and fear about being promoted or retained. It is not surprising to find inter-personal problems surfacing among students and staff at this time of year as tempers grow short under the strain of wrapping up another year and facing the unknown beyond high school.

It is no coincidence that many school shootings have occurred at this time, and beleaguered administrators who are struggling with their own year-end issues often dread the "short time" spring syndrome that can lead to major disruptions on their campus.

I was in my car when a call came in from a frantic school adminis-trator with the message to be at Hollyhills High School the next day at 7:00 A.M.—"and bring some of your staff." I learned that the situation was very tense because a White male student had written an article for the school newspaper that angered Black students. In it he castigated his peers for being lazy, slovenly, complacent, and materialistic: "All you care about is yourselves. Stop being followers and learn to spit in the face of authority! Care more about your hygiene and wear deodor-ant. People who use rollers on their book bags should be teased for be-ing nerds. And there are too many fights around here. People run to see them when they should be going the other way. Next time there's a fight, don't stand around watching like a bunch of monkeys!" Unfortu-nately, this last sentence appeared as a caption under an accompanying photograph of African American males at the school.

The next morning two members of my staff—Latasha, a twenty-seven-year-old African American woman who had graduated from Hollyhills, and Bradley, a twenty-eight-year-old African American man whose sister attended the school—joined me in the principal's office. Accompanying us were a senior school district administrator and the teacher responsible for organizing the school's multicultural activities. Robert Drake, the prin-cipal, was around fifty and was fighting to maintain the impression that he wasn't going bald by letting the shock of grayish brown hair on the left side of his head grow and combing it across the sparsely covered top. He had been at Hollyhills for less than a year, after serving as principal at a large, racially diverse middle school that had a distinguished record of multicultural activities. But running a high school is another world, and Bob Drake was learning that.

"What happened to the boy that wrote this piece?" asked Mary Pines, the school administrator.

"He's waiting outside. I haven't decided what to do with him yet," replied Bob, who was poring over a carefully worded apology written for him by his boss, an assistant area superintendent.

"What are you going to do with that?" demanded Mary.

"If it's all right with you, I'm going to read it on our morning television show in a few minutes."

"That would be good," said Mary, "but we still have to decide how we're going to handle this thing and what we're going to do with the kid who wrote that piece . . . what's his name?"

"Stanley."

"Yes, Stanley. Was that him sitting in your office?"

"Yes. His mother doesn't want him to go on TV. She's afraid it will bring too much attention to him. She's afraid for his safety."

"Well, that doesn't surprise me in the least after what he did. You said you had him escorted home yesterday after the paper was circulated?"

"You bet I did," replied Bob. "I wasn't going to take any chances. There are a lot of angry Black kids out there. I think he should make some kind of apology to the school."

"Well, I'm not sure that he meant it as a racial slur," I interjected.

"That doesn't matter," said Mary. "The fact is, that's the way it was taken and now we've got to do something about it. Why don't you bring Stanley in and let's hear from him."

Bob left the room and Mary turned to me from the other end of the conference table where she was sitting.

"I'd really like to hear what the kid has to say, but that picture and caption are pretty damning. Perhaps he should go on the air and apologize," I said.

"We can't put him in a spot like that," said Mary. "It's not fair to him. He's got to sort this out in his own mind and take appropriate action, but I am concerned for his safety."

Bob returned with a six-foot-tall youth with curly black hair. He had on a black T-shirt and jeans. "This is Stanley Dunn, everyone."

"Hello, Stanley. I'm Mary Pines from the school district, and these other people will identify themselves."

After introductions Mary asked Stanley about the article. "What were you thinking when you wrote this piece?"

Stanley sat at the head of the table looking self-confident, not the least remorseful. "I never intended it to be racist. I was trying to shake the students up, that's all. It was not directed at any group in particular."

"What about the picture?" I asked.

"I never saw the picture until the paper came out. I had nothing to do with the selection of the picture."

"That's right," affirmed Bob. "Somehow the whole thing got by the paper's adviser, Ms. Simms. This was her first year here. When I heard about it I had all one thousand copies of the paper confiscated and the staff and I sat down and whited-out that sentence under the picture."

"The problem was," said Stanley stoically, "you could see right through the whiteout they used. It was like an arrow drawing them to that line."

We spoke with Stanley for another fifteen minutes and learned more facts about the situation before we decided, with his consent, to arrange a meeting with the students who were upset about the article. Bob recorded his prepared apology, which was broadcast over the closed-circuit TV, and he invited concerned students to participate in a dialogue that we would facilitate. Stanley was concerned about the impact the article had on students, but maintained that it was not meant to be racist. We gave him a chance to explain himself in the dialogue.

We adjourned to a room adjacent to the cafeteria where Bob had the chairs arranged in a circle with snacks placed on a nearby table.

"We're expecting about fifteen students. That's how many came down yesterday to my office to file complaints about the article. There may be a few others that straggle in after my statement and I'll have them brought here."

Within fifteen minutes the group arrived. We sat in a circle and introduced ourselves. There were eighteen students, my two staff who ran the dialogue, two African American teachers who had been Anytown advisers, Mary Pines, the multicultural teacher/adviser, and Bob Drake.

Only Stanley and a large young student with his hair pulled back and cropped along the sides were White. The rest of the students were African American, and they did not look happy. Stanley sat three chairs down to my right. On his left was a tall African American young man. On his right was another tall African American young man, and on his right was the large White student. The rest of the group was divided evenly between young men and women, mostly upperclassmen with a few freshmen and sophomores.

"Now we're gonna have a dialogue about what happened here yesterday with respect to this article," said Bradley, who sat to my left. Alongside him was Latasha. "But first we've got to have some ground rules for how we're going to behave. What rules would you all like to have?"

"Show respect."

"Be honest."

"You can't use any offensive words."

"No side talk. Just one person talks at a time."

"Is that it?" asked Bradley. "Any more? If not, then let's get on with it. OK? I'd like to know why you people are here?"

"Why are we here?" repeated Simon. "We're here because of that racist article and picture that came out in the school paper yesterday. The article he wrote. I want you to know that it greatly offended me," he said looking across the circle at Stanley who sat with his arms crossed in front of his chest.

Before Stanley could respond Marta, a well-dressed African American student broke in: "I want you all to know that I'm on the school paper and I know Stanley. He's not a racist. Far from it. I've never heard him make a racist remark. I don't feel that he's being treated fairly here." And then looking at Stanley, "But you should have been more judicious in your choice of words in the article. You should have known that all different types of students were going to read it and interpret it in different ways. You have to be more sensitive to your audience."

Stanley looked on plaintively and replied, "I'm sorry if my article offended anyone. I never meant it that way. I'm not a racist. I was just trying to shake people up. I never saw that picture until it came out. I wrote that article last November. The school paper was supposed to come out every six weeks. I used to be the editor, but they were so incompetent that I quit. I forgot all about that piece until yesterday."

"Yeah!" huffed Damian, the tall African American student to Stanley's left. "I don't believe you!"

"What's wrong with you?" asked Mark, the large White student on the other side of Stanley. "He already told you he apologized and he was sorry for the article. I know Stanley and he's not a racist. I know what some of you go through. My grandmother is Black and I've been called all kinds of names. That's not right and I know Stanley would never do something like that."

"Man, you coulda fooled me," said Damian, disparagingly. "I look at you and I see a big White boy. Ain't no one gonna take you for bein' Black. How can you say you know what it's like bein' Black?"

"I know because I've been called a nigger! I've had to put up with it."

"Look here," said JT, a well-built African American student sitting across from Stanley. "I work with Stanley every day on the television show here and I know he's not a racist. I didn't know him at the beginning of the year, but after working with him every day I know where the dude's at and he's not a racist. We have fun and kid around and I've never heard him say a racist thing. Just the opposite. He wants to put an end to those kinds of things and I think you all should take him at his word."

"Well, I don't believe him," said Damian, never looking up from his gaze at the floor. "I don't believe his story and I don't think his apology is serious. And I think he should suffer the consequences. I mean . . . I don't think you should be allowed to go to school here anymore."

"What you mean that you never saw that picture until it came out?" demanded Adrian. "You knew damn well what picture they were goin' to put there! That's a pile of lies."

Mark jumped to his feet. "I'm not goin' to listen to this anymore!"

"Sit down," said Latasha and Bradley simultaneously. Bradley continued, "They didn't like to hear what you had to say but they listened to you and now you have to do the same. Now sit back down and listen." Mark returned to his seat.

The tall African American young man on the other side of Stanley now weighed in.

"Look here, brother," he said to Damian. "The man said he was sorry. I know him, too, and I like him. He's not a racist. He meant what he said. What's wrong with you? Don't you know when a guy's telling you like it is. What's the matter with you?"

I had a bad feeling about the way things were going. Then Theo, a small, studious-looking African American, cut in: "I don't know why you're getting so upset, Damian. I believe Stanley. I don't think the article was racist, but I think it was a piece of crap! I don't know why you wrote it, but I know you could have done a lot better. That's what bothers me about this whole journalism program here [and looking at the principal]—it's a lousy program. It's so disorganized that I don't even take any courses in it. I'm a writer but I'm going to wait till I get to college to take journalism courses because this program's a waste of time."

Then looking at Stanley, "Why did you write a piece of crap like that? You could do a lot better. It looks like you did it to fill space."

Stanley smiled. "That's exactly what I did. I wrote it in November to get credit for an English course, and then I forgot about it."

Theresa, a professionally dressed African American student, spoke up. "It would have been forgotten if the staff hadn't put that picture there and Ms. Simms hadn't asked students to blacken out the caption in her office before they released it."

One of the teachers asked why the article and picture hadn't been pulled earlier, since that was the adviser's responsibility. Bob replied lamely, "She must have missed it."

"Well, I'm still not satisfied with your answers," said Damian, still looking at the floor. "This whole thing bothers me a lot."

Michelle Weaver, a young African American teacher, looked at Stanley and spoke: "I have to agree with Damian. This whole time you've been sitting there with your arms folded across your chest and a smirk on your face. And you want us to believe you when your body language sends us the message that you think this is a big joke?"

Stanley immediately shifted in his chair, put his hands on his knees, and changed his expression.

Bradley interjected, "Body language is a funny thing. We don't always mean to convey certain messages by the way we look so we have to be careful about how we interpret others' body language."

Theresa added, "I think Stanley wrote that article to shake people up. I believe him, but Stanley, you have to keep your audience in mind when you write things. I don't believe in censoring things, but not everyone understands what you were trying to do." Then, looking around the circle, "I don't know what it takes to get you to believe him. I believe him. You people call yourselves Christians. What kind of Christians are you? He said he was sorry. What does he have to do to make you forgive him?"

Her remarks cast a pall over the room. Damian looked up and turned to Stanley.

"Well . . . I forgive you. I believe you now, but there were a lot of brothers out there yesterday that wanted to mess you up. That's why I went to Mr. Drake's office and told him to send you home."

Latasha addressed the group: "Now it's up to all of you to send the message that it wasn't an intentionally racist thing to the other students. Please tell them that Stanley has apologized and appropriate action will be taken shortly."

The group agreed to meet in two weeks to discuss the effects of the meeting and the underlying racial climate at the school. When they reassembled there was none of the acrimony that characterized the first meeting. There was lighthearted banter among the twelve students and some discussion of the upcoming graduation. To all outward appearances the initial crisis had been defused, but a few days later an incident in the community threatened to undo our work.

Eight years before, in this neighborhood, an eighteen-year-old African American youth was shot and killed by a city policeman when he attempted to run over the officer. This sparked rioting in the African American community leading to numerous arrests and the destruction of homes and businesses. After the policeman was acquitted of wrongdoing, another night of violence ensued. Scars from these incidents remained and were now aggravated by a civil trial of the policeman brought by relatives of the slain youth.

Exacerbating the situation was the recent shooting of another Black youth in the neighborhood. When a student linked to a militant Black community organization attempted to distribute flyers at Hollyhills High School condemning the police action, she was suspended. The school administration contended that they asked her not to hand out flyers but she disobeyed the request.

Following her suspension, another flyer surfaced on campus denouncing the principal, Bob Drake, as a racist, and castigating him for not suspending the author of the school newspaper article that alluded to Blacks as monkeys. The flyer pointed up an alleged double standard in freedom of speech at the school—one for Whites and another for Blacks: "Well guess what, Drake—Black people do have rights. One of those rights is to call out your racist and unacceptable behavior. We will remember Marquell because it was racist cops like you that took him away from us. Furthermore, we will defend any and all students that take a stand for what's right."

When the jury delivered an innocent verdict exonerating the policeman and declined to award damages to the family of the youth slain eight years before, there was a night of civil disturbances. Rocks and bottles were thrown at cars. A few people were injured and several houses burned. Approximately twenty people were arrested, but there were no problems at Hollyhills. I applauded the students and their parents for their restraint when I addressed them at their graduation two weeks later.

Schools are not responsible for all the social problems that afflict our society, and teachers cannot become social workers and counselors. But educators must recognize the extent and gravity of the problems our children confront, and that it is impossible to separate or compartmentalize issues such as hunger, shelter, abuse, and prejudice from other facets of their lives—including education. To the extent that children must contend with these issues, they will be more or less ready to assimilate the information they are scheduled to learn.

Rigid approaches that prioritize testing and the attainment of specific skills by stipulated dates are, by necessity, eclipsed and preempted by the harsh realities of survival. At the end of a workshop for administrators about the importance of introducing human relations concepts in schools, a middle-aged gentleman politely pointed out, "You're right that we shouldn't forget these kinds of things, but I've found that for many kids getting their next meal or a place to sleep for the night is their first priority." Such realities take precedence over how to conjugate verbs or solve algebraic equations. Certainly, schools can't be all things to all students, but they can be safe places where kids are respected, acknowledged, and valued—even if they aren't at home.

# 3

## Stereotypes: Nobody's Born a Bigot

The imaginations people have of one another are the solid facts of society.

—Charles Horton Cooley, sociologist

Imagine living in the world of adolescents today. It's a place filled with sensations and temptations that promises, and often delivers on, instant gratification. Activities that were forbidden or only dreamed of in the past are heralded in their pop culture through music, videos, movies, and television. And while children are physically maturing earlier, their emotional maturation lags behind. Still, they are frequently capable of far more than we assume, having the capacity for leadership and to engage in community action. At the same time, their impressionable, growing minds take cues from the media and significant others at home and in school, which can impede logic and rational behavior. It is vital to have good adult role models to instill positive values to block the proliferation of stereotypes that demean so many and pit one against another.

This chapter focuses on the most contentious issues in school: gender, sexual harassment, race and ethnic relations, sexual orientation, bullying, and gossip. Stereotypes pertaining to these issues are rampant in society and schools, where they find expression through the cliques and social pecking order that permeate all levels of our educational system, making the lives of many students miserable.

There is an insidious side to stereotypes. While they may be derived from factual incidents, generalizations based on them are untrue. The mind, in its attempt to process and simplify information, is susceptible to stereotypical thinking, which lumps people into neat categories to facilitate predictions. From the time we are able to comprehend our environment, we are bombarded with cues that reinforce and perpetuate stereotypes. The pernicious characteristic about them is that social pressure and conformity to group norms leads us to continue using them—even when we know they are untrue.

Research has long shown the pervasive influence of stereotypes on marginalized groups. Paradoxically, stereotyped groups often accept the designation ascribed to them—even when it's unflattering and impedes their academic success (Clark & Clark 1950; Steele 1999). Adults also buy into these misperceptions. During a break at a teacher workshop a middle-aged African American teacher related the following story: "I hate to fly. It's always a bad trip for me. I took this trip recently to the Midwest. I was very nervous, fidgeting the whole time in my seat. We had a stopover at another city and they changed crews. I saw a Black pilot get on and it really set me off. I was terrified. After we landed I got mad at myself and this society that made me feel that way."

Stereotypes are ubiquitous in school, with kids being labeled for virtually everything from their body shape and size to clothes, skin color, religion, social class, and sexual orientation. Children need to learn that stereotypes are false representations of reality, but this is often complicated by the fact that many teachers labor under the same misperceptions. And since children and adolescents often lack the maturity to deflect stereotypical insults, they may lash out verbally or physically at their tormentors, escalating the conflict.

Saving face among one's peers is also an impediment to rational action. Having heart and not being chicken all too often leads to suspensions and expulsions. That is why it is so important to teach children about their culture and help them realize how unique and important everyone is—to create a respectful community in the classroom and on campus. For example, the teacher who is afraid of flying and lacks confidence in the ability of African Americans to master aviation might study and teach about the Tuskegee Airmen and their outstanding record during World War II. Knowing that you are a decent, competent person helps diminish the power of stereotypes.

The following exercises raise children's self-esteem by helping them learn more about their ethnic/cultural groups and create mutual respect. The trick is to get children to behave beyond their chronological age. This can be accomplished by creating an environment that prioritizes self-respect and respect for others. Establishing such norms helps counteract the negative dehumanizing and stultifying environments of overcrowded classrooms and buildings, which feed into portrayals of students as dehumanized stereotypical units.

Allowing students to learn about and share their cultures and discuss critical issues of mutual interest and concern debunks stereotypes and infuses awareness of humanity and emotions into an otherwise sterile bureaucratic environment. Students begin to realize that the outsiders being ridiculed have likes and dislikes similar to their own. They have feelings and wants, and desire to be treated with dignity and respect. We can create such caring communities in our schools if we model this behavior and establish boundaries and rules that reinforce positive images of self and others—even when these are not being reinforced at home. When we expect a higher level of emotional maturity from our children and create an environment conducive to it, they respond to our expectations.

One can introduce students to the topic of stereotypes with a humorous video like *Cultural Baggage*, about a mythical baggage claim area at an airport where passengers searching for their luggage assume the dialect, ethnicity, and purported behavior of the bag they touch. Another good video is *The Lunch Date*, which places an affluent elderly White woman in a booth with a poor Black man in the cafeteria at Penn Station.

After seeing and discussing the video students get into groups of six to eight and list stereotypes about teachers. It starts out humorously, as middle and high school students take revenge on their erstwhile tormentors. Below are typical responses gathered from the exercise:

| | | |
|---|---|---|
| mean | strict | ugly |
| fat | boring | talk too much |
| favoritism | move on girls/boys | prejudiced |
| don't know how to dress | dumb | attitude problem |
| old | child molesters | ugly feet |
| gay | try to be funny | they don't try to |
| only think about | grouchy | recognize |
| themselves | annoying | what Black students |
| mental problems | get on your case | achieve |

try to fit in with younger
   people
give detention for no
   reason
base your grade on your
   siblings
boring
have teacher's pets
blame people for their
   problems
don't realize when
   they're wrong
think they're always right
Whites are more
   intelligent than Blacks
   (in their eyes)
discriminate against each
   other (cliques)
try to take away your
   personality by telling
   you how to act and
   what to wear
considerate
fun
lies
cranky
administrators are racists
   against Blacks and
   Hispanics
all teachers think Asian
   kids are smart and
   well-behaved
overworked and
   underpaid
smart alecks
petty
careless
too strict (enforce things
   that aren't important)
corrupt

think they are superior
make fun of students
stereotype people (races)
sexist (think boys are
   troublemakers)
don't care about students
give lots of homework
always tired
flirt with each other
all White teachers are
   prejudiced
most guy teachers are
   perverted
they assume Blacks
   cause trouble, don't
   follow rules
rude
act retarded
hate kids
throw books at students
bad and unacceptable
   language
slower than students
too high expectancy
deaf
hate kids
teachers watch us like
   we're babies
pedophile
child molesters
perverts
homosexuals
gossips
nosy
anal retentive
no encouragement
intolerant
lesbians
can't teach subject
psycho

challenge you
pick out one person to
   intimidate
brag
weird
overdramatic
hate their job
don't listen to students'
   ideas
all White teachers are
   mean
all White administrators
   are harder on Black
   people
antisocial with students
dorky (living in the '80s)
complain about their pay
don't let you express
   yourself
bad role models
well-preserved
meathead
tells insane stories
too cheery
mood swings
have no life
talk about students
   behind their backs
smelly
drug addicts
caring
dedicated and motivating
drunk
two-faced
hypocrites
lazy
jealous
male teachers favor girls
act like our parents
out to fail us

| | | |
|---|---|---|
| coaches are sexist | smoke too much | some are too easy |
| bitchy | attitude | bad |
| they're here for the | can't admit when | dykes |
| money, not to teach | they're wrong | understanding |
| egotistical | abusive | nice |
| smoke weed | disorganized | cool |
| burned out | smart | bad breath |
| tacky (somebody needs | bitter | |
| to take them | | |
| shopping) | | |

While the kids obviously relish poking fun at their teachers, some ideas occur with disturbing regularity. They were not listed here for their shock value—but because they, or responses like them, appear *every time we do this activity*. While the overwhelming tenor of the remarks is negative, a few positive notes occasionally surface as students recognize and appreciate their teachers as caring, helpful, and nice. But we can't overlook the frequency of words that reflect deep racial and ethnic divisions—racist, prejudiced, stereotypes. Nor can we ignore the children's perceptions that they are perhaps being treated differently by teachers and administrators based upon their race and ethnicity: Blacks disciplined differently and more often; Blacks causing trouble; White teachers are prejudiced.

Along with feelings of unequal treatment among children of color are comments like "they are rude," "bad tempered," "mean," and beliefs that many teachers don't care about them. Sometimes kids' naïveté comes through in the occasional jibe that "teachers are just in it for the money," but we can't take much solace in their oft-stated belief that many teachers are lazy or burned out.

Another disconcerting set of responses centers around frequent mention of alcohol and drug abuse among teachers. How accurate these perceptions are may be debatable, but they reveal disdain and contempt for people who are ostensibly functioning as adult role models. It points up an important area for image improvement.

Even more disturbing are the references to unwanted sexual activity on the part of teachers. Again, while the accuracy and interpretation of that behavior as perceived by students may be challenged, the subject cries out for more careful scrutiny. It certainly points up the need for specialized in-service staff training and more conscientious attention to this issue.

After they have a chance to vent, we turn the tables and ask students to list the stereotypes they think their teachers have about them:

stupid
disrespectful
sluts
slobs
obnoxious
smell
too revealing
jocks are stupid
not trustworthy
unattractive
sexist
pain in the neck
self-centered
dropouts
wild
no work ethic
we're animals
delinquents
honest
Black students are rude
spoiled little rich kids
blow their minds on
   weekends
think we're always
   wrong
cheerleaders are dumb
   whores
generation X
good kids
only go to the bathroom
   to smoke
wearing black means
   you're a devil
   worshiper
all couples sleep together

weird
no desire to learn
slackers
rude
uncontrolled
sarcastic
drunks
kind-hearted
gangsters
satanic
liars
lazy
violent
no morals
no future
no control
bad upbringing
ignorant
dishonest
sex-crazed
honor students can
   be trusted
Whites are smartest
girls are smarter and
   better students
know-it-alls
cheaters
thugs
minorities are not
   capable of being in
   honors programs
wearing gold means you
   stole it or are a drug
   dealer

unattentive
drug users
scary
clueless
immature
vulgar
smart
trustworthy
attractive
racist
gossip
sexually active
druggies
stupid
unclean
low values and morals
hell-raisers
irresponsible
mature
baggy pants equals
   being in a gang
failing means not trying
quiet people are either
   dumb or make the
   best grades
immature
no manners
no goals
all have personal
   problems
all Black males sell drugs
Black kids who drive
   nice cars are drug
   dealers

This only a partial list, but the most obvious conclusion is students believe teachers view them negatively. It's hardly surprising, since many of the messages adults and the media send about teenagers reflect such images. As one teenage group wrote, "They always think the worst of us."

Once again racist feelings emerge, particularly directed toward Black males, who, some students believe, represent a threat to teachers. While some positive statements were interspersed in their teacher lists—for example, "good students"—they are rare, and one wonders whether the exercise is itself responsible for evoking negativity. It probably plays a part in the tone of their responses, but the frequency of such comments deserves consideration.

During workshops with teachers, none of their lists ever contain prejudiced or racist stereotypical attitudes about students, or a preponderance of negative stereotypes about them. Students and teachers obviously live in different worlds, and until we create opportunities for candid discussion between them, classroom interaction and education will continue to be driven by and suffer from the myths and stereotypes that each generation has about the other.

Perhaps the most painful part of the exercise occurs when students list stereotypes they have of one another. Now a host of racial, ethnic, and classist phrases are unleashed as students pour out their feelings onto the newsprint. While there is some bantering, this part of the workshop takes on a noticeably serious air. They know how cruel stereotypes can be. Most have experienced hurt and anger from them. They are asked to be honest and open, and not to accuse so we can learn how to dismantle prejudice as we get better acquainted. They don't spare any group and have names that sometimes defy logic and mystify adults.

Asians eat cats and dogs
all Black students dance well
all Black students play basketball
White kids' wet hair smells like a dog
kids with shaved heads are racists
kids who dress well are rich and snobs
girls who wear baggy clothes are sluts
boys who wear baggy clothes are in
    gangs
Whites have big noses
four-eyes
all Black people can rap
all short-haired girls are lesbians

girls who play sports are butch
preppy dressers are snobs
senior guys think freshman girls are
    easy
if you don't have a car you're poor
if you have a boyfriend you're
    having sex
all guys want is sex
if you don't smoke or drink you have
    no life
Whites can't dance
Spanish girls are whores
skaters are druggies

everybody with a lisp is gay
if you're rich you're a snob
White kids are physically inferior
all Black people are thugs
smart people are dorks and nerds
gothic people are devil worshipers
blondes are dumb
button-down shirts are for preps
Blacks and Latinos wear stolen gold
   or get it from drug dealing
if you have a beeper you're selling or
   buying drugs
football, basketball, and baseball
   players get treated specially by
   faculty and administrators
cheerleaders are airheads
dancers are hos
Black girls are hoochie mamas
if you're light skinned you're mixed

gothic women are lesbians
if you wear chains you're in a gang
football players are dumb
all Blacks can fight
Whites who hang around with Blacks
   are "wiggers"
Black men have longer penises
White girls want to try it with
   Black boys
fob (fresh off the boat)
kids in the band are nerds
all Asians know karate
all Asians are smart
all Spanish people are poor
Black boys sell dope and White boys
   do it
Whites are crackers
Hispanics are spics, chicos

Once two boys were giggling while we talked about different religious stereotypes.

"What's the matter?"

"He wants to know what a Jew is," said one.

"Do Jews believe in God?" asked his friend.

At a middle-school youth conference in a county with a growing Asian population, a girl of about ten or eleven called me over.

"You should ask Lin about her stereotype. She's got a bad one."

"What did you write?" I asked the little Asian girl.

"My mother taught me to hate all Vietnamese."

"Why is that?

"I'm Cambodian and the Vietnamese killed my father."

Sixty students at a high school in a rural county were asked to list positive things about the groups they had just negatively stereotyped. They were dumbfounded, unable to think of anything. After squirming for several minutes they wrote essentially the same stereotypes, except that now the remarks were inverted to reflect a positive bias. For example, Jews, previously labeled as cheap, were now said to be good with money.

African Americans, who were hung up on rap music, now had "good rhythm." Asians ate dogs and cats but on the positive list were creative with food. Native Americans were initially lazy but later characterized as having an environmentally responsible culture and living off nature. Europeans (Whites), first depicted as bossy and stuck-up, became disciplined, well-organized, and good leaders with a strong work ethic. Latinos, initially characterized as criminals and gang oriented, were listed as knowing how to have a good time, driving fancy cars (earlier referred to pejoratively as low-riders), having big families, and sticking together.

Many of the stereotypes didn't change. Asians often remained smart, had nice skin and pretty hair, and were good with technology. Latinos were still seen as great lovers and world-class baseball players. African Americans were fine athletes, dancers, and singers, and ate soul food. Native Americans were spiritual, cared for nature, and made jewelry. Europeans were rich, designed and wore nice clothes, had political power, and controlled things.

The exercise demonstrated how stereotypes create barriers in school and communities. Most students didn't catch on until one young man accurately pointed out the problem.

"I thought you were teachin' us to stop using stereotypes. It's wrong to put people into categories. Many of the listed things are still insulting to some people. Everyone must be judged as an individual." His group then wrote across their sheet of newsprint in large letters:

STEREOTYPES ARE BAD!
THERE ARE NO GOOD STEREOTYPES!!

Walking the halls of middle and high schools can be an eye-opening experience. You never know what you'll encounter. Two things are certain: there's a lot of noise, and it's very crowded. If you can manage to squeeze through and hear above the din, you might see kids laughing, shouting, or taunting one another, couples kissing, some pushing and shoving, perhaps even fighting. One high school was built for a thousand students but had eighteen hundred. All the kids had to make their way out to the buses through a central corridor that looked like the Black Hole of Calcutta. In the middle of the exodus a fight erupted between two young men, but you could hardly tell there was a disturbance in the midst of the tumult. We were trying to extricate ourselves from the mass of bodies when we suddenly started choking and coughing. Outside, we discovered the cause of our discomfort was dust released into the air by the students stomping on the carpet.

You see a lot of sexual harassment going on in the halls: boys pinching, pawing, and pushing girls. Bitch, ho, slut, queer, lesbian, dyke, and fag are part of the vernacular. It goes both ways. Some girls may be able to deflect unwanted comments or advances, but many resent being constantly accosted. And it can lead to assault.

Kids rarely reflect on the damage their labels and name-calling do. But they appreciate an opportunity to talk about such issues, especially gender-related ones. The young men and women are separated, and each group lists what they feel the opposite sex thinks about them, followed by ways they would like to be thought of. The two groups then come together and present their lists. Participants must follow the ground rules they established at the outset, and they are reminded this is not a debate but a dialogue. They are asked to listen and try to understand one another, because it is a rare chance to discuss such issues candidly.

Many hot buttons are pushed in the ensuing discussion, and it sometimes gets raucous because the boys don't take it as seriously as the girls. The young women often become outraged over their immature, callous, sexist remarks. Boys' smirks and giggling often belie their immaturity, but in a more profound sense, reflect their fathers' and society's condescension toward women. The discussions often become heated and accusatory, with women singling out a young man known for "hit and run" or gossiping behavior.

At times it's difficult to settle them down, even when we impose the eraser or marker rule—no one can speak unless he or she has the eraser or marker. This activity is difficult to use in middle schools because of their immaturity, yet there is a great need to discuss such issues among that age group and interrupt the formation of gender-related stereotypes. Below are a few examples of student lists:

**How Women Think about Men from the Men's Perspective**

| | |
|---|---|
| slobs | don't do house chores |
| dogs | don't work hard enough |
| want only sex | not romantic |
| players | liars |

immature
pigheaded
sexist
all the same
not responsible
not as intelligent
unorganized
eat too much
never serious

possessive
jealous
controlling
perverts
sex machines
studs/stallions
poor hygiene/smelly
afraid of commitment

## What We Want Women to Think about Us

romantic
loyal
make her feel special
organized
mature
responsible
clean
handsome
hardworking
not sexist
able to commit

smart
respectful
understanding
compassionate
sympathetic
caring
strong
gentlemen
motivated
serious
useful

## What Men Think about Women from the Women's Perspective

weak
tedious
pestering
always on PMS
possessive
inferior
bitches
too emotional
controlling
bad drivers
disposable
not equal
have no opinions

teases
deceiving
gullible
helpless
spend too much money
gold diggers
too committed
maids/housewives
sex objects
judge us by our looks
can't play sports
baby makers

## What We Want Men to Think about Us

worthy of respect
ladies

partners
friends

| | |
|---|---|
| intelligent | not just sex objects |
| viewed for what we are | have good minds |
| liked not just for our looks | can be good managers (at home and |
| good at sports |    work) |
| committed | not always barefoot and pregnant |
| independent | respected for who we are |
| good people inside and out | trusted |

From these recurring themes it's obvious that both sexes want to be treated fairly and respected, and that their perceptions of one another are similar and fairly on target. At Anytown, we follow this activity by reading a series of statements for the men to consider, and then one for the women, and we ask group members to stand if what they hear applies to them. It is one of our most powerful exercises. Here are a few of the men's statements:

Please stand silently if

- you have ever worried you were not tough enough
- you were ever hit to make you stop crying
- you have ever been called a wimp, queer, or fag
- you have ever been hit by an older man
- you ever exaggerated or lied about a sexual experience
- you ever felt you needed to put a woman in her place in front of other men
- you ever saw a man you look up to hit or emotionally brutalize a woman
- you were ever wounded by a knife or a gun

Examples of the women's statements:

Please stand silently if

- you have ever been afraid you were not pretty enough
- you ever changed your diet or exercised to change your body size, shape, or weight
- you ever pretended to be less intelligent than you are
- you were yelled at, commented upon, whistled at, touched, or harassed by a man in a public place, in your workplace, or at school
- you were ever called a bitch, a slut, or a whore
- you have ever been afraid of a man's anger

- you ever said yes to man when you wanted to say no
- you ever saw a man hit or emotionally brutalize a woman

At first there are a few snickers and chuckles, but most take the exercise very seriously.

After the lists are read, their faces are solemn. They realize what they have been doing to one another and the price a status-conscious, acquisitive society has been exacting on us all. During the discussion that follows there is no laughter or teasing. Inevitably, there are questions about abuse and neglect, usually beginning, "I have a friend who . . ."

Staff provide information about where they can get counseling and help, and remind them that they don't have to stay in such relationships — that they deserve and should expect respect. We no longer read the statements during youth workshops in schools because many young women make disclosures about abuse, rape, and incest in front of the group. When student-planning committees request gender activities (and most do), we ask that a social worker be present.

On several occasions, student disclosures have led to the arrest and incarceration of parents. Not long ago at a high school workshop, a seventeen-year-old who had attended Anytown the previous summer declared in front of two teachers and several students, "I'm doing much better now that I told you about the way my father sexually abused me. He's in jail now and my mom and I are flying out to Philadelphia next week to testify at his trial so we can keep him there. I'm still going for therapy, but my life's straightening out." Frequently the young men are taken aback by how serious the women are about the way they are viewed and treated.

Another subject that frequently comes up in discussions about gender and stereotypes is sexual orientation. Widespread myths and stereotypes about lesbian, gay, bisexual, and transgender (LGBT) individuals surface, and all too often find expression in cruel, tasteless comments that should be — but aren't — offensive to the group. This, despite the fact that many adolescents are discovering and questioning their own sexuality and have little factual knowledge about others' sexuality in the group or their school, but they are quick to ridicule and label peers who don't conform to their stereotypical images of straight society.

The Gay, Lesbian and Straight Education Network (GLSEN) National School Climate Survey of 2005 (Kosciw & Diaz 2006) included information from 1,732 LGBT students aged thirteen to twenty from all fifty states and the District of Columbia. The report revealed that 75 percent of the respondents heard homophobic remarks in their schools frequently or often. More than a third of the respondents experienced physical harassment at school on the basis of their sexual orientation, and more than a quarter experienced harassment based on their gender expression. Almost a fifth were physically assaulted because of sexual orientation, and another 12 percent were assaulted because of their gender expression.

LGBT students were five times more likely than other students to report having skipped school in the previous month because of safety concerns. The average grade of LGBT students who were being physically harassed was half a grade lower than LGBT students who were not being harassed. In an earlier survey GLSEN found that 80 percent of teachers reported negative attitudes toward gays and lesbians, and in GLSEN's 2003 National School Climate Survey it was reported that 83 percent of LGBT students said faculty and staff never or only rarely intervened when they heard homophobic remarks (Kosciw 2004).

The U.S. Department of Health and Human Services found that 28 percent of gay youth drop out of high school to escape violence, alienation, and harassment. Further, harassed youth were found to be four times more likely to have attempted suicide seriously enough to be treated by a medical professional (Gay, Lesbian and Straight Education Network 1997).

Yet precious little is being done to protect LGBT students from bullying and harassment around our country. GLSEN's 2004 State of the States Report, the first systematic measurement and comprehensive analysis of statewide policies to ensure the safety of all students regardless of sexual orientation or gender expression, revealed that only two states received letter grades of A, while forty-two received an F. Grades were awarded based on six categories: existence of statewide safe school laws; statewide nondiscrimination laws; support for educational or sexual health and sexuality; local safe school policies; general education issues, for example, graduation rates; and existence of laws stigmatizing LGBT individuals. The report concluded that the vast majority of students do not have legal protections against anti-LGBT bullying and harassment.

Despite the presumed conservative fundamentalist bias in southern schools, talk about sexual orientation is allowed in our workshops if students initiate the discussion or if the planning group requests it. This happens frequently, since boys' vocabulary is peppered with pejorative words about gays, leading to discussion about harmful stereotypes and the violence committed against students who are presumed to be different. We frequently show the first fifteen minutes of *It's Elementary*, the award-winning documentary on the topic.

In one school district a homophobic school board member pressured the superintendent to remove the film from our workshops. Ironically, one of the more conservative districts allowed us to pilot a workshop on homophobia that became an integral part of Anytown and is very successful in schools. We never received a complaint from a teacher, administrator, student, or parent about the workshop.

After these activities, students sit in a circle and talk about how stereotypes can lead to conflict and violence. This has become particularly sobering since the Columbine tragedy. Many students (and teachers) have a heightened sensitivity to the effects their words can have on others, yet abusive language and behavior is still widespread. We also talk about ways of eliminating stereotypes, and students work in groups to develop projects for improving relationships. It's also useful to create a banner at middle schools and ask students to sign: "I pledge that I will not use stereotypes at school. I will not engage in fighting, and I will work to keep the peace." Then it's hung in the cafeteria.

In schools where a dedicated teacher or committed principal gives students support, there have been some notable outcomes. Two violence-prone high schools and a middle school in different counties cut fighting, suspensions, and referrals to the principal in half within a year of our workshops. In a third county, all the high schools began multicultural leadership clubs after our visits, and scores of students went to Anytown, formed a countywide youth council, and regularly do community service activities.

We can't erase the reality that many children must deal with, so it's understandable that those of the same gender and ethnic background hang out together. It's natural to gravitate to like-minded and similar-looking people. Myths and stereotypes about the opposite sex and people who are different from us could be defused, creating more congenial and safer schools, if sufficient opportunities existed for students to interact. (See Tatum [1997] for a discussion of racial identity development and why African American children congregate together.)

At the start of every term, teachers should engage their students in meaningful dialogue about themselves. The students should introduce themselves to one another, share their likes and dislikes, and talk about career aspirations. Developing a sense of community in the classroom helps kids realize that those who are different have similar values and goals. Despite the differences, they are thinking, breathing human beings who have families, pets, friends, relatives, hopes, joys, and fears—just like them.

Prejudice appears in many forms in our schools and society. Griggs High School reflects what America will look like in the not too distant future, but its students were wrestling with some contemporary weighty issues. The student body is composed of 40 percent Latinos, 20 percent African Americans, 10 percent Asians, and 30 percent Whites. Entering the long, flat building, one can see kids milling about everywhere and hear Spanish and Asian languages being spoken. This morning seemed especially hectic. The principal seemed anxious as she walked down the hall, walkie-talkie held close to her ear.

"Base to three. How are things going there?"

The power went off just as students were arriving. "Please leave the building and wait outside until the power is restored," came a directive over the intercom.

The library had auxiliary lights on, but student helpers were unable to get in to prepare the room for my workshop. "I have got to get in to set things up for the workshop," said Lara, a Russian émigré.

"I'm sorry," said the media specialist. "Only faculty can come in." Lara waited outside, exasperated. Five minutes later the lights flickered and came on.

Tony Green is in charge of activities like mine at Griggs. He's a former track coach in his early fifties. The kids like him; there are always a few hanging around his office.

He stayed in the back of the room as we went though our icebreakers. From time to time a teacher wandered in and hovered around the homemade Danish baked by the cafeteria staff for the occasion. They'd listen in for a minute or two, grab a Danish, and leave—except for Barbara Manning, a middle-aged history teacher who was captivated by the dialogue that followed the noon break. The afternoon session began the way most do, with students sitting in a circle talking about school-related issues.

"What can you do when your best friend is an atheist and you want to help her?" asked Nina, a pert blonde senior.

"I want to answer that," said Lisa, an Asian student sitting opposite her. "She's talking about me and she knows what the answer is—leave me alone."

"But you need to hear His message . . ."

"I don't want to hear any messages. I'm perfectly happy being who I am. I don't need God or angels to help me out. After I'm gone from this place that will be the end. I don't know or care about your heaven or afterlife."

"But you've got to believe we love you," said John, a big kid with close-cropped blond hair.

"I don't want your love either," snapped Lisa. "There are too many conditions, too many demands. All you ever do is try to convert people."

"You don't understand us," said John with evident emotion.

"That's right," said Sarah, an African American across from him. "We want to be your friend."

"What is it with all you Christians? I don't even know some of you."

"We want to share Christ's gift with you," explained John. "It's a gift of love—because we care about you, not that we want anything from you. God loves you, and we want to save you from hell."

"I'm tired of all this lovin'," quipped Tyrone. "Can I change the subject?" A rumble of agreement arose from those who sided with Lisa.

"Okay, okay," continued Tyrone. "I want to know what to do when your best friend tells you he's bisexual?" Most of the kids laughed, but three or four didn't join in. Dennis, a tall and dignified-looking student spoke up.

"It's really not funny. I mean, I've got gay friends, and I wouldn't want to have to take the abuse they put up with."

"Well, they bring it on themselves," replied Irena. "The way they dress and swish around." Laughter. "You know what I mean."

"I do," replied Dennis. "But that's an unfair stereotype. Not all gay people are like that."

"But some are," interrupted Andy. "I've got a friend who's bisexual. This morning he said, 'I like that shirt you have on. You look good!' I told him, 'Hold it! Don't go any further!'"

"How do you know he was comin' on to you? Maybe he was just being polite," said Tian, an Asian student.

"I don't know, but I wasn't goin' to find out!"

"I know some gays, and they don't fit in anywhere. Can you imagine what that's like?" said Dennis.

"It's a very serious matter," I interrupted. "One of this country's leading causes of suicide among people your age is over sexual identity. And we're not even sure who's gay. A lot of the time we stereotype people and subject them to physical and verbal abuse, ostracize, and ridicule them."

Tony had been listening intently from behind the librarian's desk and jumped in.

"We had a student here a few years ago who shot himself right in class. It was before most of you came here."

"I remember," said Alicia, "It was in Mr. Ritter's class."

"He was an Eagle Scout and an outstanding student," added Tony. "I guess the pressure got too much for him. He took out a gun and shot himself in the head. A girl put her fingers in the bullet hole, trying to stop the bleeding. Blood was everywhere. The EMS guys got here and pronounced him dead. He was the first student to kill himself in a school in this county."

There was a momentary lull in the discussion until a choral group joined us. Several had participated in the workshop.

"Since this is a multicultural activity, we'd like to sing you a few songs from around the world," the director announced.

The first three in French, Spanish, and German were about Jesus Christ. Did the music teacher grasp the concept of multicultural education? While her naive insensitivity about diversity might be overlooked, it's difficult to ignore some of the more blatant affronts to students and colleagues perpetrated by overzealous, self-righteous teachers.

Several years ago I served on a panel along with a multicultural adviser from a large urban school district in Florida. The audience was composed of twenty schoolteachers from around the state who had been selected as outstanding teachers from their districts. They were participating in a week long training on cultural and religious diversity sponsored by the Florida Humanities Council. The panelists were to present different perspectives about the role of religion in public schools.

The panelists had just been introduced when a discussion ensued among the teachers in the audience about how they incorporate religion into their schools. "Before every faculty meeting we all get together and pray," said a middle-aged White woman. "It sets the right tone for our deliberations."

"What about teachers who aren't Christian or don't want to pray?" I asked.

She looked stunned and replied, "Oh, nobody ever says anything about that. They all participate."

"Are you sure everyone there has the same beliefs as you do?"

"We don't get any complaints."

Another teacher interjected, "We do something similar in my school. We have prayers for teachers before school starts in the morning. But it's voluntary."

"That's the best way to go," said another from a large city in south Florida. "We wanted to do it for all the teachers and students, but the principal warned us that there were some Muslim students and we might get in trouble."

Their lack of sensitivity was matched by their ignorance of the First Amendment. I could hardly believe what I was hearing. I delicately tried to inform them about the law that allows teachers to teach *about* religion but prohibits compulsory or coerced prayers of a specific religion. Most were not able to get past their own myopic view of the role of religion in education to understand the distinction.

Apparently, some school administrators misunderstand the law also. From Hernando County, Florida, we learn that the principal and a few teachers at an elementary school recently prayed together in school for their students and blessed their desks with prayer oil in an attempt to improve students' scores on the upcoming Florida Comprehensive Assessment Test. The oil was still on the desks when school started, leading some teachers to think vandals had been at work. "It was greasy. It was oily," said one teacher.

School administrators were not going to investigate the incident because they did not believe any violation of the law had occurred. "We also can't discipline against folks who want to practice or live within their religious practice, as long as it's not disruptive," said the school district attorney (Marshall 2007). An odd interpretation of the law, but not surprising coming from a district that had a major upheaval years before when a Jewish school board member called for public hearings to consider abolishing prayers before board meetings. In addition to losing his seat on the board in the next election, his family was harassed and he received death threats. (For information on how to address the issue of religion in schools go to www.firstamendmentcenter.org and www.freedomforum.org.)

Sexual orientation is a vexing issue in schools, especially in the south, where White and Black fundamentalist churches cling steadfastly to doctrines that often disparage LGBT inividuals, condemning them for what they consider to be an immoral lifestyle—a morally depraved choice that will damn them for eternity. (The most extreme expression of this view is represented by Fred Phelps of Westboro Baptist Church in Topeka, Kansas.) In the face of hostile remarks and actions by students, teachers, and administrators, it takes a lot of courage for a gay teenager to come out or for a straight kid to stand up for the rights of gays. Some areas have a less-than-enviable record in this regard.

When Sandy Freedman was mayor of Tampa in the early 1990s, she led the fight for recognition of gays and lesbians, pushing through an equal protection clause in the city's antidiscrimination policy. Hillsborough County had a similar provision, but less benevolent forces led by the American Family Association of Florida (AFAF) mobilized public opinion against the ordinances. Hearings in 1992 to consider repeal turned out hundreds of angry demonstrators, mostly in favor of repeal, spurred on by the inflammatory rhetoric of the organization's director, himself an admitted former pornography addict.

A number of weapons were confiscated from would-be testifiers. One of their pamphlets bore the headline "Sodomy Is Not a Civil Right" and warned parents about the "homosexual agenda" that purportedly included teaching the "homosexual lifestyle" in schools, allowing homosexual couples to adopt children and to recruit in public parks and restrooms.

The effort was known as the Take Back Tampa campaign. Opposition from liberal groups and clergy prevented them from turning back the clock in Tampa, but they did manage to convince the Hillsborough County Commission to repeal its sexual orientation policy. Flush with that victory, the director of the AFAF led an assault against AIDS education, focusing on the Hillsborough County School Board. One evening he harangued the board, warning of dire consequences if it adopted a more liberal sex and AIDS education curriculum. Noting that "condoms are ineffective in stopping the AIDS virus," his presentation was almost as bizarre as the ACT UP guerrilla theater's demonstration in favor of more AIDS education.

The board decided to leave its modest program in place for juniors and seniors, despite the fact that its district had one of the highest rates of teenage pregnancy and HIV infections in the nation.

The homophobic assault on educational institutions received a boost from some prominent politicians, including a conservative Republican state senator. As the head of one of the most important education committees in the legislature, he threatened the president of the University of South Florida with cuts in state funding to prevent Olympic diving champion and acknowledged gay Greg Louganis from speaking on campus. When his caustic letter was published in a local paper, he was deprived of the opportunity to deny it. The president refused to interfere with the students' decision, and Louganis spoke as planned. A liberal public radio station that criticized him didn't fare as well—he succeeded in cutting nearly $100,000 in state support for the station, but a fund-raiser replaced it.

Against such a backdrop of misinformation and bigotry, it's not hard to understand the fear and anxiety that gay and lesbian students face. A gay activist who helped organize the Gay Rights March on Washington called one day.

"I've been asked to come up with some kind of education plan for a couple of kids who are harassing gay students. The judge decided to withhold adjudication and asked me to try to get them in a program to sensitize them. Do you have anything?"

"Not offhand, but I'll work on it. What about the school system? They should work with things like that."

"I called the chairman of the board of education and told him about the problems gay and lesbian kids are having. He wasn't very receptive and said he didn't think it was serious. So I asked one of our staff specialists to call him, but he won't take her calls."

Some of the more courageous students will not be silent. Peter was only fifteen when he came to Anytown. The first evening he asked us if we were going to discuss homosexuality. Then he reeled off a number of facts about gay teenagers' problems. "I've got some files with me that may be of use," he said. For the next five days he prodded the staff to include more pertinent information.

To the surprise of very few, on our final night, Peter came out. We hoped he would be treated respectfully by the other teenagers, but we never anticipated the outpouring of affection and support he received.

They hugged him, embraced him, and cried with him. There wasn't a dry eye in the place. Yet Peter knew the real battle was ahead—the fight for his parents' acceptance. They weren't as understanding. Within a year he moved out and eventually put himself through college.

A growing number of teens are becoming increasingly vocal about the harassment and abuse gay, lesbian, and bisexual kids encounter. They have begun to form support groups, gay/straight alliances, in schools— much to the chagrin of some teachers, administrators, and school boards who would prefer to pretend it's a nonissue or a fad that will go away. Students at a magnet school in a large southern district tried to start such a group, but the principal discouraged them. When another group sprang up at a large high school nearby, two Anytowners asked us to speak with their classes to reduce hostility toward them. After it was cleared with two school board members and an assistant principal, our scheduled visit was cancelled by the principal, who said, "You are always welcome on our campus, but we'll take care of the situation in-house."

The kids were disappointed, and the harassment continued. They invited us back after clearing it with their teachers. We met in a classroom with about thirty students; all but one were White. She sat off in a corner. There was a combination of classes, including student government representatives. Supposedly, they had been briefed about the nature of the presentation. We began by discussing the history of our organization and how we work to improve understanding and respect for all people in our society. Because our country is more diverse than ever, racism and discrimination must be stopped if we are to survive.

"That goes for the treatment of women, too."

A couple of the young men snickered.

"What's the matter? You think I'm being funny? I'm not trying to be. How would your mother or sister feel if they had to take the abuse women face—the pinches, looks, trash talk?" Silence.

"Do you know what it's like for a woman traveling in this country? When you come to a stoplight, which way do you look? If you're a man you probably look all around at the cars to see who's driving. If you're a woman you look where?"

"Straight ahead." The women in the room replied in unison.

"That's right, because if she looks at a strange man, establishes eye contact, then it might bring on unwanted advances. Do you think about what streets you'll drive down when you go out? Whether it's safe to go out after a certain time? Well, women do, and so do elderly people and the disabled. No one should have to live in fear. No one. And that's true for gays and lesbians and bisexuals, too.

"Many of you have been taught that homosexuality is a sin. But every religion teaches that we must respect one another, that we shouldn't mistreat anyone. Even in the Old Testament there's a section in Leviticus that says 'As you were strangers in the land of Egypt, so should you welcome strangers among you.' Every person, regardless of age, race, religion, ability, or sexual orientation must be treated with dignity and respect."

They listened attentively and watched when we showed *It's Elementary*. They saw how children in the third and fourth grade acquired stereotypes about homosexuality, and how innovative teachers were dealing with the subject—not like some of their own faculty, who made disparaging remarks about their peers in the campus support group.

The following week one of the students called to thank me and said the atmosphere had improved.

A few months after the shooting at Columbine High School in Littleton, Colorado, I was invited to serve on a committee on civility for a large southern school district. Nearly twenty specialists from the school district—principals from elementary, middle, and high schools; psychologists; social workers; representatives from programs that target special needs children; and system administrators—met in a conference room at a large high school. The initial two-hour meeting led the group on a three-year odyssey that entailed monthly meetings, the creation of a student survey assessing school climate, the formation of a subcommittee on bullying and training of personnel and students throughout the district, and the subsequent creation of a subcommittee on LGBT students.

Most of the original committee's work had been accomplished during the first two years. The training of representatives from each school to help identify and respond to bullying (one of the paramount factors that led to Columbine and a host of similar incidents) was completed, along with the posting of a civility policy statement in each school and an information section about it on the district's website. Although other innovative ideas, such as an anonymous interactive chat room for students and parents concerned about bullying, were offered, the district chose to offer more traditional alternatives. Nevertheless, its approach was recognized by other regions around the nation who sought advice on creating similar initiatives.

I do not know if these policies and procedures created a more civil school environment, or if incidents of bullying decreased during the height of the campaign. Obviously, the program helped to make the problem more salient and was commendable. Ironically, a woman who heads a conflict resolution program in the district confided to me that her own child had been victimized by a bully at school during the campaign and she did not gain satisfaction from his teacher or principal. The child, like thousands of others around the nation, refused to attend school and had to be transferred.

Identifying the problem is an important first step. Creating awareness and understanding must follow. But prejudice, discrimination, and bullying are not always visible even to trained professionals, let alone teachers who are preoccupied with dozens of other children and the pressures of their jobs. One must be constantly vigilant and create a climate of trust where children have the opportunity to discuss such issues. The expression of this philosophy is perhaps most relevant to the harassment of LGBT students, and that is where the committee's mettle was tested.

Of all the -isms that afflict our society, homophobia is perhaps the most socially acceptable form of discrimination in some communities. This district was particularly troubled about gay rights because many of its clergy regularly assailed gays as sinful and unrepentant. In early 2004 a public opinion poll revealed that 72 percent of the people in the region were opposed to gay marriage (Lush 2004). Several vicious assaults on gay men occurred in 2003–2004, including the murder of two gay men.

The civility committee recognized the need for a proactive approach to the issue and created a subcommittee to suggest action for improving the status of LGBT students in the district. For more than a year we met to review the situation. We talked, read reports, debated various proposals, and then decided to have a series of trainings that would include all administrators in the district. This would take place in November 2003 and would be completed within a few weeks.

Following the sensitization of administrators, principals, and assistant principals to the issue—including the legal ramifications of indifference—a team would undertake a three-year project that would ultimately reach all students and teachers in middle and high schools.

The subcommittee had collected and reviewed reams of material pointing to the issue as a recognized national problem, and most committee members agreed that something had to be done. But the climate in the last two meetings seemed to change as support for the project waned. One could apprehend increased wariness, even dismay, as we tried to concretize our plans. "I think we should proceed, but we need to do it slowly," a committee member, who was also on the board of education, said. "I'm not sure that we need to do all this training," added a high-level administrator. "I know we need to do something, but we should take this one step at a time."

When asked if they had received negative feedback about the plan from other administrators, they said no, but the tenor of their remarks implied otherwise. Months passed, and those in favor of doing the training exchanged exasperated e-mails and waited for the new committee chair to reconvene the group. It never happened.

Workshops were periodically held for district employees, but nothing was conducted on the scale of the subcommittee's proposal. Then, early in 2004, one of my staff received a call from a district administrator who supervised a group of school counselors. He summarized the conversation for me: "She called and asked if we could do an in-service for her staff. She said they needed to learn more about the problem. I asked her what she meant and she hedged around. I knew what she wanted to say, but she had trouble even saying the word 'homosexual.' She means well, but she's got a problem with it herself."

Martin, my staff person, was a twenty-five-year-old gay man who works with LGBT youth in the area. He's a strong advocate for these young men and women, having endured the insults and injuries all too common among them. Martin's exuberance and industriousness are well known, but he sometimes behaves like a bull in a china shop.

A few weeks later Martin and I met with the administrator and about forty of her staff in the media center of a middle school. People were seated around small tables. I let Martin take the lead. He began, "I'd like everyone to repeat after me: gay, lesbian, bisexual, and transgender."

The words were mouthed with some trepidation and you could see some people squirm in their seats. If Martin intended to make them feel uncomfortable at the outset, he succeeded. And he followed that up with a definition of the terms "so we're all on the same page." Unfortunately, many of them weren't.

Despite their ostensible support of the workshop, many were clearly anxious and uneasy. As Martin cited statistics about the harassment and abuse of gay students to illustrate the gravity of the situation, you could see eyes darting in all directions and hear deep breaths from the back of the room.

Not all participants were reticent. "We know there's a problem," said a young female counselor. "We want to help. What can we do?" she asked plaintively.

"Well," said Martin. "You've got to create a safe place for LGBT students, a place where they can come and talk if they have to. Many of them can't even talk to their parents and they're afraid of talking to other students. But they need to talk and must have someone they can trust.

"Why don't you make your offices a safe space for them? You could paste a rainbow above your door. That's a universal sign of welcome for the gay movement. Or inside your office. You probably have pictures of heterosexual families. Why don't you put up some pictures of gay families?"

The administrator had been trying to contain her emotions but now threw her hands up in the air and screamed, "Not in our school district!"

At that point I rose from my seat and intervened. "Martin is a bit exuberant. He means well, but I realize you have some constraints."

"That's right!" said a middle-aged man sitting across from me.

"Even if we wanted to do something like that, we'd be putting ourselves out there all alone," said a middle-aged woman. "You don't realize what parents might say or do, and we wouldn't get backed up by our administration."

"Look," I said. "You know what kind of environment you have to work in. I don't want you to risk your jobs, but you've got to realize that there are a lot of hurting kids out there. They need your help now."

Again, there was a chorus of "Tell us what we can do." Martin and I reiterated the necessity for creating an accepting environment: providing support, counseling, and guidance, and, most of all, an adult who cares about their welfare. In whatever way they could, they must convey these feelings and create a safe school environment.

We left after two hours. The administrator said she would call to arrange further training. The next day I ran into an assistant superintendent for the district and related our experience: "You know there are court precedents concerning harassment of gay students. Your district is a suit waiting to happen."

"I know," he said. "I'll speak with the person in charge of curriculum and instruction and have him give you a call." And that is the end of that story.

This school district is still struggling with the LGBT issue. In June 2005 the county where it is located made headlines in the *New York Times* because the Board of County Commissioners, in a 5–1 vote, approved a policy "to abstain from acknowledging, promoting or participating" in gay pride recognition or events. Furthermore, the commission voted to require a supermajority to overturn the policy. One outspoken commissioner reported being influenced by the actions of some librarians who were distributing pamphlets, "and they referred children to youth groups outside [the] County to explore their sexuality" (Waddell 2005).

The subsequent debate spilled over into the school board. A group of parents asked the board to deny the establishment of a gay/straight alliance in their children's school—despite the fact that a number of the clubs already existed in area schools and they were functioning well. The parents expressed fears about the recruitment of students into the "gay lifestyle," and exposure of their children to sexual material and issues they believed to reside within the purview of their families and the discretion of parents.

The board was aware that court precedent was on the side of the students. The Equal Access Act of 1984 applies to all public secondary schools that receive federal funding. It stipulates that a school that allows student-initiated non-curriculum-related clubs to meet in school groups during lunch or after school cannot deny other non-curriculum-related student groups access to the school or otherwise discriminate against the group due to the content of the students' proposed discussions (*Board of Education of Westside Community School v. Mergens*, 496 U.S. 226, 271, 1990).

A federal judge summed it up: "The Board Members may be uncomfortable about students discussing sexual orientation and how all students need to accept each other, whether gay or straight . . . [but] defendants cannot censor students' speech to avoid discussion on campus that cause them discomfort or represent an unpopular viewpoint" (*Colin v. Orange Unified School District*, 83 F. Supp. 2d 1135, 1148. C. D. Cal. 2000). Under the Equal Access Act, if a public school allows at least one non-curriculum-related student group to use its facilities as a meeting place during noninstructional time, it cannot deny other students the same opportunities and facilities. (These cases are summarized in National Center for Lesbian Rights [2003].)

Knowing the status of student rights on the issue, the board sought to placate vocal conservative parents who opposed the clubs by requiring parental consent. After a year and a half of deliberation, and with recommendations by a subcommittee investigating the issue that cautioned against parental notification (which would have been required by all clubs to satisfy legal requirements but would have exposed students to possible negative ramifications with parents who did not know their children were LGBT, or defeated the very purpose of the clubs by discouraging them from joining and receiving support), the board voted not to require parental consent but to require parents to sign off if they didn't want their children to join a club in school. (Nationwide there are thousands of gay/straight alliances, but this region is recalcitrant. A school district just seventy miles away is going through the same ordeal.)

We need to create a positive environment and model the behavior that promotes it. At Taylor High School in a nearby, but slightly more progressive school district, students formed a gay/straight alliance. When news of it leaked, the director of the American Family Association of Florida went on the offensive, organizing a campaign that deluged the school board with letters, most from outside the county. He was ostensibly protesting because the group met during school hours and received public funding. The school board rejected his efforts to kill the project, noting that harassment and violence against gay students had decreased since the formation of the group.

Stereotypes die hard, and as fate would have it, we had scheduled a workshop the day after the tragedy in Littleton, Colorado, in a school that bore many similarities to Columbine. It was in an upper-middle-class White suburb with just a hundred Black students and only a handful of other children of color.

Here are the stereotypes the kids used to describe other students and themselves:

| | | |
|---|---|---|
| golddigger | freaks | dikes [*sic*] |
| devil worshiper | oreo | half-breed |
| phony | stuck up | nerd |
| bitch | hoochie | slut |

chink

homo

player

chunky

all Whites have no rhythm

all White people are rich

Arabs own Quickie Marts

girls that wear tight clothes are tricks, whores, stink

Blacks like loud music and rap

girls who won't have sex are prudes, dick chasers, and stingy

women are chicken heads

Latinos are fence hoppers

rednecks

Whites can't dance

dudes

Blacks are drug dealers

all gay people have AIDS

students who aren't in the magnet program are dumb

people with pagers or cell phones are dealing

teenagers don't know how to act

slutty, easy girls wear tight clothing

blondes are ditzes and airheads

all Black people can run fast

hick

queer

all Asians are smart

all Jews are cheap

all Black males are good in bed

all Latinos and Black women have nasty attitudes

all Black guys smoke weed

porch monkeys (Blacks)

Blacks speak Ebonics

Blacks have big families

Blacks are rude

all Asians do nails

all Asians are in gangs

men are dogs and scrubs

Latinos drive low riders

Whites are trailer trash

greedy

skaters

White girls are anorexic

hood rats

Egyptians ride camels

Black students can't get a 3.0

FOBs (immigrants are fresh off the boats) or JOBs (just off the boats)

Blacks only listen to rap or booty music

ESOL (English for speakers of other languages) students dress bright and tacky

wops

fag

all Blacks steal

all Whites are racist

all Black guys can play basketball

all guys want is sex

guys that wear baggy clothes are gangsters

sandniggers (Arabs)

terrorists (Arabs)

"dot heads" (Arabs/ Indians)

Blacks have gold teeth

nigger

all Asians take pictures

Chinese restaurants cook cats

men are lazy

all Latinos are gang members

preppies

surfers

Whites are gothic

all White males with a shaved head are skinheads

just because you care about your appearance then you are high maintenance

Whites listen to heavy metal or country

all Asians know martial arts

athletes are dumb jocks and do drugs

kikes

Eurotrash (exchange students)

One group of students put asterisks by queers, dikes [*sic*], fags, and witches (goths), noting they will burn in hell.

All said they had heard those terms used on campus this year, and most acknowledged that they hurt. When asked if they thought there were students who felt isolated and ignored like the ones who did the shooting in Colorado, most agreed. Nearly all of them thought it could happen in their school. We visited six other high schools within three weeks after Columbine, and students at every one believed the same.

The thoughts, feelings, and stereotypes that led to the estrangement and isolation of the shooters in Littleton and elsewhere around the country are widespread in our schools. The U.S. Department of Justice's School Crime Supplement reported that 12 percent of all students ages twelve to eighteen were targets of hate-related words and 36 percent saw hate-related graffiti at school during 2001. The percent of students reporting such incidents was fairly consistent among Whites, Blacks, Hispanics, and other ethnic groups (National Center for Education Statistics 2005, vi).

One stereotype gaining acceptance among African American students is the belief that White males are dangerous mass killers because most of the shootings on school campuses in recent years was perpetrated by them. Until we create more opportunities for students to discuss their concerns with their peers, teachers, administrators, and parents, conflict and violence will continue.

Nearly all mass shootings at school have been perpetrated by angry White males against predominantly White students. But shootings in or around inner-city school campuses have been going on for decades. Perhaps now that middle-class Whites are targets, more attention will be given to the underlying causes. Let's hope we have more success here than we have had with drugs, which didn't receive much attention until they penetrated affluent White communities.

The potential for future conflict increases every day as our population diversifies. In 2002, the ratio of Whites to people of color seventy years and older was 7 to 1. For people aged thirty to thirty-nine it was 3 to 1, and for infants to nine-year-olds it was 3 to 2 (Cole 2002). Some middle-class White males feel victimized by affirmative action programs, passed over, or left out by society. What will happen in the future as their percentage of the population shrinks and people of color become the new majority? Obviously, we have much work to do.

# 4

## Teachers: I Don't Get No Respect!

Now here, you see, it takes all the running you can do to stay in the same place!

*—Alice in Wonderland*

The research is undeniable. The most important factor for the success of children in school is their teachers' expectation for them.

—Raul Yzaguirre, President, National Council of La Raza

Hey, teacher, leave those kids alone!

—Pink Floyd

I worked with a team for four years in a school district to heighten awareness about the relationship between students' cultures and academic success. Forty to fifty teachers, principals, and resource officers joined us on day-and-a-half-long retreats. Many were apprehensive, afraid it would be "touchy-feely," but left enthusiastic about the experience.

More than five hundred teachers attended. They laughed and cried together, and although we didn't get through to everyone, we knew many would try to use what they learned in their schools. It was obvious, though, that despite their commitments, they were physically and emotionally drained by their work.

"We don't even have time to go to the bathroom. Teachers have the highest rate of bladder infections of any occupation. How can we hold more meetings to discuss these things? I get up at 5:00 A.M. and don't finish until 9:00 at night," said an exasperated woman. Her sentiments were echoed by others, who complained of increasing federal and state mandates that demanded their time. Each underachieving student must now have a personal improvement plan designed to help him or her improve performance to avoid dropping out. Many states are struggling to meet the federal No Child Left Behind mandate to achieve adequate yearly progress and have all teachers qualified in the subjects they're teaching.

For example, the Florida Comprehensive Assessment Test mandates that every third-, eighth-, and tenth-grader must pass writing, math, and reading tests to be promoted. This requirement has placed an enormous amount of pressure on teachers, students, and administrators. Schools and teachers in Florida are evaluated on the academic performance of students on the FCAT. Parents of those at underperforming or failing schools may use a voucher to send their child to a private school. Successful schools are given extra money; failing schools may be closed. Unfortunately, this puts a disproportionate burden on teachers and schools that have traditionally underperformed.

These pressures are being experienced by teachers nationwide. The National Education Association compiled a report, "NCLB/ESEA: It's Time for a Change!" (2007), which presents the impassioned pleas of teachers from every state begging for changes to NCLB because of its deleterious effects on teachers and students. And while the U.S. Department of Education has made some modifications and relaxed standards in some states, there is still widespread dissatisfaction with the law, which is up for renewal in 2007.

An analysis by Fischer and Dougherty (1999) revealed a high correlation between low test scores and schools that have large numbers of children living in poverty. The relationship between socioeconomic status and educational attainment has been documented for decades, and a school's FCAT grade (A, B, C, D, F) can, in most cases, be predicted based on this association without using the test. Further, giving monetary rewards to schools with high student FCAT scores perpetuates inequality of resources. The principal of an affluent virtually all-White upper-middle-class school confided, "We got $150,000 from the state because we were an 'A' school, but the money was needed more by the 'C' and 'D' schools. I don't mind having the extra money, but it's not right."

The FCAT is having a devastating effect on teacher and student morale in Florida and around the nation. Beleaguered teachers are being pressured to increase student achievement as purportedly measured by standardized scores. This has led some teachers to focus exclusively on the tests, to the detriment of other subjects. Labeling schools by student test performance has reinforced the stigmatization of schools with high proportions of minority students and those of low socioeconomic status.

Some teachers have rejected bonuses offered for high student test scores because they believe the practice does not recognize the effects that other important factors (e.g., parental influence) have on disparities in student achievement (Hegarty 2003). Penalizing teachers who toil in schools with students from disadvantaged backgrounds is seen as a disservice to dedicated staff in these underserved areas.

Educators have long known that the home environment is an important factor in determining academic success. Yet national representative surveys of teachers reveal that only 20 percent of high school teachers say parental involvement is strong in their schools (Johnson & Duffett 2003). Furthermore, teachers rated urban schools with high percentages of minority students as having the worst working conditions and least parental involvement. Only 11 percent of teachers said they are very confident about achieving success for hard-to-reach children by the end of the year (Farkas, Johnson & Duffett 2003).

This finding reveals an interesting paradox. An increasing number of children of color are populating our schools, and they fall within many teachers' definitions of hard-to-reach children. Further, many of the newest and least prepared teachers are the ones who are assigned to challenging teaching positions, according to a national survey of high school principals, yet research indicates that beginning teachers are not as effective as teachers with more years of experience.

A recent study of more than one thousand K–12 teachers for the Harvard Civil Rights Project found that the teaching labor force in the United States was becoming segregated (Frankenberg 2006). The report concluded while White teachers comprise the vast majority of the nation's teachers, they were the least likely to have had much experience with racial diversity and were "remarkably isolated." This conclusion was bolstered by the author's finding that 72 percent of White teachers work in schools whose students are more than 70 percent White and faculties are more than 90 percent White (p. 13).

The report noted that schools with high concentrations of nonwhite and poor students tend to have less experienced and qualified teachers. Nonwhite teachers were often found to be teaching in schools that were more difficult to teach in, despite the need for experienced, qualified teachers who can help needy students. Despite the need for highly qualified teachers in inner-city schools, Ball, Hill, and Bass (2005) found that teachers in high-poverty areas had less mathematics knowledge than teachers elsewhere in the system. They termed the aggregation of teachers with higher qualifications in non-minority areas "shameful."

To sum the situation up, there is a nationwide shortage of teachers, especially teachers of color. Large numbers of teachers are still teaching subjects outside of their area of expertise. Although the public pays lip service to the importance of education and teaching, teaching remains a low-status, underfunded profession. The newest and least-experienced teachers are being assigned to high-poverty, high-concentration areas of minority students, the most challenging assignments. The turnover rate of new teachers is 30 percent in the first three years and 50 percent in the first five years. Richard Ingersoll, an expert on teacher turnover, contends that the "best and brightest" young teachers, those with the highest SAT and National Teacher Exam scores, are the most likely to leave (Ingersoll 2004). And the Alliance for Excellent Education (2005) estimates the cost of teachers leaving schools to be $4.9 billion annually.

It stands to reason, as Susan Moore Johnson (2006) found in a study of first- and second-grade teachers, that they will stay only if they feel successful and receive support from colleagues, administrators, and mentors.

In view of this situation, it is small wonder that the study found that nonwhite teachers and teachers who teach in schools with high percentages of poor and minority students were more likely to report that they were contemplating switching schools or careers.

With this backdrop, let's take a look at Orange Blossom Middle School. Located on the outskirts of a large city in central Florida, Orange Blossom is home to a diverse population of fourteen hundred children, about 70 percent African American and the remainder White, Asian, and Latino. In an attempt to modernize, the district recently rebuilt the school, but its reputation as one of the toughest teacher and administrative assignments was borne out by its suspension record, perennially the highest in the district.

I had been there many times prior to the construction of the new building. I suppose the administration had hoped that the exterior transformation of the building might have a salubrious effect on the activities within. Unfortunately, that was not the case.

As I drove into the faculty parking lot, everything looked peaceful and tranquil in the crisp spring air. The school year would end in two weeks, but things at Orange Blossom were very unsettled. I was responding to an urgent call from the administration to work with a school specialist on multicultural affairs to assist the faculty.

Prior to my arrival I was briefed about the situation. In the last two years, some of the most talented teachers had retired, along with a beloved principal who had tried to hold things together there for many years. My task was especially difficult in light of the intransigence of many of the faculty, who, I surmised from previous visits, did not have a warm spot in their hearts for the kids who attended the school. Some of the teachers had expressed to me their disdain for the families who sent children there and they openly showed disinterest, even contempt, for my diversity workshops. But I thought that under the young new African American principal, with a beautiful new facility, the school would be embarking on a new era.

At 8:00 Monday morning, we met with seven administrators in a conference room.

The principal outlined the situation for us: "This has been a very difficult year at Orange Blossom. The kids have been unruly. Discipline has declined to the point where there are frequent fights in the hallways and classrooms. We've had six thousand discipline referrals to the principal's office."

"Six thousand!" I gasped. "There are only fourteen hundred kids on campus."

"I guess you get the picture. For some students there isn't much learning going on here. And many of the teachers don't feel comfortable here, either. There are forty-one new teachers here this year. Many have never taught anywhere before coming here."

"What do you think is the cause of the problems?" I asked.

"It's a combination of many things. Lack of parental support is right up there. But the school's overcrowded. It was built for one thousand, but this year four hundred students were added. Most of them are special education students, sent here because other schools didn't want to deal with them. Sixty percent of the seventh- and eighth-grade students were also

new because of school choice—they either selected this place or were assigned here."

Taken together, these factors led to chaotic conditions at Orange Blossom. We decided to meet with the teachers to get their perspective. The
multicultural specialist and I were given a small room for the day. The faculty was invited to visit with us during their planning periods. They were
told that the names of teachers who spoke with us would not be used in
our report.

It was Tuesday. The school year ended in another week. We settled into
our room around 8:00 A.M. Within minutes the parade of disgruntled
teachers began. Virtually every new teacher stopped in to see us during the
day. They were unanimous in depicting the children at Orange Blossom as
incorrigible, and they all said they were requesting a transfer to another
school—in the predominantly white part of the district.

School choice, the court-approved method for maintaining desegre-
gated school districts by offering magnet and specialized schools in otherwise unattractive areas populated by ethnic minorities, was blamed for
bringing maladjusted children on campus. Parents were depicted as uncaring, negative, confrontational, and quick to play the "race card." Many
teachers said they had been called racists by students and parents. African
American teachers were also appalled by the lack of civility and violence.

One young African American woman who had finished college the year
before noted, "The first semester was hell, but then I learned to deal with
the violence and aggression. I learned that I have to draw the line. They
don't teach you how to deal with these kinds of disciplinary problems in
college." In all, twenty-eight teachers complained about the violence and
lack of civility among students. "Help!" said one harried teacher.

But some of the older, more seasoned teachers took the changes in
stride. They acknowledged that it had been a challenging year, but they
did not evince the defeatist attitude of many of their younger colleagues.
Instead, they offered a variety of techniques they used to improve the
classroom learning environment, from talking daily with parents, to group
work, short assignments, quick feedback, no unstructured time, clear expectations, consistent enforcement of policies, field trips, and treating students with respect and, perhaps most important, patience.

Twenty teachers said that they would be happy to share their classroom
management techniques with their younger peers—if they were asked.

Despite the challenges they faced, many were willing—even anxious—to turn things around and share their expertise. "Whatever it takes! I'm committed to helping," said one veteran. After hearing one beleaguered teacher plaintively exclaim, "Nothing worked for me this year," we wondered about the utility of a management system that did not encompass regular faculty meetings to discuss problems and share experiences and solutions.

I got my first whiff of looming problems with the school choice program when I met with forty teachers for a workshop designed to encourage them to think about valuing diversity. In hindsight, it was a poor choice of days—the Friday before Labor Day. The teachers were as restless as the children. One would have thought that these supposedly "superior teachers" who work at this inner-city elementary magnet school for the arts would have demonstrated more interest and respect for the topic, especially since the neighborhood in which their school is located was the site of racial disturbances.

The school had only four hundred children. All but a handful were white middle-class kids who were bused in from around the county to take advantage of the specialized curriculum. As I stood in front of them outlining the status of children in the nation, with special emphasis on the disadvantaged to bring the point home, several young white teachers sitting directly in front of me (there were only two teachers of color on the faculty) carried on a conversation. Finally, I stopped, looked directly at them and raised my voice: "These are serious statistics. The lives of millions of children in this nation are pathetic. I'm sure you have some of these kids in your classes."

"I've got a Black boy in my fourth grade class," offered a middle-aged woman in the back of the room. "He's from this area and he's very difficult to control. I don't know what to do with him. I guess we'll have to leave him back."

"I've got two of them," shouted another teacher. "I've tried everything I know and I still can't reach them."

"Me, too," said another. "I've got one boy who keeps disrupting my class. He doesn't seem to want to learn. What can I do?"

School choice was allowing neighborhood children to avoid bussing and attend this local school that had been a haven for many elitist, culturally incompetent teachers. Instead of reaching out and trying to make the local children feel welcome, they created a hostile climate that began the cycle of failure for many of these children.

When I finished the workshop, the woman who headed the multicultural program at the school and had invited me there approached me: "That's just what we needed. We need to have you back for more."

The principal smiled broadly and voiced his approval of the activity. A year later school choice brought more local children into the school, but I wasn't invited back. Nevertheless, if we implement policies that bring staff, students, and parents into new situations with possible sociocultural conflict, we must also implement programs that prepare them, so their interactions will be positive. Dialogues and workshops stressing cultural competency and candid communication should rank high on the agenda to break the cycle of despair and self-fulfilling prophecies that continue to condemn children of color to limited opportunities and inferior lifestyles.

Culturally and educationally unprepared and unsophisticated teachers often complain about the amount of time they spend in nonacademic endeavors. Forty-three percent of teachers in a national survey said they spend more time trying to keep order in the classroom than teaching (Johnson & Duffett 2003). An overwhelming majority of high school teachers said things would be better in their schools if students treated each other with civility and respect—and it is reasonable to assume that the climate would improve if teachers also practiced those virtues.

This situation is not restricted to middle and high school students. For example, a first-grade teacher characterized the situation thusly: "I'm the one [who] has to teach them manners, respect, how to tie their shoes, what their last name is, what their phone number is. These kids come in first grade not knowing that . . . we have to teach them all that, and how to read and how to write and how to do math." This teacher worked in a *middle-class* district (Farkas et al. 2003, 12).

In light of the significant challenges teachers face, one might question the wisdom of utilizing standardized tests as methods for evaluating teachers and schools as well as students. Surveys of teachers indicate that 88 percent feel their districts are paying more attention to standardized tests, and 53 percent (55 percent of principals) believed the tests are a seriously flawed measure of student learning. Only 18 percent thought the tests are meaningful and are being used well by their district. A majority of teachers opposed incentives based on students' scores (Farkas et al. 2003).

It is not surprising that only 15 percent of high school teachers rate the morale of their school as high (Johnson & Duffett 2003). Yet states are forging ahead with standardized tests and the results are alarming. In 2003 nearly a quarter of all third-graders in Florida, forty-three thousand, failed the reading portion of the FCAT, and by May of that year thirteen thousand high school students hadn't passed the test despite six chances. A disproportionate number of these children were Black and Hispanic. According to state law, they are supposed to be left back.

Jeb Bush, then Florida's governor, believed that this was good policy. "There should be more retentions. If you ask Florida parents, do you believe we should pass kids on when they haven't learned to read, they say 'no'"(*St. Petersburg Times* 2003). His view is supported by national surveys of parents—four out of five are opposed to social promotions (Johnson & Duffett 2003). Yet research indicates leaving children behind has a negative effect on them and their subsequent academic success. The National Association of School Psychologists (2003) concluded that "[t]he retention of students . . . is in large measure not substantiated by sound research. The cumulative evidence indicates that retention decisions cannot be validated using any standardized or competency-based tests and that retention can negatively affect achievement and social emotional adjustment."

It seems obvious that children should not be penalized for the failings of their parents and teachers to provide quality educational opportunities for them to learn. Furthermore, many school districts in Florida are struggling with severe overcrowding problems. Retaining even a small percentage of students exacerbates that situation.

An unintended consequence of enforcing Florida's FCAT failure requirement may be an increase in the state's dropout rate—already the highest in the nation. Some middle and high school students are dropping out because they do not believe they can pass the FCAT, or because they do not want to be placed in remedial FCAT preparatory classes because of the stigma associated with them. Similar problems are occurring nationwide (Civil Rights Project 1999; Orfield & Wald 2000; Coleman 2000; Glickman 2004, 151–98).

As if the pressures generated by standardized testing are not enough, teachers are besieged by parents, students, administrators, and legislatures. They are subjected to dangers that range from deleterious working conditions to violent students, parents, and co-workers. Forty percent of teachers (and 25 percent of students) believed a violent incident causing severe bodily harm would occur in their high school within two years, and 40 percent of students reported that serious fights occur monthly in their schools (Johnson & Duffett 2003).

The subjects of ridicule and scorn, teachers in the United States are often the brunt of jokes, their intelligence impugned by cynics and their sanity doubted by colleagues who know the stress and anxiety they endure. "Stand by Me," a 2003 national study of teachers conducted by Public Agenda, revealed that more than three-quarters of the teachers surveyed felt unfairly blamed for school shortcomings.

During a workshop I conducted several years ago for twenty teachers at a prestigious private school, a teacher became hysterical and had to be helped from the room. At the break, her colleagues confided the discussion caused her to flash back ten years, when she taught at a public school where two students went on a rampage, killing an assistant principal and wounding two others. The principal perpetrator was a student who had been undergoing counseling before his family's health insurance expired and his treatment was terminated.

Diverse students pose a variety of challenges for teachers. Millions of students have a physiological or psychological impairment. Nearly 6 million students have limited English proficiency, and 10 percent of schoolchildren have parents who are illiterate. Our schools and curricula were not designed to accommodate the resulting mix of students and problems, and our teachers and staff are too often unprepared to deal with them. Many are wedded to systems of rules, regulations, and traditions from another era.

Change threatens teachers' normal way of doing things, their values and beliefs about themselves and society. Most teachers have been trained in the Eurocentric tradition, with its emphasis on lectures, conformity, and obedience to authority. They are accustomed to having bells and buzzers regulate every move in schools that more closely resemble factories or prisons than learning institutions. They have not been prepared for, nor do many expect to perform, the multiple roles they are called on to play as surrogate parents, disciplinarians, social workers, psychologists, sociologists, nurses, nutritionists, and anthropologists.

Children today mature physically at an earlier age. They are more restless, inquisitive, aggressive, and sexually active than those of previous generations. They are being reared in a culture where competition is paramount under a system that shortchanges many children before birth. Millions lack adequate food, health care, and shelter as well as basic knowledge about hygiene and civility. Many have low self-esteem and don't consider the consequences of their actions. Schools sometimes become battlegrounds where the struggle for power and privilege is fought, creating mental and physical anguish for children and teachers, and forcing many teachers into early retirement—or worse.

In the early 1970s, less than 5 percent of fifteen-year-old girls and 20 percent of fifteen-year-old boys had engaged in sexual intercourse (Jarrell 2000), compared to nearly 50 percent of ninth- to twelfth-graders in 2005 (National Youth Risk Behavior Survey: 1991–2005). The Institute of Medicine's 1999 Report on Adolescents, published by the National Science Foundation, stated that teasing and physical fighting is more frequent among thirteen and fourteen year olds, and violent criminal activity peaks around the fifteen to seventeen age group. It was also found that about 25 percent of the adolescent population is at high risk for psychosocial problems and poor developmental outcomes such as academic failure, alcoholism and drug abuse, delinquency, and violence. The report estimated that 20 percent of adolescents have a diagnosable mental disorder sometime during adolescence—the highest rate for any age group.

Kevin Dwyer (2000), past president of the National Association of School Psychologists, has noted that adolescence now begins as early as age nine. Adolescents experience emotions more intensely than adults and process information and make decisions differently. He concluded that it is imperative that evaluators (teachers?) be skilled in recognizing potential problems among youth.

For all their work and commitment, teachers are still held in low regard. One survey of the prestige ranking of 250 occupations showed teaching placed 164, behind teacher's aide (111), janitor (154), and maid (157). What would you expect from a society that ridicules the profession by saying, "Those who can't do, teach, and those who can't teach, teach teachers."

In a culture that stratifies occupations based on financial compensation, teaching falls low on the ladder. Parents and students openly berate it.

"It's hard to get their respect," said a teacher at a distinguished urban high school. "Students in Porsches and BMWs see what we drive and the clothes we wear. All they hear at home is how poor we are, so there must be something wrong with us."

In the Ups and Downs game I play with fifty to sixty students in my school workshops, students are asked to stand if they are the oldest child in the family; were born in another country; choose pizza as their favorite food; want to be doctors (ten stand), lawyers (four to five stand), or teachers (usually no one, and if someone does, she is laughed at); want to be millionaires (everyone stands).

"What do you want to be when you grow up?" is a category on our icebreaker culturegram chart. Kids fill in career plans that range from being athletes to neurosurgeons; teachers often put "retired."

"I'm ready to retire right now," proclaimed a teacher at one of our meetings. "I've had enough. Five more years to go and I'm out of here. I just don't think I'm making a difference."

Such feelings are widespread, and so are protestations that "kids aren't the same anymore." If that is so, why do so many cling to antiquated methods and materials? Perhaps it would be best if those middle-aged dinosaurs followed through on their threats so that new people with fresh ideas and enthusiasm could take their place. The profession must attract more intelligent, qualified people, and until we increase their social and economic status and improve their working conditions, we'll continue to wrestle with mediocrity.

The demand for new teachers is enormous. Nationwide there is expected to be a shortage of more than 2 million in this decade. For example, in 2006 Florida needed to hire an additional thirty-two thousand teachers, but many teachers are nearing the age of retirement. Nearly fifteen thousand teachers, or 10 percent of Florida's public school faculty, retired in 2003.

Even when teachers are available, they often teach in areas out of their specialization. Nationwide, six out of ten middle school students in English, foreign languages, math, science, history, and bilingual education, and six out of ten high school students in physical science, chemistry, geology, physics, history, and bilingual education were being taught by teachers who did not hold certification and a major in the subjects they were teaching in 1999–2000 (Seastrom et al. 2003). Given these facts, the No Child Left Behind legislative mandate of having a qualified teacher in every core subject area by 2005 had to be moved to 2007, and even that date was too optimistic.

Finding full-time qualified teachers is difficult, but finding substitutes is even harder. Many places around the country have hired substitutes whose only qualification is that they passed the mirror test. Some Florida counties require only a high school diploma. Compensation for substitutes rivals that of burger flippers, further assuring a paucity of qualified applicants.

Considering the number of teachers and substitutes who are unqualified to be working with students, and the pressures they face in hostile environments, it is not surprising that multicultural activities are not a high priority. Yet those pursuits help calm students and involve them in the learning process. Given the challenges that teachers and substitutes face, many of them find their workplace anomic. This feeling may intrude into their attitudes and behavior, which, in turn, influences students' perceptions of themselves and the institution.

"I must say I'm feeling very stressed out," said a middle-aged woman in a workshop. "I can't do any more than I'm doing right now." Many teachers are so obsessed with ritual and requirements, they overlook truly important teaching opportunities. A month into the 1999 war in Kosovo, at a workshop for seventy teachers in a large middle school with a history of racial problems and one of the highest suspension rates in the region, participants were tense.

"We face more challenges getting along here than they do in Kosovo. What do your students say about it?"

The room was full of blank faces.

"How many of you think your students don't know anything about what's going on?"

All but five raised their hands. We asked them to spend fifteen minutes discussing the war so their students might learn how children their age were dying because they hadn't learned to live together. At the end an assistant principal announced, "I don't know how many of you heard about what happened yesterday afternoon, but I want to tell you everything I know about it. Someone pointed a gun through a classroom window at a student. It was seen by several kids. We're pretty sure it was someone from the outside, and we're trying to find out who. But the kids got pretty scared. That's why some of them weren't here today. That's all we know. We'll let you know anything else we find out, but Mrs. James [the principal] and I wanted you to have the facts so you can answer questions. I wouldn't bring it up unless they ask about it."

Some teachers don't understand that creating a more congenial environment at the beginning of a class can facilitate their objectives. When children don't feel good about their school environment, when they don't feel part of the community, they aren't ready to learn. To make this point, we ask teachers how many know all of their students' names. They all raise their hands. When asked how many know all their colleagues' names, perhaps three or four raise their hands. Hopefully, they begin to realize how little they know about one another and how this can lead to stereotypes and conflict among staff and students.

Some teachers recoil at the thought of engaging in activities that may elicit emotions. Yet their classes are filled with adolescents and prepubescent children with racing hormones and wildly vacillating emotions that spill over into their interactions with one another and affect their academic performance. If we ignore this reality, we fail to provide a supportive and respectful learning environment where students can take risks without fearing derision and retaliation.

Before classrooms can become places of tolerance and understanding, much work needs to be done with teachers so they can model behavior that demonstrates respect for everyone. We conducted a workshop for the faculty of a large high school in a rural, almost entirely White upper-middle-class area. The school had barely a hundred African American students, and two Black teachers—a man and a woman—out of 140.

"Do we need multicultural education?" The first two teachers answered no.

After speaking for a few minutes about the virtue of multicultural education, we showed a video about prejudice. While they were watching, we read their culturegrams. The last question was "What do you want to be when you grow up?" One answer stood out in large letters: "RESPECTED." It was the African American man. When the video ended we invited them to take a careful look at the chart and consider how many students felt the same way at their school.

We weren't invited back for four years.

A similar situation happened at a large urban high school with a high proportion of children of color. The principal, a strapping White man with a shock of blond hair, was a strong proponent of the multicultural program. He assembled the 160 faculty and gave them a brief pep talk about the importance of my work. Their enthusiasm was muted. During our introductory remarks, a dozen teachers were reading newspapers or writing. How would they react if their students behaved that way?

We managed to engage most of them in small problem-solving groups. Then an elderly White man rose and spoke: "This is nothing but a waste of my time. I'm too busy to be concerned with such nonsense. I'm a biology teacher, and I've already got too much to do. I can't be bothered with this stuff!"

The stigmatization of multicultural education as punishment can be disheartening, especially when you discover that you've been designated the disciplinarian or break man for burned out teachers and administrators who don't know what to do with troublesome students. Take Green Pines High, a large school with two thousand mostly well-heeled White students. The student planning committee was in disarray. Its adviser, a middle-aged White teacher who got the task by default, eavesdropped on our meeting while standing in the doorway to monitor her classroom.

At the workshop the following week the students were raucous and rude. Whenever we engaged in a serious discussion, someone would do something disruptive. The adviser remained out of sight, while an elderly volunteer tried to quiet them so we could discuss sexual harassment. When the room became quiet during a critical exchange, someone passed gas and everyone laughed.

Two hours into the workshop an athletic-looking aide entered the room: "I heard you were having problems with them. One of the teachers called and asked me to help. I'll hang around and give you a hand."

He leaned against a wall and watched menacingly, but the kids were unfazed. Their disrespect mirrored that of the staff who came in on breaks to munch on the food. A lot of time was spent asking students to listen to one another. A burly police officer entered and offered to throw unruly kids out. We declined because we wanted to treat them differently. Nearly all were in a dropout prevention program and had been ordered to attend as punishment. After they left, their adviser was fumbling with a bottle of pills.

"Headache?"

"No, Xanax. I've got to get out of here."

The following stories are indicative of the discipline problems teachers encounter. These incidents are not isolated, and their severity could be magnified depending on the school and location. How teachers handle discipline affects classroom climate and ultimately determines whether students will be able to learn. Classroom management is crucial for establishing trust and mutual respect between and among students and staff.

The Great American Teach-In is held in November. Community volunteers visit schools and talk about their occupations or matters of interest to students. On the one hand, it's an attempt to give kids insight into different careers and issues; on the other, it gives schools an opportunity to show off. It allows visitors to see what the American educational system is really like. Sometimes what they see can be eye-opening, like my visit to Freeman Middle School.

"You'll be working with me today," said Dwayne Wilkins. "I teach science — at least that's what I'm supposed to do. We'll see what happens. By the way, what's your field?"

"I'm the director of a human relations organization that helps people get along with one another."

"We could use a lot of that here."

About forty students were waiting in his portable classroom. Some were walking around, others gathered in little cliques.

"What will you talk about?" he asked in a whisper.

"The kind of work I do, and I'll show a video they can talk about."

"It might work with this class, but I'm not sure about the next one. We'll see."

The students were pretty well behaved and seemed to follow the lecture and the video. We even let them play Hello Bingo, which they liked. When the bell rang, Dwayne came over: "Pretty good job. Now let's see what happens with the next class. They're a pretty difficult bunch. I just don't know . . ."

He seemed genuinely concerned, even fearful. They came in a few at a time — loud, boisterous, and rude. Many were chewing gum, and Dwayne went around the room holding a piece of cardboard for them to spit it upon. The noise went on unabated, even when he tried to introduce me.

"Let's be quiet so you can hear our guest. What he has to say is important so show him some respect."

"You mean the way we show you respect?" said a boy sitting in the first row with a smirk on his face. Dwayne cringed.

The presentation wasn't going well, so we let them play Hello Bingo. It worked for about fifteen minutes — then chaos. We couldn't get them back in their seats. Dwayne had no control over them, and they couldn't have cared less about me. At last we got them settled down enough to show the video. About half of them watched. The rest talked. Then—disaster! The VCR ate the tape! What followed was the longest ten minutes of anyone's career.

We saw how some teachers manage their classes at my next stop that day. Johnny Franklin, a Vietnam veteran, is a well-built African American who taught history at another large middle school in the same district. His room was spotless, with kids sitting silently in neat rows. If anyone got out of line he'd be over in an instant, arms draped around the kid, whispering in his ear. Then he'd take him out into the hall. In a minute or two they'd reenter and the kid would sit quietly. What he said is a mystery, but they were quiet, and he spent most of his time keeping them that way.

During the third presentation I apologized for repeating myself.

"That's okay," said Johnny. "They don't remember anything."

On another Teach-In we spoke at an old working-class high school where we squeezed through a sea of students on the way to the portable classroom where we were greeted by Darryl Davis, a thirty-year-old dropout prevention teacher who doubled as the soccer coach. He had a good sense of humor and seemed genuinely interested in students. Darryl explained that the thirty-five students were from two dropout prevention classes combined for this workshop. Many of them didn't want to be in school and it was his job to keep them there.

How sad to see kids in their early teens with no goals or long-term vision. Worse, many displayed no affect. They sat with their heads on their desks, passing time. Only about half seemed interested in the presentation. When a couple came up and asked questions, we were flattered. Then Darryl took a switchblade from a student.

"I told you I never wanted to see that again."

"My father gave it to me," said the boy.

"Why did you bring it back to school? None of the others have knives."

"Oh yes they do. I know four in here that have 'em."

"Go on. I'll speak with your father myself," he said, then turning to me, "I took it away from him about a month ago and gave it to his father."

"Maybe you should ask them why they feel he needs one?" I quipped.

If you observe many classrooms you'll find wide variations in teachers' approaches to managing conflict and crises. Some teachers are respected for their honesty and flexibility. Others set codes of conduct and enforce rules uniformly. Successful teachers are not afraid of children or diversity. They are able to tap students' creativity through innovative strategies that involve them in the educational process.

Active learning necessarily commands students' attention. Passive learning leads to boredom and disengagement. Some teachers have lost sight of the mission of education and are stuck in the business of classroom management—gum collection. For them, going through the methods and process of teaching takes precedence over content, a pitfall perpetuated by standardized testing. And 84 percent of teachers in a national representative survey believed that they would end up teaching to these tests (Johnson & Duffett 2003).

These teachers are often disinterested and even afraid or uneasy around children, especially those from different cultural and ethnic backgrounds. Their days revolve around going through the motions. Students sense they are mere units—appendages to the educational process. They don't see people who look or act like them in positions of power. Obligatory tributes to Black Emphasis or Hispanic Heritage months merely reflect the shallowness of their feeble, often naive attempts to placate ethnic minorities.

Teachers who understand and value children from different cultural and ethnic backgrounds have been shown to be more effective educators (Ballenger 1992; Cartledge & Mulburn 1996; Banks & Banks 2001; Gay 2000), and there is mounting evidence that teaching children about their cultural heritage has a salutary effect on their academic performance. Lessons that connect materials with students' experiences, respect the legitimacy of their culture, teach students to value all cultures, and incorporate a diversity of learning styles have a positive effect on student learning and achievement (Kilman 2006; Klump & McNeir 2005; Demmert & Towner 2003; Doherty et al. 2003; Lee 2003; Cooper 2002; Gay 2000; Ginsberg & Wlodkowski 2000; Ladson-Billings 1994).

While teachers and administrators say they believe it's important to create positive learning environments that integrate information about different ethnic groups, most schools do not have strong policies that support this position. Nor do they provide adequate training and funds to support such initiatives. In fact, pressures generated by NCLB standardized testing requirements are preventing the introduction of such innovative materials into the curriculum and reducing the time teachers allocate for discussions that would improve understanding and interpersonal relations on school campuses.

The seeming aloofness that some White teachers evince toward students of color may also appear in their interactions with colleagues. To enhance their knowledge of ethnic minorities and improve interpersonal relations among staff, diversity workshops are being offered in schools (and corporations) throughout the nation. But it's difficult to change a lifetime of attitudes, beliefs, values, and behaviors in a few hours or days. The goal is to create a sense of community among the faculty by helping them recognize and value differences among themselves and students. Sometimes the results are gratifying.

My first teachers' workshop, twenty years ago, was a big challenge. After a career as a university lecturer for more than twenty years I had an aversion to small-group interpersonal activities. Accompanied by Fred Thurow, a senior school administrator who was considering our proposal to start a multicultural program in his district, we were about to engage forty-five teachers in what might be a racially charged dialogue at Maple Hill Elementary School. We knew he'd be watching closely.

Research on job satisfaction indicates that people need to discuss their concerns in a safe, controlled environment but are seldom afforded that opportunity. These teachers wanted to talk about racism, but we were reluctant at first to let them. We would learn that we need not fear emotions, that denying their existence creates a climate that perpetuates fear, frustration, anger, and mistrust.

We met in the cafeteria. Jamie Gleason, the principal, introduced us and moved to one side. Fred sat in the rear and watched. We began talking about our organization and threw in some facts about changing student demographics. The group sat silently, and we sensed they were looking for more. Then a young White woman spoke up: "I wish people would find a way to get along better. There are so many cliques, and people don't mix."

"That's true, all right. I keep hoping I can get to know people, but it's hard. I've been here for two years and still don't know everybody. I don't think it's a very friendly place," said another young White teacher.

"What could we do to improve things?" I asked.

"How about having a party? That might bring us together," someone said.

"We did that last year," said a middle-aged woman. "None of the Black faculty came. I wanted to meet them, but they stayed away."

"You don't need a party to get to know us," said a Black teacher. "We're here all day. Why don't you just come up and say hello?"

"I've tried a few times, and you just avoided me," said a young White woman who looked hurt. "You seem angry all the time."

"Maybe you should work on your own stereotypes. I never thought you looked friendly, either. You always stick with your own group."

"Are you saying I'm prejudiced?"

"You never went out of your way to talk to any of us."

"I can honestly say that I never meant you any disrespect."

"I never said anything to make you think I didn't like you."

"No, but . . ."

"But you assumed I didn't like Whites when you were the one who wouldn't take a chance on reaching out to the few of us who are here. We've been ignored by all you folks as if we were carrying some kind of disease. We didn't go to the party because we didn't think you really wanted us."

We stood silently at the front of the room, braced for more.

"I have a problem with Christmas parties," said another Black teacher. "Linda and I are Jehovah's Witnesses. We don't observe the holiday. We don't celebrate birthdays either. I know some of you don't understand, but you need to respect our beliefs."

"I do understand," said another, "but you're depriving the kids of our culture. When Halloween or Christmas comes you don't even decorate your room. The kids are missing out."

"That's not fair," countered the teacher.

"You can't avoid some things," said another, "that's why we have team teaching. I work with Marsha, and I know that at certain times of the year I've got to double up. I'm willing to help out more with holidays. She does other things to compensate. Oh, I complain at times, but I think we make a good team." She looked at Marsha and smiled.

"I'd like to get back to the Christmas party," said someone else. "I'm Jewish and I don't appreciate being invited to a party that conflicts with my heritage and beliefs. Besides, you have it at a place that's restricted."

"What's that about?" asked a young woman.

"They don't have Black or Jewish members at the club where you had your party. What kind of signal does that send?"

"We never realized . . ."

"That's why it's so important to talk like this. People are hurting without anyone knowing or seeming to care," I said.

"Well, I never thought negatively about our Black teachers," said the young White woman.

"You could have fooled me!" quipped a Black woman.

"It really hurts to know you think I'm prejudiced."

"That's the message we get when you swish down the halls like little Miss Prim-and- Proper, just walking in as if we don't even exist."

"That's the last thing I wanted you to think. I suppose I was afraid of being rejected. I didn't mean anything . . ." she began to cry.

"I guess we need to work on this some more. We've never had a chance to find out what's really on our minds. I promise you we'll continue to have these meetings," said Jamie, who was moved by the disclosures. So was Fred, and we got the contract.

The teachers began to meet regularly. From time to time we touched base with Jamie to see how things were going. The experience showed us that many teachers suppress their feelings about each other and students, sometimes creating a negative environment for themselves and the children. It is imperative that teachers have a chance to dialogue on a regular basis to discuss mutual concerns, lesson plans, and strategies for teaching and classroom management. However, only 19 percent of teachers in a national survey said they do this (Johnson & Duffett 2003).

Once the school board and the superintendent made a commitment to develop a comprehensive multicultural program, we formed multicultural committees in all of the middle and high schools and took them away for overnight retreats. There were forty schools, and each committee had ten students, two parents, two faculty members, and the principal. We took two schools at a time to a retreat center in a quiet neighborhood on four acres bordering a river. The food was edible, the rooms were Spartan but adequate, and the nuns who ran the place were thrilled to have us.

The team was joined by two other social workers—an African American man, who later became a state representative and successfully sponsored a bill that mandated the teaching of African American history in schools, and a woman who became the supervisor of social workers for the district—and a school psychologist. The day-and-a-half-long sessions were divided into segments designed to help students and adults improve their understanding of prejudice and discrimination, but especially to learn about themselves and each other. We helped them understand how the multicultural committees worked, shared ideas for activities, and gave them time to plan their own agendas.

Over the next two years we did thirty-six overnight retreats. The program expanded to include all principals, school social workers, and psychologists. Consultants came and shared their perspectives. We had children as young as twelve spending their first night away from home, getting off the bus looking scared and bewildered, and high school students who thought they were coming to party.

Of all the challenges we faced, the middle-schoolers were especially tough. As soon as they went upstairs to their rooms, we'd hear them running up and down the halls. We lost a screen when one tried to climb out a window, and once a kid kicked a hole in the wall, but no one was hurt. We never had a fight and we never had to send anyone home.

Fred would sit up in the hall until 2:00 A.M. or later to keep things under control. And he'd be the first one up in the morning walking along with a set of chimes, awakening everyone. The first time we had a large group of teachers we decided to try our ethnic sharing activity after dinner. They were asked to bring one or two items reflecting their own culture to talk about. Forty of us sat in a circle, and a White teacher in her early thirties led off. She took out an elaborate family tree that traced her ancestors back hundreds of years.

"One of my relatives lived in Virginia and had a plantation with slaves on it. I'm not proud of that," she said looking at the four Black women to her left, "but it's true."

"Well, that's all right," said one of them. "We had relatives who were slaves. My great-grandmother told me what it was like, but it wasn't your doing. You weren't around then." She laughed to relieve the tension.

Giving people a chance to get to know one another was an asset to the program. They carried the spirit of the retreat back to their schools, and asked for our help in working with colleagues. Over the next three years we conducted two- to three-hour diversity awareness workshops for seventy-five hundred teachers in the district. Days were set aside for schools that had specific problems and needs.

The committees became permanent, and until a few years ago we still ran into kids who had come to the retreats. Like their teachers, they never forgot it.

Participants were kept involved at the retreats in a number of ways. We showed videos, had small group discussions about personal experiences involving prejudice and discrimination, let them develop projects to improve tolerance and understanding at their schools, did singing and dancing, and used a host of funny icebreakers.

Late in the afternoon of the first day we'd have a young couple who were puppeteers work with the students. They showed them how to make finger puppets. While the kids ate dinner, the puppeteers glued the pieces together and assembled a stage made of PVC pipes with a black curtain. The kids wrote stories about their puppets' experiences, usually on the theme of prejudice. Some of them were poignant. The room was silent as they enacted situations that made their characters happy or sad.

During the puppet shows we began to realize the kind of baggage some kids carry. While many characters were fictitious, some were obviously not, like the stories of a little girl who was abused by her parents and an Asian boy who was beaten and ostracized by kids at school.

We also used the retreats to educate teachers about cultural diversity. It didn't take long for our team to realize how insensitive many teachers are about race relations. Whether from fear, frustration, or alienation, Whites don't like to discuss race relations. Many White teachers and administrators, state mandates notwithstanding, have an aversion to multicultural education. Perhaps it's a reluctance to change, or maybe fear of saying something that reveals ignorance about racial matters, or worse—personal biases.

There's a considerable divide between Whites and people of color, a chasm that will never be bridged until we talk about who we are, how we feel about living and working in a society dominated by White males, and how what we teach and the ways we do it affect our children. That dialogue must take place among students, teachers, parents, and administrators.

Being a White male can be an asset in conducting cultural diversity workshops, at least in the beginning. We've seen workshops where White teachers tuned out good Black trainers. You can see it in their eyes and their body language; it's reflected in their attitudes, the types of questions they ask, and the way they ask them.

Dr. Marvina Lee, an African American, and Rosaline Alvarez, a Cuban American, assisted us in a daylong workshop for 130 middle school teachers in a rural county. The time set aside for the workshop had originally been designated for teacher planning. We discovered that two other planning days had also been expropriated by the administration, creating an inhospitable climate for our workshop.

The meeting hall was filled to capacity as we rattled off statistics and embellished them with illustrations to punctuate the need for enhancing our knowledge of other cultures. We mentioned that sexual orientation needed to be addressed in our conversations because many purportedly gay students were being brutalized by peers. A man's hand shot up.

"Are you saying that we have to start teaching about homosexual lifestyles?"

"That's not what I said. It's important to recognize that all groups of oppressed people need to be treated with dignity and respect. No one is trying to make you teach about the sex life of gays and lesbians."

"What if you don't think that the homosexual lifestyle is acceptable? Why should I have to teach my students about it?" asked another, as if he hadn't heard a word.

Marvina took over and reviewed the economic implications of globalization for our children and their need to become culturally competent so they can compete in the worldwide marketplace.

"Why should I have to learn Spanish?" shouted an irate woman. "I was in a McDonalds where they only spoke Spanish. They wouldn't wait on me. Do you believe it? This is my country! They should speak English!"

"No one is forcing you to learn Spanish. I just said that today's world is changing, and our children will have to be able to interact with people from different cultures. Speaking Spanish and other languages will be an asset. Any progressive businessman who wants to increase his market will adapt to the target culture. Most Hispanics learn English. But if you don't like the way you're treated at a business, you can go somewhere that wants you."

"All those Cubans just want to take over and turn this place into their country," shouted someone from the back of the room.

Rosaline, who didn't fit their stereotypes of Latinos, stood by silently as angry teachers vented at Marvina. Then she began by discussing the difference between deep and surface cultures and the kinds of activities that children can do to become culturally competent. The group listened attentively as the White woman spoke, much as they had for me. And then Rosaline, who speaks without a trace of accent, related the story of her exodus from Cuba and subsequent mistreatment by her fourth-grade teacher in Miami.

"I didn't speak any English in those days, so she just put me in back. I sat there all alone for the entire year, not knowing what was going on. I lost the whole year because that teacher didn't take the time to get to know me. She never made any attempt to teach me, she just let me sit there.

"The next year I had a teacher who was the opposite—a nice Jewish woman who made me a star. The class decided to learn Spanish. They had been listening to an instructional radio program that was awful. I can still hear the announcer saying *repetir*. She asked if I would help teach the class, and we had a great time together. It shows the kind of influence a teacher can have." The room was silent.

Whites may have an advantage in diversity training because they're part of the dominant group, and other Whites may assume they have something important to say. The concept of privilege—that Whites have access to jobs, housing, travel, and a host of other facets of our society, including respect, based on the color of their skin—is a volatile one. We may initially have the attention of a group, but when we begin discussing differences in power in our society based on color, some in the audience become agitated. It's uncomfortable to hear you live in a society purporting to be color blind and classless that is still laced with racism and classism. (See Barnes [2000] for illustrations of "everyday racism.")

In addition to pointing out the difficulties people of color encounter in business, housing, and education, we ask workshop participants to relate their experiences. They invariably recount being harassed by police, followed while shopping, or mistreated by a racist person. Many White teachers find it difficult to believe that Blacks regularly receive this type of treatment.

White privilege can take many forms in the classroom, like emphasis on cultural contributions of Europeans to the near exclusion of those of color, or focusing on the same few token Black contributions of Carver, King, and Black athletes and entertainers. It can surface in preferences for certain children selected for special tasks, being called on or not, or being acknowledged for one's work. And it affects teachers' choices of disciplinary action for children who don't conform to their cultural norms.

That many Whites just don't get it testifies to the power of the concept of White privilege and confirms the supposition that we live in different worlds, or, as social scientist Andrew Hacker (1995) terms it, in "two nations." Because our experiences and interpretations of the world are different, it's important for students and teachers to share them, especially since four-fifths of our teachers are White and more than a third of their students are children of color. All teachers must be allowed to talk about their experiences as men and women, people of color, and all the labels that society uses to categorize us.

If we don't have the chance to develop a sense of who we are and how we relate to one another, how can we be sensitive to the many challenges our students face? If teachers don't learn to take risks with one another, how can they create classrooms that value diversity and promote an egalitarian learning community?

In a recent workshop we asked teachers to list obstacles that prevented them from doing their jobs. They outlined about a dozen when a middle-aged White male raised his hand. We didn't know what to expect because he seemed disinterested all day. He spent the first hour thumbing through a tool catalogue.

"I have one non-obstacle," he said cryptically.

"What's that?"

"Things like this. I've been here for twelve years and I've never had a chance to talk like this."

Most teachers aren't intentionally holding children of color back. They don't consciously discriminate. Those who do are easily identified. You hear it in the halls and see it in their referrals to the office. It's the well-intentioned people who steadfastly contend they are colorblind who pose the bigger challenge. They are the ones who say, "In my class, every kid is treated the same. We all work together like one big family. I respect everyone, and they all respect me. I don't see color." But that's one of the first things we observe, and to deny that is to deny someone's identity. To say that you don't see color is an insult—however unintended it may be—and to steadfastly maintain it is the height of naïveté or hypocrisy.

Studies by the national public opinion polling organization Public Agenda consistently reveal that parents believe teachers have a preeminent role in the success or failure of their children (Farkas et al. 2003). While there are many talented teachers, not all are doing a great job, and for many children, including Whites, the experience of school is unpleasant and unsuccessful. This sentiment is reflected in the low graduation rates (the percentage of children who enter high school in the ninth grade and graduate in four years) of African American, Latinos, and Native American children. It also finds expression in the large numbers of children of color labeled as having learning disabilities; fights among students and assaults on teachers; discipline referrals, suspensions, and expulsions; and high rates of absenteeism and tardiness.

Of course, we can't attribute all of society's ills to teachers and the education process. Many teachers are quick to point out that a student's home life is an even greater determinant of his or her success. But the fact remains that children spend much of their lives in school, and their experiences there have an important effect on character and personality development.

How many of us remember an outstanding teacher who shaped our lives? If love, affection, praise, and moral development are lacking at home, can't kids get some at school? If home is a place of abuse and neglect, can't schools be havens offering respect, protection, and enrichment?

We have tried to convey such ideas to teachers with limited success, because some of them are comparing what they do now to their own educational experiences. They fail to see the necessity for qualitative change. They practice their profession as they did decades ago, using outdated, noninclusive materials, concepts, and methods that inhibit learning among children from different cultural traditions. A complete overhaul of our materials and techniques is needed. Few school boards, administrations, and teachers have the desire or courage to undertake that. So we read about the small successes here and the many failures there—and continue to back into the twenty-first century.

These points were driven home to us once again at a day-and-a-half-long retreat for thirty-five teachers and principals from four schools. Our team of six trainers worked for days developing a curriculum designed to help them learn about cultural diversity so they could aid underachieving students. We wanted the participants to develop a sense of their own ethnic identity. The activities were structured to become more challenging and personally involving.

The participants seemed to be enjoying the experience as they selected items from magazines and catalogues that represented their interests and identities and pasted them on their name tags. Following this insightful and humorous introduction they were invited to write entries in their journals reflecting on the activity. Next we began a discussion about community partners that schools can draw on to enhance educational experiences.

Things were going well until one of the trainers asked them to assemble in a line based on the month and day of their birth. They laughed and joked as they arranged themselves with only a couple of people out of place. Then she asked them to do the same thing by height. That took a little longer, since many people were of similar stature. Next, she asked them to arrange themselves by skin color. There were stunned looks on many faces, hesitation, and nervous laughter. After a minute they formed a line representing gradients of complexion.

When we discussed the activity, several people complained that they felt uncomfortable.

"I didn't like being put at the end of the line," said a Black teacher. "It reminded me of the old days when we had to go to the back of the bus."

"I didn't feel it was a good exercise. It forced us to compare ourselves on skin color and that's wrong," said a White teacher.

The facilitator compared the activity to the preceding ones.

"Why are we so reluctant to address questions about race and ethnicity? The assumptions people have about their place in line may reflect those of society. No one designated a front or back of the line, yet some people clearly perceived the situation that way," she said.

The next exercise was even more challenging (threatening?). Participants stood in a straight line facing one of the team who read a series of statements. If it applied to individuals they were asked to step forward or backward: for example, "If your family income was over $100,000 when you were a child, take two steps forward. If it was less than $25,000 take two steps backward. If your family ever received welfare, take two steps backward. If your father was a lawyer or a doctor take one step forward."

As often happens, by the end of the statements you will find the White males in front with White females behind them and people of color at the back. Frequently participants are distraught because it so clearly demonstrates the effects of class and privilege. Discussion usually produces disclaimers by the Whites who contend that they were embarrassed by their parents' affluence and tried not to let it affect their relationships. Those at the back may be tearful, recounting obstacles they and their families had to overcome.

It is an eye-opening experience. (We don't use it in most youth workshops, but we do at Anytown, where we have sufficient time to examine the implications of the activity.) Some participants are uncomfortable, and that is our intent—to force them to consider their past and present positions in society. Some things they had no control over—their status was largely ascribed. However, we also point out that some managed to overcome formidable obstacles to achieve their present status as professionals.

One White female complained, "I don't feel that because my parents earned a lot of money, I was privileged. I try to be fair with the kids in my class, and I just don't think there's such a thing as White privilege." Then she broke into tears and left the room. (See McIntosh [1990] for a discussion of White privilege.)

Telling our stories helps heighten our awareness and appreciation about social and cultural differences. We were joined by Harold Johnson and Rosaline Alvarez for a three-day workshop for forty teachers from a large urban school district. Harold did a couple of hours on stereotypes. Rosaline talked about deep and surface culture, and we discussed prejudice and discrimination. The first day went well, although we were nervous because we were being scrutinized by members of the administration who were unsure about the process. The teachers seemed reserved but interested as we went through the exercises.

On the second day we set aside two hours after lunch for ethnic sharing. People were asked to bring items representing their cultural heritage and to describe them to the group. Each had three minutes. The activity sometimes takes longer, but this group became so engrossed in the stories that only a third of them had spoken after three hours. They were genuinely moved by learning about one another's heritage and life struggles. Many were in tears as they listened. We agreed to continue the next day.

When we arrived that morning, people were chatting, gesticulating, and hugging one another. Several Cuban Americans found out they were related. One woman brought her mother. Others brought food, family albums, genealogical materials, hairbrushes, straightening irons, and all sorts of personal artifacts. We couldn't cut them off. Though we had prepared other activities, what they were learning was irreplaceable. They continued for the entire day.

The group was scheduled to spend the last two days of the week on curriculum matters. We stopped in to say good-bye, but before we could, a man asked to speak. We didn't know what to expect.

"I've been a teacher in this school district for twenty-seven years. Do you know how many workshops I've been to? This is the best one ever!" And the rest applauded.

We all have stories, and we need to tell them.

# 5

## Setting the Tone: How Policy Makers Affect School Climate

In time, every post tends to be occupied by an employee who is incompetent to carry out its duties.

—The Peter Principle

There are many levels of people who formulate and implement the policies that establish the climate in our schools. They bring their personal, political, and theological proclivities into the educational institutions they control. Even when teachers and administrators do graduate work, some are still unprepared to manage classrooms and schools because they lack the interpersonal skills and commitment that are essential for creating cooperative learning environments in culturally diverse settings. As with teachers, the majority of policy makers do not reflect the diversity of students they are responsible for educating. This can have a stultifying effect on school climate, the educational process, safety, and student achievement.

School districts vary from postage-stamp-sized ones with a school or two to countywide megadistricts encompassing hundreds of schools and tens of thousands of students. The principal policymaking body in a school district is the school board. While some benefits are associated with economies of scale, the single-county district system has created enormous bureaucracies that are plagued by waste, inefficiency, and sometimes fraud.

A common criticism teachers have of "the administration" is that it is often long on administrators who are short on knowledge and hands-on experience about actual classroom activities. While such criticisms may be apropos (many administrators have a teaching background but may not have served in the classroom for years), the criticism is especially relevant to school boards that are largely populated by individuals from varying backgrounds, too infrequently education. While this should not a priori disqualify many well-intentioned "concerned citizens" from serving on school boards, it also attracts a fair share of people who have little knowledge of contemporary education, finances, and the social and cultural changes in schools. In many parts of the country, anyone can run for their district's school board. Terms normally last four years, with no term limits. It is not uncommon for boards to have members who have served for a decade or more. Two-thirds of the districts around the nation do not pay school board members. Nationally, only 20 percent of school boards that pay members offer more than $10,000 a year.

Many well-intentioned citizens vie for the chance to mold our nation's children by defining their educational experience, but there are those among them who seek to impose personal agendas. Several years ago the Lake County School Board in Florida passed a requirement that children in that district must learn that the United States' social system was superior to all other countries. A persistent, sometimes successful strategy of school board members is to impose fundamental Christian beliefs through Bible study courses or posting the Ten Commandments to infuse Judeo-Christian values in the presumed hedonistic void left by their parents.

Such myopic views of education reveal the incongruous relationship that may exist between board members and the children they ostensibly represent. This incongruity is also reflected in the ethnic composition of boards, which are overwhelmingly White (over 75 percent) and male (61 percent), with more than half having an average age of fifty or more. Although some board members (there are usually between five and seven per district) pride themselves in keeping abreast of the latest educational developments, learning about and promoting policies that foster better understanding of cultural diversity and relationships among students is not a priority. The obsession with finances and standardized testing has pushed cross-cultural concerns further back on the agenda.

In the aftermath of Columbine, fearful board members throughout the nation imposed "zero tolerance" policies that required the suspension or expulsion of students for a wide array of disciplinary issues that had heretofore allowed for discretion. In the spring of 1999, a prominent citizen called about a high school senior and three of her classmates, all honor students, who were expelled for a semester because an unopened six-pack of beer was found in their car. They had driven the vehicle to a Friday night football game. The interior overhead light malfunctioned and caught the attention of a school administrator, who peered in and saw the beverage. All the students, including one who stood to lose a full academic scholarship to a leading university, were suspended and sent to an alternative school for the remainder of the year, despite the fact that this was their first offense, and that there was no evidence that drinking had occurred or that they bought the beer. A school administrator explained, "We can't do anything about it. There's no appeal."

From around the nation we hear of similar inspired decisions where elementary, middle, and high school children have been suspended or expelled for having pills, penknives, toy guns, even wearing certain clothes or colors, or uttering or muttering comments that were threatening or perceived by someone to be sinister. Such draconian policies appear excessive, but may seem justified in the beleaguered context of today's schools.

A year ago, in leading a discussion about conflict in school with twenty high school students in a media center, a middle-aged principal was interrupted by a loud argument between several students and staff on the other side of the room. As we ate the carefully prepared meal she remarked, "That was nothing. This morning we had a bomb threat and we had to evacuate the school. About an hour later the fire alarm went off and we had to evacuate them all over again. We couldn't find anything wrong with the system so we let them back in. Half an hour later it rang again. Everybody had to leave the buildings. We checked every device and found one alarm that was defective. Just a normal day, I guess," she said resignedly.

Despite financial exigency and societal events that pressure school boards and administrators to initiate punitive policies, the diversity of students and the uniqueness and complexity of their lives calls for greater rather than less flexibility. In the face of rising enrollments and decreasing resources, many board members, desperate administrators, and staff have taken the path of least resistance, imposing arbitrary and what seem (to many students and parents) capricious policies for the sake of maintaining the status quo, while failing to perceive that more of the same is not the solution to the new dynamic in our schools.

The American Psychological Association criticized zero tolerance policies for creating inflexible school environments filled with tension and suspicion (Elias 2006). Such policies have had deleterious consequences for minority students, especially African Americans, who have received a disproportionate amount of suspensions and expulsions. (See Advancement Project and the Civil Rights Project of Harvard University [2000] and Dell'Angela [2005] regarding Native American students.) These inequities led the American Bar Association to adopt a policy against zero tolerance in 2001 (American Bar Association 2001).

If school boards are the policymaking bodies that establish the climate in schools, superintendents are the chief administrative officers charged with implementing them. School district superintendents have exceedingly demanding jobs. They have responsibility for the overall functioning of the district's schools, students, personnel, and physical plant. Aside from the ubiquitous and vexing problem of providing resources in these financially trying times, the magnitude of the interpersonal problems is enough to send anyone into early retirement, and that's exactly what has been happening around the nation. For example, in a recent year, two-thirds of Florida's school superintendents retired or resigned, to the pleasure (or dismay) of their boards and staff.

Having stability at the helm is imperative, especially in turbulent times. Superintendents provide the leadership that guides the system, setting the tone. The signals they emit, the practices they endorse, and the encouragement they give to staff can mean the rise or fall of new educational initiatives that will find their way into classrooms. Despite the oversight responsibility of the school board, the superintendent has enormous power, for he (and 84 percent of the superintendents in the nation are males and 90 percent of all school superintendents are White) has far more knowledge of the intricacies of the system. Although some board members may think they formulate policy, much of their deliberations are influenced by the superintendent's recommendations and those of his staff, who are more attuned to pedagogical developments. Even in their financial oversight role, board members frequently depend on documents supplied by the superintendent's staff and make decisions trusting that they have done their homework.

In some states superintendents run for the office. This practice may politicize the position, in contrast to the more common approach in which the school board appoints the superintendent. But both forms of selection can become political, given the many constituencies they must satisfy. Further, their evaluation is predicated upon their ability to exact excellence from diverse departments—a monumental task in good economic times. Consequently, boards, as well as teachers, parents, and students, may find themselves in less-than-congenial relationships—a condition complicated by differences in age and ethnicity.

While power may be shared at the top between the board and the superintendent, it is the principal whose job is to implement policies at the school level. As if students' lives aren't already complicated enough by pressures at home, in their neighborhoods, and from academic and interpersonal challenges, bureaucratic rules and regulations enforced by principals and their assistants can make kids' academic experiences problematic.

The nature of administrative work in schools and the demands of these jobs are daunting. In addition to the principal, several assistants may be assigned to specialized tasks such as discipline and academics. Since many secondary schools enroll fifteen hundred to two thousand students or more, overcrowded conditions contribute to interpersonal conflicts when kids jostle one another in clogged hallways. Schools often resemble factories, with students marching to and fro to the shrill sounds of bells and buzzers.

Principals have a pivotal role in the functioning of schools because they regulate academic and interpersonal relations there. Two-thirds of the nation's schools are headed by males, and 84 percent of all principals are White. Nearly half are fifty years old or older. While the board may influence policy and the superintendent ostensibly implements it, the principal has the day-to-day responsibility of enforcing it.

The wide variation in teacher and student satisfaction, dress codes, and, to some extent, discipline and academic achievement ultimately rests with the principal, who is most familiar with the eccentricities of the staff, students, and plant. There may be an overall academic plan and strategy for a district that establishes theory, methods, and practices, but these can be (intentionally or unintentionally) abrogated by principals. From relations among staff to decorum among students, from dress codes to discipline, from valuing diversity to interscholastic athletics, from parking to plant maintenance to the decor of the building and classrooms—the proverbial buck stops at the principal's desk.

You have to visit schools and talk with students and staff to appreciate the impact that the principal and his persona have on the people within them. Two of the most obvious differences among schools are dress and discipline; both vary widely based on the climate established by the principal and his staff. Another less obvious condition is teacher morale, which fluctuates with the principal's demeanor and ability to create a community on campus.

Like superintendents, principals are besieged by all parties within—and many outside—their schools. Parents, students, teachers, and support staff all vie for their attention, which means their days and nights are filled with interpersonal crises that often defy logic and easy solutions. How they conduct themselves, the tone they set by demonstrating consistency in their decisions (one of the biggest complaints students have about teachers and administrators is favoritism and inconsistency in the treatment of their peers), and their ability to lead through the challenges posed by increased diversity, growth, and adversity provides the backdrop for the level of achievement and conflict within schools.

If the principal is an advocate for diversity, he or she will attempt to create a diverse staff and encourage them to promote activities that reflect and respect students. Modeling this behavior finds expression in teachers' lesson plans and the classroom atmosphere as well as in students' comfort with the school environment and with one another. The following vignettes are provided to give a glimpse of how school bureaucracies and administrators can function or dysfunction, with obvious ramifications for staff and students.

The first case illustrates the interference of a school board member in hindering the implementation of a proven cultural diversity program, and the lack of leadership among some administrators whose judgment was obscured by their own religious beliefs and indecision.

School bureaucracies are like giant amoebas oozing over the landscape, searching for new ideas. Occasionally they seize on something novel but are slow to digest and implement it. Our Green Circle Program was such a case. It is a human relations program started by Gladys Rawlins in Philadelphia in 1957. Through the use of a flannel board with felt cutout figures pasted on it, children learn to value differences and treat each other with respect.

Volunteers go through eight to ten hours of training to learn the concepts and the script used with first- and second-graders. The idea is to teach them to let other people come into their circle of caring and sharing. As more figures representing parents, significant adults, children from diverse ethnic and religious groups, and even family pets are drawn into the circle, it expands to encompass the concepts of love, peace, and understanding.

It's a popular program used around the country. We introduced it in a large county with sixty thousand elementary students and arranged for a trainer from Delaware to give a demonstration. Twenty parents, a few teachers, and a couple of key administrators watched as she led them through the framework of the program on the first day. The next day she demonstrated it with a second-grade class. The kids loved it, and so did the workshop participants, though they were somewhat taken aback when a boy disclosed that his mommy didn't want his daddy in the circle because he threatened her with a gun. It was a teachable moment for all of us. Afterward, we approached the county's head of elementary education and asked her what she thought.

"You have my permission to go ahead," she said as a slight smile creased her lips.

We piloted the program for a year at a school that prided itself on progressive teaching. The parents and staff were enthusiastic and gave it rave reviews. We received a grant from a local organization to hire a coordinator. She was very thorough and extremely competent, and made dozens of presentations to area schools, parents, and civic organizations to recruit volunteers. We spoke with school officials at every level right up to the superintendent and were authorized to begin. The trainer returned to teach fifteen volunteers, and we introduced the program at three more schools. We were off! At least that's what we thought. Then we got a call from an assistant principal at Langston Elementary.

"We've decided to put Green Circle on hold."

"What's the matter?" I asked, somewhat stunned. "I thought everything was going fine."

"I can't say there have been any problems, but it just isn't good timing now," she said cryptically.

We were dumbfounded. Had we done something wrong? We knew the kids liked the program, but we didn't know that four fundamentalist Christian parents had objected to "its secular humanist" orientation. They pressured the administration to cancel and convinced an esteemed member of the school board who held similar views to oppose it.

When we learned about their opposition, we offered to meet with the parents, to show them what it was about and answer questions. They declined and kept agitating for the program's abolition. Within days we received calls from the other two schools canceling. One principal, who had been an enthusiastic advocate, now said she couldn't support it.

"I don't agree with the values you're teaching. God is at the center of my circle," she said before hanging up the phone.

Our program coordinator looked forlorn.

"What's that got to do with our work?" she asked.

"I don't have a clue. We're trying to show kids how to live with one another. It's nothing religious. We'd never get cleared for that."

A school district administrator assured us Green Circle would be reinstated, but he wanted a task force to examine the content more carefully before approving it.

"We already went through one review. We've got a deadline for training volunteers and placing the program, or our funding will be cut."

"Don't worry. It won't take long. I'll send you a letter as soon as we're done."

Two weeks after our program was unceremoniously removed from Langston Elementary, several fourth graders were caught with cocaine. It touched off an investigation about safety and security with concomitant racial overtones (the boys were Black and the majority of students were middle- and upper-class Whites). We'll never know whether what we had to offer might have improved the situation.

Weeks passed and became months; still no word from the authorities. Our funding agency was growing restless. They realized what we were up against, but we had performance criteria to fulfill, and deadlines were approaching. Our coordinator spent most of her time updating and improving the materials, including the development of a prekindergarten program, training volunteers, and lining up prospective sites.

At last we were told that we had again passed the review. We weren't surprised, since the superintendent had used it more than twenty years before. Now all we needed was the formal letter of authorization, which we were told was on an official's desk. We waited three months for that letter.

Within a year we had a cadre of outstanding volunteers and our own training video, and had the program running in eighteen schools. More than three thousand children participated, although the principals who cancelled the program never reinstituted it. We were receiving numerous requests and were hard pressed to meet the demand. And we were collecting data about its effectiveness. Interviews and surveys with teachers and students who went through it revealed that they developed 40 to 60 percent more friends from different social and cultural backgrounds; a like number were able to demonstrate more knowledge about geography and cultures than children not in the program; and there was a significant reduction in conflict, especially fighting, among Green Circle students. Nevertheless, the program was canceled after we submitted the results. Our adversary on the school board was also on our funding agency's board.

Principals are scrutinized and criticized by students, parents, faculty, the union, support personnel, and the administration "downtown." Many try to accommodate their diverse constituencies, striving for a balance, that idealistic state of equilibrium that may prevail from time to time— perhaps on Christmas or the Fourth of July. After working with more than three hundred principals, it's difficult to generalize about their styles. Most seemed to be fair and decent, but then, we haven't worked for them or attended their schools.

Even good-natured administrators can have bad days. They must have the wisdom of Solomon and the patience of Job; the stamina of Pheidippides and the quickness of Michael Jordan to cope with the variety of problems they're called upon to solve. The hours they put in test the mettle of the best and brightest.

Although they may have graduate degrees in administration, principals may be unprepared to deal with the demands placed on them by culturally diverse students, burned-out faculty, and complaining parents. Even Gandhi or King would have difficulty resolving the problems that fill their days, which usually begin around 6:00 A.M. and often end after 10:00 P.M. A man whose wife is also a principal told me they only see each other on weekends—if they don't have other commitments.

Turmoil on campus can take many forms. An average week might have fights, some involving injuries with racial overtones. Knives or guns as well as drugs and alcohol may be confiscated. Students are sometimes arrested for committing felonies on or off campus. Both sexual assault and consensual sex are part of what principals must address. So, too, are teenage moms who need day care and social support for their children, and the moms-to-be who must be coaxed into completing their education and taught how to care for their babies.

There are decisions and recommendations to make about suspensions and expulsions as well as dealing with irate or uncaring parents. Then there are unending personnel problems—from bus drivers, cafeteria workers, and maintenance staff who barely make a subsistence living to teachers complaining about low wages, long hours, dangerous students, lack of support, and mandates from the state legislature for curriculum changes and tests. All these issues must be faced with diminishing resources and overcrowded classrooms. And of course there is the physical plant, which may have inadequate parking space, a lack of money to correct structural deficiencies, and need to be refurbished because of problems ranging from insufficient heat or air conditioning to vandalism.

Into this breach step some rather ordinary people, though even Superman would be taxed. Not surprisingly, they can make monumental miscalculations, like the principal at a lower-socioeconomic-level middle school. While we were trying to help fifty students learn to respect each other's feelings, she came into the media center at lunchtime.

"How are things going?"

"It's been interesting. Some are with it, and others have a lot of growing to do. They just don't appreciate one another. Did you order food?"

"The cafeteria made sandwiches for us." Just then a worker wheeled in a large cart filled with subs, cookies, and drinks.

"Let's get them quiet and then everyone can take something," she said. "I'll call their names, and they can pay the $1.50 as they come up."

"I thought you were picking up the tab."

"The cafeteria would lose money. It's only a dollar and a half, and those on free and reduced lunch get it for nothing."

She made her announcements and began calling their names.

"Richard Jones."

Silence.

"I see you over there. Come get your food."

"I'm not hungry."

"Rashiel Middleton."

"Don't want any."

"I know you're hungry. I've watched you eat in the cafeteria."

"Nothin' today."

"Tyrone Anderson."

"Nope."

"The National Conference will pay for lunch."

"That's okay," she said quickly. "Lunch is on me." And she left.

The kids enjoyed it. Later she returned with free ice cream sandwiches.

The poet Robert Burns wrote, "The best-laid plans of mice and men may go awry." Good intentions may not be enough to overcome past incompetence and a negative school climate. Hamilton High School had a history of problems between Blacks and Whites. But the violence wasn't totally racial. A few days before our workshop several African American girls got into it using X-ACTO knives they'd liberated from shop class.

It was Tuesday. The principal, George Baker, wanted us to show a video about young people from different racial backgrounds trying to get along. We had seven or eight kids from another school's multicultural club seated on the stage to talk about how they were working together. Five hundred kids were in the audience. It was a very courageous step on George's part, since many schools no longer risk putting so many teenagers together. It's often difficult to keep them quiet, and fights can break out. That's also why many schools have abandoned pep rallies, and some even schedule football games during daylight hours on weekdays.

George notified the media about the program to demonstrate that he was trying to improve the situation. Walking on stage he asked for quiet, but even with a microphone, you could barely hear him. There were a few boos from the crowd, and most continued chatting as if he weren't there. About fifteen teachers stood around the room, no one attempted to calm the students. They stood impassively against the wall and watched George dangling in the wind.

After a few minutes George managed to introduce the visitors, and we began watching the twenty-minute video. The kids quieted down, and most were watching attentively when a reporter and photographer burst into the darkened auditorium. The photographer climbed onto the stage, turned on his spotlight, pointed his video cam at the crowd, and proceeded to shoot as if the whole scene had been set for his benefit. When he had enough tape he turned off his light and left.

The students on stage spoke briefly about their activities. (We later learned they were being taunted by kids in the front row.) Their remarks had little effect on the group, which began to writhe and wriggle like little boys who have to take a bathroom break. Sensing it might be the right time to cut his losses, George excused the group a few minutes early. At least no fights had broken out.

We went outside and stood at the top of the stairs, looking out across the grounds. Clusters of students were talking about what they had seen and how they could deal with the problem. Many of the discussions were positive, and kids were being interviewed by reporters from different television networks.

"That's good publicity for you guys," I said to the assistant principal standing beside me.

"Great, except that the one who barged into the assembly is down there with a bunch of troublemakers getting an earful of garbage. You see that kid with him—the one with the black jacket? He just got back from a ten-day suspension for fighting. That one over there was thrown out recently for defying a teacher. And there's one of the biggest troublemakers on campus. Why couldn't that guy interview some of the good kids?"

George could have asked the reporters to leave, but he hoped they might cast his school in a better light. Unfortunately, the reporter who was being "filled in" by rebellious students worked for the most popular station in town, and it was his negative take on the event that was seen that night by the superintendent and several school board members.

George retired at the end of the year.

Some principals are caught in a generational time warp. They cling to outdated, punitive methods of discipline that may demean children, and avoid interpersonal issues that contribute to student and teacher conflict. Some even realize that they don't have the necessary skills, resources, and support to make a difference.

An anachronistic administrator may linger on in the system and hinder innovation. Ed Paine is proof that the Peter Principle can cripple a school. A student who recently attended Anytown reported that when she returned to his school she enthusiastically talked with a guidance counselor about improving race relations: "She looked at me like I was sick or something when I told her I had just been to Anytown. She said, 'That's okay, you'll get over it in a little while, so just forget it and settle down.'"

Ed was an assistant principal there and, like too many administrators, did not grasp the advantages of multicultural education. He conveyed his negativity about Anytown to the staff. Several months later the student called me.

"You'd better to talk to Mr. Paine. He was at a meeting with my mother. She's a principal, too. He told her Anytown was a cult where they practice mind control through sleep deprivation. My mom didn't know what to think. And he's going on to be principal at one of the new high schools."

The county where Ed worked is building schools faster than they can find staff to fill vacancies. When several new high schools opened, Ed became principal at one. Within two weeks fights broke out and several students were seriously injured. Parents were in an uproar and the media had a field day exaggerating the problems.

Though we had never met, I called Ed and offered to help. A few days later we talked in his office. He explained the situation: "We've had some fights all right, but nothing like the newspapers made out. There isn't anything here I can't handle. The majority of the kids are sincere students. Only a few are the troublemakers. I'm in the process of expelling about fifteen now. They didn't come here to learn. They'll be out as soon as I can process their cases."

"Have you done anything to help kids to get to know each other?"

"What do you mean?"

"Well, what kinds of things have you done with the faculty and the students to create a community? Have you tried to help the kids get along with one another?"

"No, we really haven't. Would you like to meet with my department heads and explain what you do?"

He left to address a student assembly about the violence. He paced back and forth in front of hundreds of students, only a handful of Black youths among them. The discord wasn't race related, although the press had characterized it that way. Fights were over turf—local gangs and inadequately socialized ninth graders. Students from different socioeconomic backgrounds were thrown together without the slightest attention to their prior allegiances.

Ed told them how fortunate they were. There probably will never be another school built like this one, with large rooms and accessories, he said. "I want you to know that I believe you are serious students. There are only a few troublemakers here and I'm removing them. Our school is a safe place. I won't allow anyone who breaks the rules to stay. Remember that I support you, and you can come to see me if you have a problem." He went on for about twenty minutes until he saw them getting restless and dismissed them.

Three days later we attended a conference with nine of his department heads and administrative staff. All were White except one African American man.

"Since everyone is new here we don't know one another very well if at all," I began. Several heads nodded, and a few smiles creased their stony faces. "It stands to reason we've got to create a community. People who know one another realize we're all individuals with our own needs and wants, so something has to be done to help people get acquainted. When that happens, we'll have a more congenial environment."

We discussed Anytown, with its daylong workshops on conflict resolution and leadership with students. "I've heard about it," said Ed with a grin, "but I'm glad you explained it."

"When could you start?" asked one of the women.

"Right away."

"We have to check on the financial end," Ed cut in. "I put in a call downtown to see if they can help. I'm waiting to hear, but we need something like that. And the faculty needs some work, too. We spent weeks this summer going over curriculum, but we never gave any time to human relations. I guess we missed the boat."

We never heard from him again. The fighting subsided as the year went on. Overcrowding continued, and there was talk about putting the school on double sessions one year after opening. Controversy continued to plague the school and a year later he was transferred to the central office.

Kids are like sponges. They soak up all kinds of messages from their environment. They take cues from teachers and administrators that, on the surface, may seem irrelevant or innocuous. But these convey attitudes and beliefs about minorities, women, the differently abled, gays and lesbians, social class, body size, and myriad other personal and social characteristics that define schools and the people within them. Subtle gestures, smiles, smirks, winks, whispers, or looks of discomfort or disdain do not escape students' gazes. They are captives in an environment run by adults. Powerless, they thrive on the petty insults, gossip, and rumors that add color and some meaning to their world, even though they may misconstrue the situation.

If a teacher or administrator is overheard making a derisive or disparaging remark about a student or colleague, or their behavior toward a group is inconsistent, the student grapevine quickly sends the message to the ever-inquisitive kids, who yearn for inside information that will elevate their status among less well-informed peers. Although many teachers and administrators strive for impartiality, some are outright racists—and the kids know it. They see it in their mannerisms: who they call on in class, smile at, associate with, and favor.

Sometimes students like Ronnie Chilsom, an African American in an advanced program in James Madison High School, overhear remarks. He was walking past an assistant principal. "He told a White student that Blacks shouldn't be in the advanced program because they don't have the intellectual ability to do the work." That ranks up there with the comment a French teacher made to students at a predominantly White high school that "Blacks shouldn't study French because they don't have the ability to learn it."

Being opposed to censorship, we still might have stopped one student's article from running on the front page of Ronnie's high school paper during Black History Month. It was in defense of flying the Confederate battle flag from the South Carolina capitol. Claiming that it was part of his Southern culture, the student berated Blacks for wasting time over such issues. "His [Dr. Martin Luther King's] dream has now been fully realized, at least in the sense that minorities have equal rights as citizens." He saved most of his vitriol for Jesse Jackson, whom he described as a troublemaker attempting to create chaos for personal gain. "Until Jesse Jackson starts targeting meaningful issues instead of attempting to destroy a 135 year old relic, the only day on the calendar that should be reserved for him is April 1st."

Ronnie's mother phoned our office. "My son and his friends are really hurt. Can't you do something?" We wrote the principal and offered to help. A week went by, we followed up with two phone calls, and never got a response. A tremendous opportunity had been lost to educate students about the history of the Confederate battle flag—that it had been inserted into many flags during the civil rights movement of the 1960s as a protest, and that widespread discrimination against Blacks, Latinos, women, and other groups persists, despite the works and dreams of King and Jackson.

As the cohort of administrators ages and growth in student enrollment continues, new schools are being built faster than some districts can train and place qualified administrators. This puts enormous pressure on school boards and superintendents to select quality successors and identify new administrators who can walk on water, don't need more than a few hours sleep a night, are always in a good mood, and can turn a "D"-ranked school into an "A" in a year.

Some principals, like Tom Mullens, have come to appreciate the role that multicultural education can play in school. At fifty, Tom has worked in the school system for more than twenty years. He's a caricature of the All-American Boy. Born in the Midwest, he grew up in a blue-collar family that instilled in him the merits of hard work and a competitive drive, values that have served him well. As principal of a large and culturally diverse high school (more than twenty-two hundred students), Tom is often hard pressed to get through a day without an incident, some of them major.

Not long ago, an irate student fired a gun through a classroom door. Fortunately, no one was hurt. Countless hassles occur every day in his school. Some are gang related—Asians versus Whites and Blacks, Crips versus Bloods, skinheads versus Blacks, everyone against the alternatives. Because of an altercation on campus that had racial overtones, he arrived late at our workshop for improving the academic performance of minority students.

"The thing is," he said, somewhat chagrined. "These kids were friends, but once it started others got into it, egging them on. And when they really went at it, all the racial stuff came out."

The participants told us about how and when they were first made aware of their race. Tom told a story about his days as a college athlete.

"I was raised in a pretty straight family. We never heard anything negative about other people. It wasn't until I went to college that I became aware of my race. I was a sprinter in the late 1960s. White sprinters were rare even then and wherever the team went, I was always the only White guy—parties, track meets, on the bus. Nobody believed I could be a good one, but I was damn good.

"I went to the University of Wisconsin on an athletic scholarship, the only way I could afford to go. Boy, did I catch it from all those Black guys—until they saw me run! The harder they rode me, the harder I worked. The first time I experienced racism was at my first big NCAA meet. I was just a naive kid competing against some of the biggest, most talented runners. John Carlos was there—the guy who did the Black Power salute when he received the medal at the '68 Olympics. He was the fastest sprinter in the country, and I certainly wasn't ready for him.

"As we were getting ready to get into the starting blocks, he came down the line and pointed a finger at each man, telling him what place he would finish in after him. When he got to me he shook his head in disbelief and muttered 'eighth.' Everyone finished just the way he said, with me last. I've never forgotten it.

"I worked my butt off, and the next year we met again, but I didn't speak to him before we ran. After I won I went up to him and said, 'Remember me?' He shook his head. 'Well, I hope you don't forget you just got beat by a White boy.'

"I guess that's the kind of anger that builds up in someone who's been insulted. It used to happen to me all the time—like when the shoe companies tried to get the big-name runners to wear their shoes. At the meets they'd have a room full of all the latest models, and guys stopped by to pick out whatever they wanted. They were expensive shoes, some even custom made. And underneath the paper stuffed into them there'd be money, maybe a thousand dollars. It was hard for me to get a free pair because even they didn't believe a White boy could be a sprinter. When I managed to, I'd pull out the paper and find—nothing."[1]

Tom became an all-American and was written up in *Sports Illustrated* as an oddity. "They called me the Great White Hope," he says with sarcasm. But he doesn't run anymore, and for a while he had trouble walking.

The problem started when his school began experiencing rapid minority student growth. They didn't have any special programs to attract White middle-class kids, who scattered across the county in search of them, leaving his school to serve the growing numbers of Latinos, Blacks, poor Whites, and Asians. It seemed that every group was represented by a gang, and each gang had staked out a piece of the campus as its turf. The front of the library was where the Asians hung out. The far side of the campus was home base for the skinheads. Black students were concentrated near the entrance. To complicate matters, the incoming class of five hundred ninth-graders was a particularly rough one. From time to time a bunch of kids who are exceptionally bright or challenging comes along, and many of these kids were the latter. Teachers at Tom's school attributed the problem to the inadequate socialization of middle school students. Tom asked us to organize conflict resolution activities.

"I can certainly use your help. We just had a big fight between Blacks and skinheads. I don't know what gets into these kids sometimes. Many of the ninth graders have taken up that skinhead stuff. We don't let them pass around any of their literature, but they've got it. We've confiscated some pretty nasty stuff. I don't know whether they even know what it's all about, but we need to do something."

He left our planning meeting to attend a special assembly for ninth-graders. His assistants pointed out that less than 50 percent of their entering ninth-graders graduated. We offered to conduct a dialogue among the skinheads and Black students, assisted by some kids who had gone to Anytown. We planned a series of daylong workshops involving students from diverse backgrounds. Just as we were wrapping up, Tom returned with a disgusted look on his face.

"The speaker said they're the worst group of kids he's ever met, and he tours all over the country."

A week later we met with thirty students in the media center. There were three skinheads and their girlfriends led by Pete, a junior with an iron cross hanging around his neck. Most of the kids were White, with a sprinkling of Latinos and Asians. The six Black students sat together opposite the skinheads and glared across at them. Pete and his entourage were rather subdued, even solemn, in contrast to the arrogant way they reportedly carried themselves. There were two teachers whom we had briefed ahead of time.

"It will be their show. We'll let them work it out. As long as a majority in there know how to behave, they'll control the situation. The kids should set the norms for the rest of the group. We must trust the system. It might get a bit tense, but it will work. We'll stay in the background and let them do their thing."

We looked at the group, which included the two principal combatants and their followers, and about a dozen from the multicultural club.

"We're here to see if you would like to make this school a better place for everyone—a place where you don't have to walk around angry and be watching your back wherever you go."

A few of the kids were slouched in their chairs, looking as if they'd rather be somewhere else.

"It's okay with me if you just want to let things slide along. I mean, do you like going to school here?" They laughed. "Do you think it's safe?"

"It ain't safe cause there's too many of them Black dudes," said Pete.

"Like we're the ones goin' around sayin' trash about other people?" said Antonio, a large junior and Pete's principal antagonist.

"If you and your boys didn't push people around—"

"Hold it!" I yelled. "We won't get anywhere this way. Let's set some ground rules so we can air opinions without anyone losing it." We used an easel with newsprint pad to record what they called out.

"Okay. Now I'm turning the meeting over to Shalondra. Remember these rules and just one more: You can't speak unless you have the eraser. If you want to talk, raise your hand and wait till you get it."

President of the junior class as well as the multicultural club, Shalondra was respected. She had learned how to facilitate a dialogue at Anytown. Although a bit nervous, she spoke in a steady voice.

"Let's start with introductions." She began with herself and went on. "I'd like to reduce tension on campus." Each student followed her lead until it got to Antonio.

"I'm a junior here, too, and I'm sick and tired of being called names and stuff by those skinhead honkys!"

Pete looked menacingly at him and started to get up. "Everybody stay seated or you have to leave," said Shalondra. "Now sit down. Antonio, just stick to your introduction."

"What are we here for if I can't speak my piece? There'd be no need for this if it wasn't for them shovin' people around like they own the damn school. If Pete hadn't slapped Jasmine, I wouldn'ta had to hit him upside his face."

"What you talkin' about? I never hit women, and I never hit her!" snapped Pete.

"Don't tell any of your lies. I heard how you smacked her after her and your skinny little girlfriend got into it in the cafeteria."

"Hold on a minute!" shouted Jasmine, who had been sitting quietly on the other side of Antonio. "Who told you Pete slapped me?"

"It was all over the place."

"Nobody slapped me, and I certainly don't need you to stand up for me. I can take care of myself."

"You mean it never happened?" asked Antonio incredulously.

"Never."

"Then I got suspended for no reason?"

"It goes to prove you'd better get your facts straight before flying off the handle," admonished Shalondra.

"It still doesn't give them the right to keep sayin' nasty things about us," said Antonio.

"We don't—you just think we do," said Pete.

"Oh yeah, then why do you go around with your heads shaved and wearin' that stuff?" inquired Malcolm, another Black youth.

"We like it that way," replied Martin who was sitting beside Pete. "It shows our White pride. We're proud to be members of the White race."

"Does that mean that you think Black people are inferior?" asked Martin.

"Not necessarily," interjected Pete before Martin could say more. "It just means that we identify with each other because we're White. It's called White pride. We're not against Black people. We just feel that both sides should stay with themselves. We're not racists; we're White separatists."

"Oh, I get it," said Antonio. "You want to keep us separate so you can run things. We're supposed to stay in our place and let you and your honky friends do whatever you damn please. Sounds like a return to the 'good ole days.'"

"You can't blame us for the past," said Pete. "All we want is to be left alone. You go your way, and we'll go ours."

"Maybe this is a good place for us to agree to meet again," said Shalondra. "It sounds as if we've made some progress. At least we learned that the fight started from a rumor. It's too bad we weren't talking before—we might have avoided all the trouble. What do you think?"

Pete and his buddies smiled at the suggestion. "We'll talk to anybody, any time," he responded. "We're all for keepin' the peace. That's what we're about."

"Yeah, I know what you're for keepin' all right," said Antonio. "Tell you what. We'll meet again if you and your boys stop passin' out those nasty cartoons and that other junk in your notebook there."

"I don't know what you're talkin' about," said Pete. "What cartoons? Nothing's in there except homework assignments."

Antonio grew visibly upset, challenging Pete to prove it.

"How can we continue to talk if you ain't bein' straight with us. We know what you carry around."

Pete pulled a black-covered notebook from his backpack. It was decorated with swastikas and other Nazi symbols. With a smug look, he opened it for all to see—nothing.

Disappointed, Antonio slouched in his chair. "This must be your lucky day."

"It's a lucky day for all of us because we learned we have to continue talkin' so we can get to know one another and help calm this place down," said Shalondra.

They decided to meet again the following week. After they left, Tom Mullens, who had quietly entered the room and heard the last part of the dialogue, turned to me.

"I know he has Nazi literature with him from time to time. If we catch him or any of his buddies with it, they'll be suspended."

Two weeks later, we returned for a meeting with six teachers who ran a new program for 120 ninth-grade students identified as at-risk for dropping out. They had the potential to succeed, but for a variety of reasons— low motivation, deficient fundamentals, inadequate parental support— their future was imperiled. The teachers had created a special curriculum that included a standardized series of math and English courses as well as opportunities for special counseling and outdoor class trips. They had just gone on a weekend canoe trip together.

The kids came from diverse socioeconomic backgrounds, but the majority were working-class Whites. There was a contingent of about thirty skinheads. Many had swastikas inked on their hands and arms. At the age of fourteen or fifteen, they were sending out messages to the other students that might prevent them from getting any older.

Each workshop included skinheads and teenagers from different racial and ethnic groups. Ninth-graders are difficult to work with, and they did everything they could to perpetuate that stereotype. The first group gathered in the media center and was boisterous and rude. The half dozen skinheads and their girls stood off to one side, smirking as they watched the Blacks, Latinos, and Asians do the culturegrams.

It's fascinating to see how segregated schools are. In virtually everything students do, from hanging out in halls to classroom seating and eating in the cafeteria, joining clubs, listening to music, they self-segregate. Now the Black kids clustered around a sheet of butcher paper and gave answers that were very different from those of the skinheads, who did theirs on the other side of the room. All but one of the latter said they had no religion, a statement clearly the result of peer pressure. One of the youths had until recently been a regular congregant at a local Methodist church. His mother had asked us to help steer him away from his new friends.

We spent the first two hours doing icebreakers that required them to mix. Some were silly, like having small groups make their bodies into machines and demonstrating them for the rest of us. Each student had been preassigned to a group that was intentionally diverse, compelling the different ethnic groups to interact. They interviewed each other about their likes and dislikes, hobbies, and families—all an attempt to show them that others have needs and wants similar to theirs.

Members of the multicultural club took the lead in each group. After a snack we watched a video about two boys who were imprisoned at Auschwitz, survived, and returned nearly half a century later. The faculty felt it would be appropriate because of the anti-Semitism among the skinheads. While one group of fifty students was with us, another was in a different building watching *Schindler's List*.

Later we began a dialogue about prejudice and discrimination, but the kids resegregated themselves. The discussion started timidly but heated up when Julie, a White girl, looked across at Faye, who was sitting with the skinheads.

"Why do you and your friends have to smoke up the bathroom so badly it makes your clothes stink? You can hardly see in there."

"That's right!" said Nancy, sitting next to her. "It's nasty."

Faye's face turned beet red in sharp contrasted to her long blonde hair.

"None of your business what I do!"

"It sure is."

"They don't give us any place to smoke. What are we supposed to do?" shot back Faye. Both their voices were rising.

"They should keep it off campus and let us use the bathrooms so I don't need a shampoo and clean clothes every time I've been in," said Julie. "What's the matter with you anyway? I used to be friends with you until you started hangin' around with those guys."

"They're my friends. We think the same," replied Faye.

"Think the same? You never used to say those things about Black people."

"A Black man killed my brother last year." Faye stared directly into Julie's eyes. "I can't ever forget it. He's gone, and I hate all Blacks."

"Why hate everyone for what one person did?" Julie asked.

"Because that's the way I feel. They understand that and you don't."

"That isn't the right way to think," said Julie.

A hush came over the kids as they listened to the former friends agonize over the tragedy. The discussion ended when the bell sounded. As the students left, a teacher who had been listening came over.

"That was pretty intense. It's amazing what some of them have experienced. But we all have had trouble. Last year my son was abducted by two Black men. They robbed and beat him and took his clothes before dumping him on the street. In the hospital he had a Black nurse who took such good care of him. When I thanked her she took me out of the room and said she understood what I was going through. One of her sons had been kidnapped and beaten by White men. So you see, we have to learn to live together and to forgive."

"Too bad you didn't share that with the kids."

We complained to Tom Mullens that some students had to return to class because their teachers wouldn't excuse them.

"It's hard to make them realize that it relates to teaching. Some of them just don't see the connection."

He arranged for us to address his teachers a week later. We met in the closed media center.

"You're aware that we have a security problem here," said Tom. "Donnie [a former NFL football player] can't handle it all by himself, and I don't have the money to hire more security people. I'm asking for volunteers to assist."

Nobody raised a hand.

"I don't mind saying I don't feel safe here at times," said one of the women.

"We're working on it," he said. "How many kids do you think were sent to my office by midyear?" Silence.

"Thirty-four hundred, and we only have twenty-two hundred students."

He held up an inch-thick folder and dropped it onto the desk in front of him. "These are the kids that have been arrested here for felonies so far this year. Now Dr. Kaplan would like to ask for your help in releasing students to attend his workshops."

"You want us to let them out of class," said a math teacher, "but we have to get them up to state requirements. How can we do that if we keep letting them out for everything that comes along?"

"Look, I know that. If you work with me, I can help you."

Many around the room looked skeptical. Others appeared bored and burned out. You could sense the fear and tension that gripped many of the women, who dreaded coming on campus to confront the great unknown each day.

"A lot of those kids aren't able to concentrate on your subjects. If a kid doesn't feel good about himself, is having trouble at home, or is angry at someone who's called him names, he's not ready to learn what you have to teach. If you let them come we can work with them. It may not solve all your problems, but at least give it a try."

"Ah, most of them just want to miss class. They were eating pizza outside the library when you were here last time, and I heard them talking," said a portly middle-aged man.

"Let him have another chance," snapped a young woman who had volunteered as the school's multicultural club adviser. "What do you have to lose? They're not learning anyway."

Two weeks later we returned to conduct another workshop and stopped in at the office to see Tom. He rose slowly from his chair and limped over to shake my hand.

"What happened to you?"

"I tore my knee up trying to stop a fight between two girls in the cafeteria last week. One of the assistant principals got hurt, too. She's going for therapy on her back, and I'll be having an operation."

"It must have been quite a fight."

"A Black girl came into the cafeteria and went to a table that had an empty chair. She asked a White girl if she could sit there and was told it was reserved. But they can't do that and she challenged her. Then she walked away and glared over at her. That's when the White girl picked up the chair and yelled, 'Here, take the f…in' chair!' and threw it at her. It took all of our strength to pull them apart."

The door to the media center had a sign saying, "Closed again for the multicultural club." It might as well have been permanently closed, since the media specialists discouraged anyone from using it. You seldom saw students there.

Judson, a tall Black youth who was one of the club leaders, pulled me over: "Did you know they expelled Pete? I guess Mr. Mullens had enough. He went to Timberlake High School down in south county and I heard he got punched out by a Black kid while he was waiting in line in the cafeteria."

We conducted six workshops for the ninth-graders and eventually the faculty got behind the program, the violence decreased, and the suspension rate was cut in half. Judson became the head of the club, which now had more than two hundred members. Then he mysteriously disappeared from school for a week. He had "borrowed" a teacher's car from the parking lot, and the police found it in front of his house. He never returned to school but was allowed to enroll in a GED program.

Most of the skinheads and their wannabe friends dropped out and drifted away. Assisted by a few middle-class parents, a movement developed among some of the faculty to turn the school into one that stresses fundamentals, eliminating most of the working-class and at-risk kids who couldn't qualify academically. The multicultural club adviser was despondent over the prospect.

"Where will they go? What will become of them? Nobody seems to care."

Following many meetings, the movement failed. After two operations, Tom Mullens got the spring back in his step, and life goes on at his school. The turnaround could not have occurred without his leadership and support for our work and the teachers who lobbied for increased emphasis on cultural diversity activities. The interventions were so successful that the faculty voted to incorporate cultural diversity activities in the coming year's School Improvement Plan—the document that establishes the program of learning for the school. Although Tom shared his experiences with colleagues in other schools, and the multicultural adviser who drafted the goals for inclusion shared her success with other teachers and administrators at retreats we conducted, it was difficult to enlist the support of principals who were prisoners of the old-school approach that emphasizes standard curricula and preparation for mandated standardized tests. Many administrators and teachers are still reluctant to embark on activities that detract from the drills to improve test scores. The link between interpersonal relations and cultural competency among and between students and staff and academic achievement has not yet been accepted by many teachers and administrators, despite success stories like Tom's, abundant research (Howard 1999; Aronson 2000; Perry 2000; Landsman 2001), and the continued abysmal dropout rates and low academic performance of poor Whites and students of color. More of the same is evidently still not enough.

Sometimes a crisis can be the catalyst for change among administrators. School violence can be a strong motivator for increased human relations activities, especially when traditional methods fail. The director of a county agency that funds programs for children asked us to create a task force on the growing violence in schools. A number of violent confrontations had occurred, and the newspapers were filled with stories about them. Parents were enraged, and it seemed as if the climate was right for change.

We formed a culturally diverse team to ascertain the causes of conflict and recommend solutions, focusing on a sixth-grade center, two middle schools, and a rural high school. The team spent more than a year working with students, teachers, administrators, and parents. We held meetings in the surrounding communities during and after school, and conducted daylong and overnight workshops for faculty and students. We even took the high school teachers on a bus ride through some of the communities where their students lived.

Problems began to surface when a near-riot occurred at Johnson Middle School. Located in an upper-middle-class neighborhood, Johnson's twelve hundred students were crammed into a facility built for eight hundred. To complicate matters, the ethnic composition was changing too rapidly for a faculty and administration ill prepared to deal with the children of color. The situation challenged their traditional way of doing things.

An article in the newspaper described Black students going on a rampage, hitting and pushing White students in the halls, injuring some, and terrorizing the campus. The newspaper noted that a special meeting for parents was scheduled for that evening. The parking lot was full and the cafeteria was brimming with wall-to-wall bodies, half Black and half White, and they were all mad. Television cameras recorded every word for the eleven o'clock news.

In the front of the room stood the beleaguered administrators and a school resource officer who tried to respond to parents waiting in a long line at the microphone.

"I want your assurance that my children will be safe here!" demanded a well-dressed White man.

"You have it," replied the principal, Beth Daniels, a fastidiously dressed middle-aged platinum blonde.

"How can you say that after what happened?"

"Nothing will happen to them while I'm in charge," she insisted.

"But it did happen! My son was beaten up right in the hall. What are you doing about that?"

"Officer Marshall is in the process of compiling the facts, and charges will be filed. The students involved will be punished," she said, managing to stay calm.

The man walked away with a disgusted look on his face. A large Black woman spoke next.

"Do you only care about White children? What about my kids? We've got rights, too. I want to know why our boys were strip-searched."

"No such thing was done."

"That ain't true!" yelled another, who was standing against a wall. "My son told me he was searched for weapons. That they took him and some others into your office and stripped them and threatened to beat them with whips."

The principal turned to Officer Marshall.

"He can tell you that nothing like that was done."

"I was there the whole time, and that never happened ma'am."

"There were other police besides you," she countered. "My son told me they had different uniforms. Some were green and some were blue."

"Those were city police and sheriffs deputies who were called in, but nobody did a strip search."

"You were busy chasing kids. You don't know everything that went on."

"You've got to trust us," replied the principal.

"Why should we? You don't even want our kids here."

The discussion grew more acrimonious. You could feel the tension between White and Black parents, and all of them were berating the principal and her staff.

"I'm the district supervisor and I can assure you this school is safe," said a balding middle-aged man. "We are doing everything possible to get to the root of the trouble. I stand behind Mrs. Daniels and her staff. We will continue to provide your children with a first-rate education."

Many of the Black parents jeered, and some White parents left the room. A Black man approached the microphone: "You can't duck the issue like that. We want to know what you are doing about the racism among the teachers and the way our children are treated!"

A chorus of "Yeah!" came from around the room.

"And that woman," he said, pointing at the principal, "is to blame. Try talkin' to her if you can. Listen to my son."

Ms. Daniels looked anguished.

A young boy stepped forward.

"The police came on campus. We was running away so they couldn't git us. Some of them grabbed me and a few others and took us in her office and threatened us with their belts. They told us to strip so they could see if we had any weapons."

"Officer Marshall will tell—" Ms. Daniels struggled to keep her composure.

"I don't care what you say. I believe my boy!"

By now half the parents had left, exasperated.

We offered to mediate the conflict by holding a session so parents could discuss their issues. Ms. Daniels seemed relieved, and promised to have representatives from the police and faculty there to answer questions. We decided on an evening the following week.

As the last parents left the room I approached her: "That was the toughest group I've seen. I don't envy you."

"They are scared and need reassurance."

"The first thing we need to do is restore a level of trust. A lot of the Black parents think there's a racial problem. Is that true?"

"No, but I think we have a communication block. Some of their kids are real problems. I wish they always gave them the kind of support they showed here tonight. We can't get them to come to PTA meetings. Many of their kids can't handle school."

"What exactly did happen?"

"There wasn't any riot. If you believe the papers you'd think we had an all-out war here. Actually, some Black students ran down the halls pushing and shoving White kids. A few got knocked down. One boy got badly bruised when he fell against his locker."

"What about the police?"

"Officer Marshall couldn't handle it alone and called for help to cool things down. A couple of sheriff's deputies responded. You'd think the place was under siege, but it was necessary."

"And the strip search?"

"Believe me, it never happened. The police wouldn't do anything like that. It's nothing but a rumor."

"It seems like a lot of parents don't agree. The next meeting may not be any easier."

We met with sixty anxious parents the following week. With me were the president of a civil rights organization and her husband, Rita and Harold Johnson, both outstanding human relations trainers and respected members of the African American community. We decided to let the parents list their grievances and concerns and posted them on the walls of the cafeteria. They were brutally candid about the school and its personnel.

"There's no communication," said one father. "I heard about the fighting and tried to get in touch with my son, but they wouldn't let me."

"It wasn't an emergency," said Ms. Daniels. She looked haughty and very White to the lower-class Blacks, who viewed her with distrust and contempt.

"How can you say it wasn't—police were all over the place!"

"Only to maintain order. We have an obligation to keep things under control. At no time was there a serious threat to the safety of your child."

"But my son was injured!" snapped the man who had just spoken.

"Minor injuries—not enough to warrant calling you."

"Who made that decision? Are you a doctor?"

"It was a judgment call and—"

"You decided to keep him on campus although he was bruised and threw up several times. And you locked the kids in their classrooms," he said, finding Black parents siding with him.

"It's policy to do so when a disturbance occurs."

"What caused it?" asked a mother. "Does this kind of thing go on regularly?"

"Certainly not."

You could see she and several of the others didn't buy it. Harold Johnson took over.

"Maybe there's more here than meets the eye. Let's break up into small groups and list what needs to be done. If we don't make some changes, I don't think our kids will get the education we all want them to have. Ain't that right, brothers and sisters?"

Harold is a big round man of many talents—a poet, musician, scholar, bon vivant, and top-flight diversity trainer. He is known throughout the region, and he knows what it's like to be a Black student in a White school. He related an incident that happened to him when he was in elementary school in Delaware.

"I wasn't doin' that good in school, and thought I could fool my mama. So I took my report card and changed a few grades. I was just a foolish kid. I didn't think anything would happen. Even later when I handed my report card back in, no one said anything. Then the principal called a special assembly. We didn't know what it was all about. He stood there and called out my name. 'Harold Johnson, come up here.' I walked down the aisle in front of everyone. I didn't know what was going on. And when I got there he grabbed me and pulled out my report card. He told everyone what I had done—how stupid I was. He did that in front of the whole school."

The wounds we inflict on children may heal, but the scars last forever. Harold and Rita were committed to healing wounds. They were great. We had the parents sit down together and talk. It was the first time something like that had been done at the school—maybe the first time some of the Whites and Blacks had ever spoken candidly together about anything. A list of proposals to improve communication, administration, teaching, and student life emerged. The process was painful at first, filled with mistrust and apprehension. But the dialogue revealed that they were all concerned about the well-being of their children—even, to some parents' surprise, the teachers and administrators.

Our work had only begun. We formed a parental task force and had five more meetings. Specific recommendations were made about installing more pay phones so children could call home (office phones were often off-limits), creating activities during which students could learn to value and appreciate the increasingly diverse school population, conducting diversity-awareness teacher training, forming a multicultural club, and developing ways of defusing rumors to avoid the types of problems associated with the recent incident.

Over the next two months we learned that many African American students didn't feel like they were part of the school, and neither did their parents. They were bused in from a transitional neighborhood about eight miles away. The area around the school was virtually all White, with expensive homes, neat green lawns, and luxurious shrubs. Many of the Black students were from densely populated apartments miles away.

Trouble commonly occurred during February, Black History Month. The level of knowledge about the subject is low. Black students complain about the mundane way in which Black contributions are treated by teachers. They want a more thorough exploration of their culture and its impact on society, while White students often resent the special attention they get at that time.

Black teachers have staged elaborate assemblies depicting everything from slavery to contemporary achievements of African Americans. Many White students and teachers feel left out—even offended—by the ostentatious presentations of literature, art, and music that may seem alien to their own dominant culture. We mediated a dispute at a high school after an African American teacher allowed Black students to recite inflammatory prose and give a Black Power salute over the school's closed-circuit television that went into every classroom. It took many months and the teacher's transfer to mend those fences.

For many kids it's like a contest—whose culture is more important? Black or White? Latino? Asian? And the poor biracial kids don't know which side to take (but most White kids know where to put them). When working with children, teachers must convey the idea that honoring one group doesn't mean denigrating others. Yet it's hard for some adults, let alone kids, to grasp that point. Maybe one day we'll have an integrated curriculum that accurately portrays contributions made by various ethnic groups in our pluralistic society.

Harold thought it would be a good time to celebrate the diversity of the students, so we had about five hundred kids at a time in the cafeteria, where he did a rap, complete with music he composed. Several African American kids performed, and the students were singing and dancing in the aisles, having a great time. Some administrators were getting nervous—they'd never granted such freedom. Nevertheless, it was memorable. Hopefully, they'd learn to trust the process and empower students, but a lifetime of old practices changes slowly, and we were asked not to take such "risks" there again. We later learned that three White students, one of them in the gifted program, left campus and went across the street to a convenience store, vowing never to return.

Hearing from students, teachers, and parents, we found that troubles at Johnson had come to a head when some of the alienated Black youths decided to vent their frustrations on Whites during "Cracker Days." It was a display of contempt that led to "wilding"—running down crowded halls and knocking kids over. Not a riot, but it was wrong. And the parents who attended task force meetings, Black and White alike, gradually accepted the facts of the incident and moved on. Others, too steamed up and unwilling to dialogue, dropped out. By the time of our last meeting, four months later, eight people were still attending.

One mom became an unofficial leader of the Black parents and started attending PTA meetings. The problem was that she worked, and the meetings were held at 10:00 A.M. in the morning, so she had to resign.

Some of the frustration the African American children were experiencing came from feeling unwanted, some from their inability to achieve at the level of the middle-class Whites and the smattering of Asians and Latinos whose parents were professionals. And some of their anger was the result of the inability or unwillingness of teachers to accept them. We offered a diversity awareness workshop for the faculty—all sixty-five of them. This was done with the full support of Principal Daniels, who was still smarting from the public rebuke she sustained earlier.

We gathered the teachers in the media center, sitting at tables scattered around the room, but we wouldn't let them segregate. We moved them into small groups, created interactive conversations, and tried to interject some humor with things like Harold's version of Freudian slips, asking them to reply with the first word that popped into their heads after hearing a given word, for example, White, teacher, principal, Black, student, school.

They seemed interested, and had fun. We even went about ten minutes past the official ending time. On Monday a friend in the district's central office called and said several teachers had complained about the workshop. "One or two even called the superintendent. What the hell did you guys do?"

"I don't know. I thought it went over all right. We did the kinds of things we usually do. They like it everywhere else. Harold put a lot of work into his presentation. We even ran a little bit over—"

"You kept them late? You never do that, especially on a Friday!"

Obviously, some of the teachers weren't interested in the program. We got permission from Beth Daniels and the central administration to take fifteen of them on an overnight retreat. Of course, the people who volunteered were the ones who least needed it. But together with a like number of teachers from a sixth-grade center that was having similar problems, we talked, and planned projects to help all the kids feel better about themselves, one another, and their schools.

We started working with Ellie Dunn, who was getting her doctorate in education. We put together a multicultural club with twenty active members. Ellie developed a monthly calendar of events marking cultural festivals and ethnic contributions, and disseminated it to the staff. The kids held regular meetings and cultural fairs. Within a year things had changed dramatically, although there were still some disillusioned staff sulking around. That didn't include Ms. Daniels, who worked hard to overcome her negative image in the community. To some extent she was successful, but the stress and strain took its toll. Within eighteen months she was diagnosed with cancer and left to fight a bigger battle, which she eventually won. She retired shortly thereafter.

Today Johnson is a school where minorities are in the majority. Ellie got her degree and left, and with her went the driving force behind the multicultural club. Officer Marshall was promoted to detective and left, but a great biracial guy took his place. He became a catalyst for change on the campus and a regular advisor at Anytown.

Our team also worked at Shore Lakes High School, which had been the scene of innumerable fights in recent weeks. The principal, Joe Stansfield, was in his late fifties and looked stressed out. A former football coach, he had been in the job for seven years, but the recent rash of problems seemed to have pushed him to the point of early retirement. Joe was ready for help, and though he didn't quite understand our methods, he was willing to try something new. He spoke in a slow Southern drawl.

"Here's the situation," he said. "We've got two thousand students here comin' from different communities. This is a rural area. Nobody lives near the school, so they get bused in from all over. I've got 139 faculty, including a migrant specialist who works with the Hispanic kids. We have about four hundred Hispanics, some three hundred of whom are migrant children, mostly Mexican American. They're good kids, and so are their parents.

"They work hard to get their kids educated, but it's difficult because they often have to take care of their brothers and sisters or work in the fields with their parents to make ends meet. And they are frequently yanked away when their parents go north to pick other crops. They may have 30 or 40 absences during the year or just disappear. We get 250 to 300 absences a day, and six hundred students withdraw or return every year. But last June we had forty-seven graduate.

"We don't have a large Black population, and most of their students are bused in from King Village. They're decent kids who work hard and earn good grades. They don't cause trouble."

"So what's the problem?"

"It's gangs and turf battles. We had over seventy-fights here before Christmas. About four hundred of our lower-class White kids live in trailer parks, and there's terrific rivalry among them and the Mexican Americans from different neighborhoods. You must have seen the news about the shootings. There's gunfire over drugs, women, and I don't know what else. A lot of that carries over onto this campus. I even had a kid who was accused of killing the brother of another student sitting right here in class, awaiting trial while relatives of the victim were going here. We've had shootings at the building and in the parking lot."

"You mentioned gangs . . ."

"Oh, we've got them. There's Stand and Deliver, the Black Angels, the Latin Kings, Bay Boys II. We try to keep them apart, and Officer Poluso, our SRO, has a pretty good read on the situation. We had 180 suspensions here in the first three months of the school year."

"How about your migrant-education worker? Does he have a good relationship with them?"

"That would be Mr. Clark. The kids love him."

"He doesn't sound Latino to me."

"He's not; he doesn't even speak Spanish, but he communicates."

"Are many of these kids in the Limited English Proficiency program?"

"Only about 30. I don't know why more of them aren't, but we do have about 225 in special education—kids with learning disabilities or emotionally handicapped kids. And we've got about 40 who are court-ordered. They've been sent here and told to stay in school or else."

Our team included Rita Johnson, who had worked with us before, a social worker from a well-known migrant organization, and a Mexican American professor who lived nearby. We began by conducting focus groups with students from different ethnic backgrounds.

White students told us the atmosphere was strained because of friction from class differences. They felt staff lacked compassion and seemed uninterested in students. "They were just putting in time," one girl observed. They also believed that teachers often exacerbated problems.

"They're unskilled in handling crises," said a girl who was an honor student.

"When something starts they either head the other way or panic. They don't know what to do and more often than not do the wrong thing. They wind up scaring everyone because they overreact, and they don't give us enough information. We don't know what actually happened, so rumors get started. That makes things worse."

"What do you think is the matter?" asked Rita.

A thin girl with long dark hair looked her straight in the eyes.

"A lot of kids couldn't care less. All they want is their diploma. They're lower class. That's why we're called Hicksville."

"They treat us differently," a boy complained. "The football coaches favor Blacks and some kids get away with anything."

"If you could change one thing here, what would it be?" I asked.

"Get the drugs out."

"Stop the fighting."

"Give kids values and ethics to believe in."

The Latinos were more caustic in their remarks. The professor asked them in Spanish what they thought about the school. They laughed.

"We all speak English," a boy responded, "but they need more Spanish-speaking staff. Only four or five teachers are Spanish and there's no one in the office. Most parents don't speak much English and they need translators. They don't like coming here."

All communications were sent home in English. When parents called, secretaries had to grab a passerby from the hall to translate. It often resulted in long waits and miscommunication.

"There's hatred all around," a dark-skinned boy exclaimed. "It's in the bathrooms, everywhere. A classroom even has 'White Power' on the wall. They tried to get it off. They painted over it but anyone can see it."

"Everybody looks down on us," continued another girl. "Whites get special treatment here. They hang out with their own group and act superior, but cheat off each other and ask us for answers. That's the only time they talk to us. As for the Black kids, there's not many of them, and they stay pretty much together. It was great to have a Black homecoming queen this year."

"We need some kind of orientation program for Hispanics," said a girl. "The kids come over from River Edge Middle School, and they don't know what's expected of them. And they should help seniors prepare for college. They need to show them how to fill out forms and stuff."

"Another thing," said a muscular boy: "There's no activities bus for people who live in south county, but there's one for the Black kids so they can play sports. There's no Hispanics on the football team, but some of them could play. The coach is biased. All he wants is Black kids. It's not like he doesn't need help. They haven't won a game in years."

"Same story with soccer," said a girl. "They can't play even if they want to since there's no way to get home unless they drive. And very few do. You know what they say about Mexicans who have cars or wear gold."

"Isn't there a Spanish Club?" asked Rita.

"Oh, yeah," said a girl derisively. "Some club. All the members are White. The Spanish kids go to the Bilingual Club. My Spanish teacher doesn't speak it, and they discourage us from using it in the halls. We had a Spanish teacher last year who wanted to put on a special event like the Black kids got to do. They wouldn't let her, so she left."

The African American students were congenial and relaxed and liked going to school there. All were bused in from King Village, a well-kept community with a tradition of caring for its children.

"The dress code is unevenly applied," said a girl. "The preps get away with anything. Fights come from attitudes some kids have. You hear racial talk in the halls."

"We don't get into many fights, but we're blamed for them," said a boy. "One day before Christmas they stopped our bus and lectured us about fighting. We didn't even know why."

"And another thing," a girl added, "They call ours 'the project bus.' How'd you like to come to school on the 'project bus'?"

"I don't know about anyone else, but at least I do feel safe here," said a girl.

"Me, too," said a well-built boy. "But I wish they paid more attention to us. It just seems they don't have any time for us. No one encourages students to study more. And they shouldn't announce negative things like lock-outs over the intercom. The principal got tired of people comin' in late, so he started callin' for the rooms to lock their doors at 7:30. They have to report to the office and serve a detention. That's hard on some of them if they miss the bus and their parents don't have a car. And servin' a detention means they have to walk home, maybe ten or fifteen miles. If you cut detention you're suspended for three days and lose points from your grade."

"They even surveyed the students about school problems but then didn't pay any attention to us," continued a girl. "There's also trouble comin' from River Edge. Some of the migrants get held back and they can be seventeen years old when they get here."

River Edge Middle School was about two miles from Shore Lakes. The students came from the same communities, but the principals were very different. Bill Jones, the principal at River Edge, was in his mid-fifties. He was a bit portly with a ruddy complexion and curly black hair. His Spartan office was barely lit by a single desk lamp when our team visited him. He spoke cautiously and we sensed an air of distrust, even suspicion, about our project. Coming with the blessing of the central administration and outside funding, it was difficult for him to turn down our offer of help. "We don't have anything much wrong here," he said as he sized us up.

"How large is your faculty?"

"We've got one hundred teachers, plus four who work in our exceptional education program. There are 1,561 students in the seventh and eighth grades. Three hundred sixty are Hispanic, 103 are African American, 9 Asian, 12 American Indian, and 1,077 are White. That's as of right now, but the figures change almost daily."

"How many of your teachers speak Spanish?" asked the professor.

"Five."

"When you have trouble, what do you feel is the source of it?" asked Rita, the civil rights leader.

"I think here, as well as at the high school, it's a matter of rivalry among Hispanic students. A lot of it starts in their communities—it's often among family members and sometimes is gang related. Things boil over into the school. You need to focus on them. They're the problem, not the Black and White kids. This year we've had to expel thirteen kids so far. Here it is January and we usually expel about three all year."

We left and met with Richard Clark, the non-Spanish-speaking migrant counselor at Shore Lakes High School.

"Much more could be done if we could get the kids before they arrive here," said Clark. "So many of the Hispanic kids need extra help. We were planning for over three hundred more from River Edge to enroll, but they never came. And because of the language barrier, many parents are unfamiliar with the way things are done. Suspension letters are sent home in English to post office boxes that may be checked once a month."

We held meetings for parents of children in the two schools, and for the first time, invitations went out in Spanish and English. Our first meeting was held in a farming community civic center with a tin roof that clanked as rain pounded it during a thunderstorm. Local people had been terrorized by gang warfare over control of the drug trade, and many teenagers, mostly Latinos, had become victims of vendettas associated with bad deals.

"I know things wouldn't be so bad if we were able to raise our kids the way we were raised," said a middle-aged White woman. "We need to get prayer back into school. That's where we went wrong. We need to give kids respect for God. That'll straighten them out."

"And parents have to be in control and take more responsibility for their kids," joined in another.

"And they shouldn't be giving out condoms," added an elderly White man.

I looked at him quizzically. "They don't." He said nothing further.

A man holding a small child said something in Spanish. The professor moved to his side and pressed him for more information. She turned to us: "He doesn't think the children are adequately prepared to go through the transition from River Edge to Shore Lakes. There ought to be older students appointed to advise newcomers—like Big Brothers/Big Sisters."

"I'm an elementary teacher, and I don't think the teachers in those schools care enough. We spend more time with the kids."

"That may be so," replied Bill Jones, "but look at the numbers involved. Our schools are twice as big. We just can't do things the same way."

"Suspending or expelling kids gives them what they want—out of school," said a Hispanic woman. "For some, it is a badge of courage. We need in-school suspension."

Five days later, in a small-town recreation center, we held another meeting. It was attended by migrant workers and poor Whites who expressed concern for the safety and education of their children. "The kids don't even have textbooks to take home," complained an exasperated parent. "And there's safety issues at both schools."

"There's been some fighting at River Edge, but I assure you we haven't any organized gang activity," Bill Jones sounded defensive.

"I find that hard to believe," said an elderly White man, a citrus grower from a large nearby farm.

"My son has seen weapons at school," added a woman with a fearful look on her face.

"We've confiscated a few but we have the situation under control," replied Jones.

Joe Stansfield from Shore Lakes looked away, and a few parents rolled their eyes. No one mentioned the reports of shooting in school parking lots, or trouble caused by a few White students who antagonized the Latinos by flying Confederate flags on their cars.

"Why do Black and Hispanic kids have to take different buses from the White kids when they come from the same place?" someone asked.

"I'll answer that," said Stansfield. "It's got nothing to do with segregation. It's for safety. There was too much fighting on the buses, so we decided to separate them for their own good."

"How will they learn to live together, to get along, if you do that? Are they separated in school?"

"No," replied Jones.

"That's not exactly right," said the professor. "Most of the Latinos are in special remedial classes."

"We're working hard to bring them up to passing. We're graduating thirty-four this year," Stansfield said with pride.

"What about those who have to work?" asked the grower.

"We've got a real problem there, that's true. We have about three hundred absences a day and a hundred more sign-outs because of family needs. Until we cut down on that there's not much we can do."

"It would help if you sent messages home in Spanish," said the grower.

"Many of them can't even read in Spanish," replied Stansfield.

"That's true, but you have to try. Why, you don't even have a Spanish-speaking secretary in your main office."

"I'd like to hire one, but we don't have the money. I'm hoping to get some funding for one."

Our team set up a meeting for parents from the predominantly White rural community that sent students to both schools. Only two women attended, but we had a productive exchange. They complained that disciplinary actions weren't evenhanded.

"And we never know what's going on," said one. "Either we don't get the information or the bulletins arrive too late. When we go, some of the teachers don't show up."

"My son's English teacher showed videos for the first six weeks because he wasn't qualified to teach the course," the other added. "Who knows what he did after that."

"Why haven't you brought such matters up at PTA meetings?"

"There is no PTA at the high school," she replied. "They can't get anyone to go to meetings."

When we met with parents of the African American students they all expressed concern about rival groups of Black teenage girls at the middle school not getting along, but they were particularly incensed over alleged favoritism.

"For two years now our kids haven't been allowed to take a trip to the Museum of African American Art, but they let other kids go all over," complained a woman. "They need to work with their staff. There's a lot of racism there—especially with the bus drivers. They need to be trained how to treat our kids."

"The problem is at the top!" shouted a Black man who had been sitting quietly until now.

A few days later our team sat down with both principals and reviewed our findings. We made several proposals that included creating a parents' task force to rejuvenate the high school PTA, diversity training for the faculties as well as overnight retreats for teachers and students, and the formation of a multicultural club for students at both schools. We would provide the funding. They consented to the plan, but Bill Jones was skeptical about the benefits. On the other hand, Joe Stansfield was willing to try anything that might reduce conflict and prevent him from being transferred or sacked.

We got permission from Stansfield to conduct diversity training with the entire Shore Lakes faculty—all 139 of them. Neither of us liked working in their auditorium, with its theatre seating that inhibited small-group discussion. The hour we were promised turned out to be forty minutes after a time-consuming number of announcements by Stansfield. It wasn't a total loss; most of them stayed awake. And except for the eight or ten who were grading papers or reading while we spoke, they seemed interested. We'd barely scratched the surface when four o'clock rolled around and they walked out.

"It's in their contract. They only have to stay till four, but you can come back next week," said a somewhat sheepish Stansfield. "It's also in their contract that I can have one faculty meeting a week and they have to attend."

"We'd like to focus on the Hispanic students."

"Now there's something we can work on," declared Stansfield. "We'll try to educate the faculty about these kids, give them a better idea of where they come from and what they're up against. We could charter a bus and take them on a ride through the places where they live. Let them see for themselves."

He found a few teachers who were familiar with the area, and we took the entire faculty on a two-hour tour of six of the areas that send kids to Shore Lakes. It was September and it was hot. Unfortunately, neither Stansfield nor any of our team could go, and that was a source of aggravation. The buses weren't air-conditioned, and we never heard the end of that. But at least some of the teachers realized that the kids had to ride that way every day.

These comments about the trip, from their faculty newsletter, are revealing.

*What was something positive that you got from this trip?*

- The opportunity to see a migrant camp
- Better understanding of the diversity of homes
- We really draw from a large diverse area

- Every area unique adding to Shore Lakes climate
- Realize why they hang around before and after school
- Insight
- Something we all needed to see in dealing with our students
- I really had no idea what our area looked like
- Realizing the poverty
- Seeing why some act the way they do

And then there were these:

- Nothing (2)
- It's not as bad as S. Alabama and Central Ga.
- I don't know
- Zero
- The sleep
- The end (2)
- I lost 20 lbs.
- Getting off the bus
- Pulling into the parking lot at Shore Lakes High

*What is the most negative thing about the trip?*

- The sad living conditions of some of our students
- The distance that some students have to travel
- Conditions of migrant camp
- We need to reach out to a lot of the poor people in our community
- The extreme poverty level and quality of life
- The bus ride for students must be grueling
- Empathy for students
- We didn't see any nice areas

And then:

- I was sick. It was unfair to make us sweat for two hours.
- Do we get comp time?
- Getting on the bus
- Too long
- The implications were insulting
- Bring Dramamine next time
- Recruiters let us down—not enough food

- The situation bordered on abuse
- It was a waste of my time
- Listening to all the teachers' bull . . .
- Being on the bus with negative people
- Teachers can be the hardest audience
- Other than the rudeness of other teachers on the bus, I found no real negative activity.
- I've come to realize that I work with some very self-centered obnoxious people.

*How can this experience impact my classroom interactions with my students?*

- Help me relate with the students better
- Open my eyes to a lot of things
- No community feeling where they live so no wonder no unity at Shore Lakes
- Being less judgmental, less critical in attitude to lower socioeconomic backgrounds
- Help me be a little more giving and forgiving
- Better understanding of emotional and cultural forces on our students
- Being more open-minded about students' feelings
- Better understanding of migrant situation
- Incorporate more cultural awareness in classwork
- I can mention these places, neighborhoods, etc., in class
- See why they are tired from working late to help family
- Seeing distance kids have to travel to school
- More compassionate with sleepy students
- See why they are hungry at lunch
- Request more field trips
- Develop units and using cooperative learning for all groups to interact
- Nothing (8)
- It won't. I've seen it all before
- It was a useless trip. It will not affect me
- It will not impact me any differently
- I'll tell you when I re-hydrate.

We obviously had a problem with a number of teachers, so we decided to continue the weekly forty-minute sessions to broaden their perspectives. It was clear that they needed to discuss these issues among themselves, but Stansfield was unwilling to devote more time to the activity.

Bill Jones never invited to us to do similar work at River Edge. He authorized fifteen of his teachers to attend an overnight retreat on diversity, though only eight went. We discussed ways of working with and motivating kids from different traditions and developed plans for involving colleagues so they could share what they'd learned and start new programs.

They seemed energized and enthusiastic, and began applying some of their ideas. Joe Stansfield supported them, even setting aside a room for me one day so teachers could come in and chat about their perception of the situation at Shore Lakes. I sat alone in a tiny windowless room for three hours. The only person to come by was a math teacher who announced guys like him didn't need what we were offering. We were wasting his time.

We got the same message a few days later from Bill Jones. It wasn't quite as blunt, but he made it clear that our services were no longer needed at River Edge. "I think we can handle it ourselves," was the way he put it. But the problems persisted. For a while, Latino students weren't allowed on the playground with other students. It was the only way they knew to prevent violence—a unique application of *Brown v. Board of Education*. A year later Jones was promoted to a county administrative position. From time to time we run into teachers from his former school. They still regret not having had his support.

With the aid of Joe Stansfield, we kept plugging along at Shore Lakes. The human relations counselor and school resource officer (a regular Anytown adviser) helped organize about twenty-five students into a multicultural club. We took them away for an overnight retreat and taught them how to conduct student activities.

They crossed ethnic lines, built friendships, shared experiences about racism and other issues that trouble teenagers, and resolved to start new programs as soon as they returned to school. They even conducted a workshop for twenty-seven incoming freshman from River Edge. They dealt with stereotypes, peer pressure, self-image, priority setting, and problem solving. And they brought canned goods that were donated to a spouse abuse shelter.

But the best laid plans . . . The human relations counselor had to assume other responsibilities and had less time to promote the program. No formal lines of communication were opened to continue the dialogue between faculties of the two schools, despite their desire to engage one another. When some of the seniors graduated, Shore Lakes lost the leadership to carry on the program. A few students attended Anytown and became outspoken advocates of multicultural activities. The climate at the high school improved the next year—there were fewer fights and a more congenial atmosphere, and more Latinos graduated over the next few years.

Joe Stansfield left Shore Lakes to become the principal of a new high school. The school resource officer increased his youth work and was recognized as national school resource officer of the year. Problems continued at River Edge after Jones left. Sometimes, even a crisis can't break old habits.

On May 17, 2004, the nation celebrated the fiftieth anniversary of the *Brown v. Board of Education* Supreme Court decision. Despite decades of busing to achieve racial integration, the nation's schools were more segregated than they had been before the landmark case. How ironic it was to find school districts being relieved of court orders to desegregate when some schools were still virtually monochromatic—80 to 90 percent Black, White, or Latino.

The successful attempt of some school districts to have mandatory busing lifted often hinged on their attainment of unitary status—a designation meaning they had satisfied the court by achieving a semblance of racial balance. Replacing busing was the concept of school choice, which ostensibly afforded parents the opportunity to select neighborhood or other schools in the district for their children. Such policies are contributing to the resegregation of America's schools, because most of the neighborhoods in the United States are de facto segregated. An unintended consequence of such policies surfaced when I began consulting in a large urban school district that was in its second year of school choice.

The principal of a high school with two thousand students called me and asked for help. It was a clear, warm October day. On the way to his office I watched the students crowded on the sidewalks shuffling to their classes. The school, like many others in the district, was undergoing tumultuous changes wrought by school choice. An influx of local African American and Latino students opted out of busing to attend this school in their neighborhood.

The principal's office was filled with athletic souvenirs—a reminder of his former career as a high school football coach. He was happy to see me and extended his hand.

"Have a seat. I'm so glad you could make it here today."

"What's going on? You said it was urgent."

"There's been a lot of changes around here. I know you've done a lot of work here with the kids over the years and I was hoping you might be able to help us out again."

"What seems to be the problem?"

"Well, the composition of the students has changed since the district implemented school choice. We've got about 30 percent African American kids here and a growing number of Hispanics. Most of these kids are OK, but we've got a real problem with some of them. They fight on campus and off. Cut classes. I don't think that some of them even care about going to school. They want to come here to do business—drugs. Officer Bently is constantly off campus taking them to the juvenile detention center and appearing in court. We've got gangs . . ."

"I know some of your kids. Two brothers attended Anytown this summer."

"Oh, you mean the Taylor brothers. They're part of the problem. Always getting into trouble. I've never seen anything like them."

"They did a good job at Anytown. One of them even made a presentation to parents on Culture Night. I heard his speech and he seemed genuinely moved."

"I don't know if he's playing you or what," said the principal. "But they're a constant source of trouble here. The whole bunch of them ought to be thrown out. I'm trying to clean the place up, but it's hard. Do you know how many discipline referrals we've had here in the last two weeks? Thirty-four hundred."

"That must be some kind of record: thirty-four hundred referrals and only two thousand students. What does that say about the teachers? Have they given up? Don't they want these kids in their classes?"

"You've got to help us," he implored.

"The climate has to change," I said. "But we've got to start with the teachers. Get them on board. We need to get them together and hear what they think."

"That's all well and good, but I've got to structure it in such a way so they buy into it. They've got to think it was their idea. Otherwise they'll oppose it."

"Why don't you just make it compulsory? After all, the situation is pretty desperate."

"They come up with all sorts of reasons for not participating. The union, too little time, no planning dates. . . . Let me work on it and I'll help you put a plan in place so we can change things."

One year later, we still hadn't started. In the interim a White student was arrested on campus for making racist comments and threats to minority students. His home also contained White supremacist propaganda. The principal's inability to deal with the cultural changes on campus no doubt was a contributing factor in the deteriorating race relations, conflict, and chaos.

Another example of administrative inertia happened shortly thereafter when I received a call from the assistant of an African American principal at a predominantly Black inner-city school. This school also had a magnet program to attract diverse students from around the county.

"Mr. Ashe [the principal] would like you to meet with us. We've got a safety problem here and we need your help."

"A safety problem? That's not one of my specialties."

"Mr. Ashe said he knows you and he thinks you will understand."

Two weeks later I met with Sam Ashe and five of his assistant principals in a conference room on the campus of his sprawling urban school. On the way to the room I was led through a maze of offices, with waiting areas crowded with African American students awaiting the disposition of their disciplinary referrals.

Inside the conference room Ashe's staff distributed themselves around a large table: two White females, one White male, and three African American males including Ashe. Several of them had blank looks on their faces—one kept dozing off as Ashe spoke. He began slowly: "We brought you here because we think you might be able to help us. Ms. Spence probably told you that we're having a safety problem. Frankly, we don't know what to do. Some of us have worked with you before and we thought you might have some ideas."

"What kind of safety problem do you have?"

Ashe continued, "You know that the campus is being redesigned. It's very spread out and until our new buildings are ready, the place is pretty open. We've got a lot of new African American students here this year under the school choice plan. We've always had a high percentage of Black students, but it seems these new ones are a different type. There's a lot of kids cutting classes and just wandering around the campus."

"I thought there were rules against that."

"Oh there are, but we don't have the manpower to police the whole campus. That's why we've designed this new system that we're going to put in place so all the teachers will have extended time walking the campus and trying to get the situation under control."

"Tell me about the students here."

"Well," said Ashe in his patently contemplative style, "we've got about two thousand students here and the place was designed for fourteen hundred. This year we got about four hundred new Black students from the surrounding area and they just don't seem interested in studying. About half the students are at reading level 1." (Reading level 1 means that the student can't form a coherent sentence or understand the content of what he reads.)

"Reading level 1? Why, you don't have a safety problem here, you've got a reading problem. Why should they go to class—they don't know what the hell is going on there. I don't blame them for being bored. We've got to start a special reading program for the kids and get to work on the teachers so they make them feel wanted in class."

A year passed, the discipline problems continued, and no further discussions ensued. Sam Ashe was replaced, and a new young African American female took over. I joined the faculty of a nearby university and had forgotten about the situation until I saw a front-page article on the school in the newspaper. The story was a litany of problems affecting the school and contained comments from students, teachers, parents, and administrators.

The young principal was depicted as fighting an uphill battle against ungovernable and violent students who were defacing buildings, threatening teachers, and disrupting the educational process. She had requested help from the district administration and a task force was established to assist her. The district superintendent maintained that most of the students wanted an education. The problem was the result of a couple of dozen troublemakers who would be expelled or removed to another school.

Columns in the newspaper and numerous letters and stories about the school followed. Some people blamed parents for not doing their job of socializing and civilizing their children. Others castigated the school system for tolerating the mayhem and wasting money on remodeling the school because the children didn't appreciate it. Still others blamed the problem on apathetic teachers whose racist ideology prevented them from caring and ministering to the students.

In all the discussion nothing was said about the curriculum that focused on NCLB standardized testing and concepts and information with little relevance to the culture of students who attended the school. And not a word was uttered about the reading and writing deficiencies that had surfaced in my earlier experience on the campus. How ironic this was. Six months prior to the newspaper stories I had been reminded of the problem by one of my students at the university.

Ronnie Jenkins enrolled in a summer course I was teaching. On the first day of class I asked each of the thirty-five students to tell us something about themselves. When it was his turn he stated that he was a forward on the basketball team and wanted to play in the NBA. "That's a nice goal," I said, "but what if that doesn't work out? What else would you want to do?"

"Haven't thought about it," he said.

The six-week course passed quickly. I read Ronnie's essay exams. They were marginal at best. He earned a C-minus for the course. In the fall he enrolled in an independent study reading course under my direction. We spoke about the reading assignment in my office. I asked him to begin by reading *The Invisible Man* by Ralph Ellison. I thought Ellison's novel about the struggles of a young Black youth in his quest for identity and success might give Ronnie some insight into his own situation. He agreed to meet with me periodically so we could discuss the work. I never saw him again until the end of the semester when I got a call from the athletic department.

"How is Ronnie doing?" asked his adviser.

"He's not doing anything. He's like the Shadow and that's the grade I'm going to give him."

"Wait a minute. We'll be right over with him."

Ronnie and two academic advisers appeared at my office fifteen minutes later.

"Let's meet in our chair's office. He knows about the situation and wants to speak with you. Ronnie's done marginal work for another professor and she can't be here today, so he wants to represent her."

We sat in the chair's office and introduced ourselves. Then one of the advisors popped the question to Ronnie: "Ronnie, why don't you tell Dr. Kaplan why you didn't complete the work for him?"

Ronnie squirmed in his seat and said softly, "I have a reading problem."

"Well, why didn't you tell me earlier? I wouldn't have assigned you a five-hundred-page book. We could have done other things."

The department chairman looked at Ronnie and his advisers, and said solemnly, "I don't blame the student for this. I blame a system that let's this situation come about."

Ronnie received an incomplete in the course and promised to finish his work after the basketball season. He was a senior and needed the credits to graduate. But Ronnie received national recognition for his athletic accomplishments and dropped out. Three months later he gave interviews in the local newspapers and on television in anticipation of the huge signing bonus he anticipated. That never happened. Ronnie was passed up in the NBA draft. He tried out with two or three pro teams without landing the dream job he wanted. Ronnie was one of Sam Ashe's students.

It's easy to criticize beleaguered school administrators. Today's megaschools are like small cities and often mirror the values and behaviors found in the larger society. But that is precisely why public schools must become self-contained communities with rules and regulations that reinforce humanistic values and behaviors so students and staff can pursue the goals of becoming good citizens.

It takes well-rounded administrators to create caring learning communities: men and women who are flexible, creative thinkers; people who are comfortable interacting with students, staff and parents from diverse backgrounds; people who grasp the big picture—that schools must be places where people feel safe and respected; people who are good managers and, above all, good listeners.

In the pursuit of the knowledge that will make them better school administrators, thousands of educators annually enroll in graduate educational leadership programs around the country. Having a master's or doctorate in educational leadership is often the key to unlocking the door for advancement within the school system. It brings the promise of increased status, upward mobility, and money. And with the demand for school administrators increasing as baby boomers retire and new schools are built, the market for school administrators is booming.

Arthur Levine (2005), the president of Columbia University's Teachers College, studied educational leadership/administration programs around the nation. Noting that nearly nine out of ten of the school principals in the United States have studied in such programs, he contended that few of the 250,000 school leaders are qualified to handle the complex demands of their jobs. Even more alarming is his conclusion, after studying master's and doctoral programs in educational leadership, that "credentials have come to overshadow competence." Present programs have little value and should be overhauled or abolished. Ironically, Levine surveyed educational leadership graduates, who acknowledged that their coursework was of little use to them.

The need for competent school administrators has never been more urgent. We can expect more crises on school campuses as the complexity of human relations increases and school administrators continue to be picked based upon traditional résumés heavily laden with useless courses and degrees.

## NOTE

1. Price (1997), in a study of White middle and high school students, found that Whites shy away from football and basketball because they are perceived as Black sports. White athletes don't want the competition or feel they aren't respected by players and coaches. They believe the stereotype that Blacks are superior athletes. That creates a self-fulfilling prophecy by discouraging White athletes, and, as Hoberman (1997) shows, the obverse holds for their view of Black intellectual ability.

# 6

## Special Education: I'm Not Stupid!

I always tried hard in school, but I had trouble with math so they put me in a special ed class in middle school. They kept me in those classes, and you all say I'm stupid. I'm not! I'm as smart as any of you in this room and I'm graduating!

> —African American male high school senior
> to seventy peers at a workshop

The president and I believe in the bright potential of every child, and the research is clear: teachers' attitudes affect student achievement. Children—no matter their race, their family income or their ZIP code—show the greatest achievement gains with teachers who really believe they can learn.

> —U.S. Secretary of Education Rod Paige in his
> March 12, 2003, speech, "Soft Bigotry of Low Expectations"

There are 6.5 million school children in United States schools with disabilities ranging from profoundly impaired through behavior disorders. Nearly 5 million children aged three to seventeen have been diagnosed with a learning disability. Public schools are required by the Individuals with Disabilities Education Act (IDEA) to offer quality remedial and educational opportunities to these children—in some instances to age twenty-one. The quality of their educational experiences varies widely, especially since thousands of teachers in special education are working without the appropriate certification or licensure.

The distribution of students by ethnicity in special education programs is striking. Nationally, a disproportionate percent of African Americans (especially boys) make up the ranks of students in special education programs labeled as behavior problems, learning disabled, and emotional disorders. In fact, Black public school students are three times as likely as Whites to be classified as needing special education services, according to research by the Civil Rights Project at Harvard University. Often these children are classified as mentally retarded. Yet Harry and Klingner (2006) demonstrate that four of the categories most often used to designate schoolchildren in need of special education are judgmental, that is, they depend on clinical judgment rather than verifiable biological data. These categories (Mental Retardation and Mild Mental Retardation; Specific Learning Disability or Learning Disability; Emotional Disturbance; and Speech and Language Impairments) comprise high-incidence categories because the majority of children in special education programs are placed in them. And there is clear evidence of ethnic disproportionality.

Harry and Klingner provide case studies of teachers and administrators to document their conclusion that these categories and classifications "do not necessarily reflect real disabilities within children." In actuality, they are the result of social processes that result in definitions of children and ethnic groups that "reflect a set of societal beliefs and values, political agendas, and historical events that combine to construct identities that will become the official version of who these children are" (2006, p. 7). A National Academy of Sciences study concurred, noting that high-incidence disabilities are nearly impossible to separate from culture and school context (Donovan & Cross 2002).

A report of the Civil Rights Project of Harvard University, *Racial Inequity in Special Education*, concluded that "[m]inority children with disabilities all too often experience inadequate services, low-quality curriculum and instruction, and unnecessary isolation from their non-disabled peers. Moreover, inappropriate practices in both general and special education classrooms have resulted in overrepresentation, misclassification, and hardship for minority students, particularly black children" (Losen & Orfield 2002, p. xv).

When students are unable to function normally in school, they are frequently labeled with a special education designation such as MR (Mental Retardation), ED (Emotional Disturbance), SLD (Specific Learning Disability), EMR (Educable Mental Retardation), or LD (Learning Disability). There is a veritable alphabet soup of labels for kids who can't or refuse to make it, and they adhere like bumper stickers on cars. With a label goes stigma that stays until one graduates—or drops out.

Special education students are frequently avoided by other students and teachers. They might be segregated in special classes or areas reserved for problem children, or put into centers to isolate them. It's difficult for kids to work their way out. Some are too volatile and unpredictable to attend regular schools. They may have assaulted someone. Others lack the motivation or ability to make satisfactory progress toward graduating. Occasionally special education students reenter regular schools only to be returned in a day or two. That scenario was described in a workshop for the twenty teachers at a special education center.

Ray: "Tommy's a good teacher all right. Remember how he got those two Black boys ready to go back to Clements High last spring. Got 'em so they could participate in classes, or so he thought."

John (laughing): "Yeah, those boys sure liked Tommy. But it wasn't two days before they were here again. They didn't give them hamburgers to reward them for being good the way he did."

Academic progress in a special education center is problematic. The disproportionate designation of children of color to special education classes and centers is contributing to the resegregation of schools, along with tracking, magnet and charter schools, vouchers, international baccalaureate programs, advanced placement, honors and gifted programs, and specialized curricula that cater to White children. Public schools are becoming increasingly stratified, leaving many children of color at the bottom of the educational ladder.

A study by the Harvard Civil Rights Project concluded, "While the public school enrollment reflects the country's growing diversity, our analysis of the nation's large school districts indicates a pattern of growing isolation. We find decreasing Black and Latino exposure to White students is occurring in almost every large district as well as declining White exposure to Blacks and Latinos in almost one-third of large districts" (Frankenberg & Lee 2002, p. 22).

Even in supposedly integrated schools, children of color are often segregated and channeled into non-college-preparatory curricula. The National Center for Education Statistics reported that in 2001, only 52

African American students per 1000 took advanced placement examinations, compared to 185 Whites. The Bridges Project of Stanford University found widespread misconceptions among high school students in nonaccelerated curricular tracks (especially poor and minorities) about college standards and expectations (Venezia, Kirst & Antonio 2003).

We saw this phenomenon firsthand at a nationally acclaimed urban high school during a workshop for eighty students. When an African American male asked the guidance counselor for information about college, "She told me I should apply to the local community college. I told her I was thinking about Harvard. I've got a 4.0." We asked if other students in the group had similar experiences, and all twenty of the African Americans raised their hands.

Many of the millions of physically and emotionally disabled children in the United States are mainstreamed; that is, they attend regular classes. Research indicates this has a beneficial effect on all students, generating personal growth, academic achievement through tutoring and mentoring, and increased social interaction. Some severely disabled children may be institutionalized or placed in specialized public schools. The Apple Center is such a school.

Located on a ten-acre campus with a pond, ducks, and assorted animals, it serves 150 children from kindergarten through high school. When students reach twenty-one years of age the state no longer provides schooling, and families must arrange for alternative services or institutionalization. The center cares for children whose problems range from incontinence to being wheelchair bound. There are affectionate kids with Down syndrome and difficult-to-manage ones with severe emotional and physical disorders. All require a great deal of personalized care and commitment by the staff of forty teachers and a similar number of aides. It takes a very special person to work there. The days are filled with challenges, the work is hard, and the children demanding.

Many districts don't provide adequate funding for such programs, which greatly imbalances student-to-staff ratios, but the Apple Center seemed to be adequately staffed. However, there was friction between teachers and aides. All but two of the teachers were White and all the aides were Black. We danced around the Black/White issue for about an hour at a workshop before a White male asked what had been on most peoples' minds: "How can we create better relationships with our Black aides with the difference in education between us? You can't expect them to understand everything we do."

"If we tell them to do something and they don't want to, that's defiance. Insubordination. But they'll cry racism if we report them," said someone else.

A number of heads nodded. There was clearly a need for dialogue between the two groups, but none of the aides were present because they rode home on the buses with the children.

"How can we get together when there's not a spare minute to do that?" asked an exasperated teacher. "It's like a merry-go-round you can't get off."

On the way to conduct a workshop at a special education center we drove through a postage-stamp-sized city that looked like a Norman Rockwell painting from the '40s. Streets lined with oak trees, small, neatly landscaped homes that lead to the business district, such as it was, with rows of old antique shops. Across the railroad tracks down a back road that dead-ends at a cemetery is Brady Educational Center. How symbolic, placing two warehouses for unwanted human beings next to each other—one for the dead, the other for unwanted children.

We'd never seen a school adjacent to a cemetery before, but the kids at Brady are, for many people in the community, educational outcasts: their future as bleak as that of the corpses nearby. Its ninety students range from the profoundly disabled to the gifted, most of them known as misfits and losers. Though pregnant students can remain in their regular schools, most in this county don't provide the necessary support for them to do so. Brady has a relaxed attendance policy and a day care center with licensed staff to care for the students' children while they attend class. The sixty female students accounted for fifty-three babies. They could stop in to see and feed their infants during the day. The moms ranged in age from twelve to nineteen. Some had two children; few were married.

Two days before the workshop Maryann Dubois, an administrator who works with us in that county, called: "One of the students whom we met on the planning visit was killed last Friday in an automobile accident—that pretty blonde girl sitting on the left side of the table. She wrapped her car around a utility pole. It's shaken up the students. They've had some counseling, but I don't know how they're going to react when we get there."

I parked my car in front of the administration building and was escorted to the media center. Brady is small, so except for the severely disabled, all the students attended. The rap on kids in special education programs is that they don't want to work or can't succeed in regular academic courses even if they tried; that they're lazy, unmotivated troublemakers who can't get along with the "normal" kids; that they are easily agitated, aggressive, and combative.

Several students were placing supplies on the floor around the empty room when we entered. The chairs and tables had been removed so we could sit on the floor in small groups and talk. It was already twenty past eight, and only a handful of kids were there. We turned to Janice Dunfy, a social worker and the adviser to the students who planned the day: "Where are they?"

"Don't worry. They'll be here soon. The moms are taking their babies to day care."

Gradually the room began to fill. Many were reluctant to participate and hesitated to fill out the culturegrams. They drifted off in cliques. Unused to the lack of structure, they waited for the daring to go first. Soon they were on their hands and knees scrawling answers across the six-foot sheets of butcher paper. Even the shy ones got into it, and the room started to reverberate with the chatter and laughter of kids having fun.

The principal came in and greeted them.

"This is a very special day for us at Brady. Today you'll have a chance to work together and learn about yourselves. You will stay in the media center all day except for lunch. I hope you'll work well with our guests and your teachers so you can learn. I know you believe, as I do, that Brady is a great school and you're great students!"

We let them roam around the room to play Hello Bingo because we wanted their workshop to be the same as other schools. Most did fine. A few sat on the floor and declined to play at first, but after a few minutes they were just as animated as the rest. For some it was an awakening. They came out of the shell they'd been hiding in. It was a revelation for some of the staff, like the spouse abuse counselor who works at Brady several days each week.

"I've never seen them like this! Some of them who haven't done anything all year are participating. There are kids who haven't spoken before actually talking."

They listed stereotypes they thought people had about kids who went there. Students read their comments. The same descriptors came leaping off the pages:

| | | |
|---|---|---|
| burnouts | wasted | never amount to anything |
| stupid | retards | criminals |
| losers | useless | drunks |
| no future | rejects | troublemakers |
| dropouts | at-risk | lazy/slow |
| sluts | redneck | freaks |
| whores | violent | dumb |
| failures | alcoholics | all the girls are pregnant |
| bad | druggies | |
| school for stupid people | | |

"My God," whispered Maryann. "I have two sons who are learning disabled. I can't imagine them believing such things about themselves. How can kids live with those thoughts?"

When they finished we sat in a circle. "You know these aren't true," I said. "I work with kids from all kinds of schools, and you've behaved better than many. You're as smart as any of them! Now I want you to list positive things you would like people to think about you."

In a few minutes they produced this list, which they posted around the room:

| | |
|---|---|
| have a future | mature |
| smart | good parents |
| capable of being responsible | drug free |
| caring moms | organized |
| good students | responsible mothers |
| hard workers | not "hos," sluts, or whores |
| mistakes happen, get over it | we're not burnouts |
| it's not dangerous | we all don't smoke |
| we all are here to graduate | we are not all easy |
| there are hardly any fights | not everyone is dirty |
| teen moms are taking | we are all winners |
| responsibility for their actions | we do our best |
| determined to graduate | going places other than jail |
| having kids doesn't mean you are dirty | not all the mothers are on welfare |

we're not lazy
most of us are normal
just because we come here doesn't mean
    we won't make something of ourselves
we don't care what anybody thinks about
    us because we're proud of who we are,
    and that's all that matters

we get the same education
we're good kids—we just have
    problems that our teachers help
    us understand
it's better to have a place to take
    your baby than to drop out

"You've proven today that you are all of those things. You are hard workers and responsible people who care about your babies. Don't ever let anyone label you or put you down! You are in charge of your own lives. You can be what you want to be. It's up to you."

They quickly came up with the following ways for changing the public's perception about the school, and agreed to meet in a week to begin working on them.

"Take people on tours of our school."

"Video tape what we do and show it to people."

"Form a drama club and put on plays around the area."

"Start sports teams and play other schools."

The cafeteria was filled with teenagers feeding their babies, table after table, three or four mothers at each. All the children were less than a year old—blonds, brunettes and redheads, and some with no hair at all. Many moms cradled their babies on their laps while they fed them. One young woman was giving her baby chocolate milk and a hot dog.

"She's a very bright girl," said Ms. Dunfy. "She was in the gifted program but dropped out. There are others who were in those programs but didn't want to do the work, or they were just too unconventional for regular schools. They missed so many days they'd never be able to graduate. We have a more lenient attendance policy, but they have to complete all the work. Some of them may take several years to graduate, but they can get a regular diploma."

Some special education experiences were more difficult, especially at centers for children with behavior problems. Using microphones seems artificial and impersonal when we're trying to make kids feel special. But this day, we could have used one at a two-year-old charter middle school for special education students. About 150 students attend the school, which shares space with the criminal investigations unit of the sheriff's department, anti-drug programs, and several social-service agencies. The facility was in good condition, but it was austere. There were no amenities for the kids because they ran the program on a shoestring budget with a federal grant. No extracurricular activities—sports, art, music, band, or clubs.

Our meeting room was being cleaned by three large African American women wearing prison-striped black and white uniforms.

"Is this a joke?" I asked one of the administrators.

"The sheriff believes they should wear those clothes. They don't mind. I think they even find it funny."

The freshly mopped floor was ready for the kids, but they were nowhere in sight. Ten elderly community volunteers were standing around waiting to help. We briefed them about their role as facilitators: "One of you work with each group, but don't take over. Just be there to answer questions and guide them. Let them think for themselves, generate their own ideas."

We waited another ten minutes and still no students. News at last: One of the boys had fallen. They thought he had a concussion and were waiting for the ambulance. They held the kids in the classroom to avoid upsetting them. Finally, two lines of students began coming from different directions and entered the room, which doubled as a cafeteria.

It's best to limit the workshop to around fifty to allow them to mingle and create a more intimate environment. It's also more manageable, especially with middle school students. But we ignored that rule and allowed all of them to participate. There was no furniture so we sat on the floor. The nineteen-inch TV was barely audible and woefully inadequate. The kids hadn't been briefed about why they were there and what to expect. All of them were labeled with learning disabilities and behavioral problems.

"Today we'll be working on making this place safer and better for everyone. It begins with having respect for yourselves and others." They were starting to fidget, so we turned off the mike.

"I don't have many rules, but when I talk you don't. When one of you is talking, I'll be quiet!" I shouted at the top of my voice. "Raise your hand if you've seen a fight here this year." Everybody's hands went up.

"How many of you would like to stop the fighting?" Only three hands appeared.

"You mean you want more fights?" That got a laugh.

"Be honest with yourselves and one another. You know fighting won't solve anything. You know disrespect causes a lot of fights. So listen to me and to others and try to understand what they're saying—even if you're 100 percent certain they're wrong. Because if somebody says something to you and believes it, then it's true for him."

The kids were restless. It was Friday, their first week back after the Christmas break. We knew we had to channel their energy so we played the Ups and Downs game and followed that with Cultural Bingo. The volunteers and teachers passed out the sheets and pencils and the kids got right into it—most of them. About fifteen boys decided not to play. Two sat in the middle of the floor and let the other kids walk around them as if nothing was going on. Several students asked what the boxes said—they couldn't read. We should have known not to try something that might embarrass them.

Most of them were having fun. After fifteen minutes we managed to bring them together and asked which questions were the most difficult. We explained about Ramadan, which was currently being observed. No one, not even the African American boys who said they wanted to play in the NBA, could identify Hakim Olajuwon as Muslim.

We talked about what makes a good job and how much it pays. Working at fast-food places might put some money in their pockets, but couldn't pay for the kinds of things they wanted. We did the math together and they agreed that flipping burgers and asking customers if they wanted paper or plastic didn't offer much long-term promise.

Most kids like to compete in contests, so we put them into small groups to make slogans for bumper stickers and posters on the theme of eliminating stereotypes, with prizes for the best ideas. The volunteers gave each of the ten groups a sheet of newsprint and markers. It seemed like pandemonium, but most took it seriously. About a third wandered around aimlessly. A small boy led me to the front. "Take a look at our slogan," he said, glowing, as he pointed to his group's paper: "Names are like rubber and glue. Whatever you say comes back to you."

In another group kids were tracing their hands together in a circle of friendship. Off on the right, five boys were working on a list of slogans: "White isn't always right. Fight racism together. Racism is only skin deep."

Near the back several girls were making a poster that took off on Martin Luther King Jr.'s words: "Don't judge someone by the outside. It's the inside that counts."

Slogans and posters were popping up all over the room. By now most of the kids were hooked, but time was up and they had to stop. But they all wanted to be the first to display their work. A dozen mounted the stage and stood on chairs, proudly holding up their posters. In about twenty minutes they had created wonderful slogans and colorful posters. You should have seen the smiles on their faces.

We asked them to sit down so we could show them a video, but they were restless.

"Can't you be quiet?" bellowed Mrs. Smith, the assistant principal. "I'm talking to you! All he's asking you to do is show some respect and pay attention!" A hush came over the group. They could see she was mad, but in a minute the noise level rose.

We tried to end on a positive note. After all, what could you expect from that many middle-schoolers on a Friday afternoon? Sure, some of them had no manners; sure, they could use more respect—but why not give them a boost for the positive things they had done?

"I want to thank you all for participating in this workshop. You did a great job! I liked working with you. Those posters and slogans were tremendous. That just goes to show you what I've been saying—you have the ability to do what you want to. Don't ever let anybody say you can't do something. You define yourselves. You can be what you want to be."

Ms. Smith was still angry. She took the mike and chastised them: "I have never been so embarrassed. Your behavior is terrible. You keep doing things like this and no wonder people ask what kind of kids go to this school. I'm telling you, this behavior is the worst. I know you wanted to go on that field trip we were planning, but I think we're going to cancel that.

"Johnny James. You keep quiet! That's right. Get up and go to the back of the room! I was saying that you all should be ashamed of the way you misbehaved here today. You showed no respect! There shouldn't be any talking while I'm talking! Jacinto! Jacinto turn around and look at me while I'm talking! Jermaine, get up and go with Coach Nelson.

"Can't you people keep quiet for a minute? That's just what I mean. This is constant. It's happened before. I'm going to have to rethink our field trip to Sea World, too. Your behavior is disgraceful. You all need to learn respect! Now I'm going to send you back to your classes. Mrs. Johnson's class, exit by the right door. Mrs. Wilson's class, go out by the left rear door. Mr. Bennett's class, go out the front."

As the classes departed, she put down the mike and left without saying a word. An elderly volunteer came up to me with two matronly women by his side.

"I wish she hadn't done that. If she hadn't said anything after what you said it would have been better. The kids tried. After all, they're only kids. They've got a lot to learn, but they tried."

Some adults have a lot to learn, too.

Special education teachers have a tough job. Working with children with learning disabilities and a host of social, psychological, and physiological problems requires dedication and compassion. Many of their students with behavioral disorders are impulsive, aggressive, and confrontational. That's why they are so closely supervised, often with a teacher and an aide in each class.

Class size is frequently not more than ten, and children are seldom brought together in large groups. Classrooms are highly structured, in part to provide order to the chaos that may characterize their lives. Many of the children are medicated, Ritalin being one of the most common for hyperactivity and attention deficit disorder. An increasing number are on antidepressants like Prozac.

One is struck by the wide range of ages among students. Nearly all the centers we have visited had children ranging from the first grade through high school. Our workshops are often the first time that thirty or more students have been allowed to work together. Sharing and cooperation are not their forte, so for safety's sake we generally have eight to ten teachers and aides scattered around the room. We have never had a problem working in a special education center, thanks to many dedicated staff who assisted us and the special children in them.

At one school, we had the entire ninth grade working together in small groups. It took several minutes to get them quiet so we could begin, but once they got started they became engrossed. A thin boy with reddish-brown hair was in tears.

"I don't want to do this," he said, pleading with a teacher. "I want to go back to my room." Another became agitated and was taken out by an aide.

One of the teachers confided that the students weren't used to such an unstructured environment, but most of them worked hard and stayed on task. The problem was getting them to stop and shift gears to begin another activity. The whistle in my briefcase was an invaluable tool. Several teachers dropped in and out during the day and marveled at how the kids were working and interacting.

Life in a special education school is highly regimented. Students we taught in a state prison had more freedom. A lack of trust, and even fear of students at these schools isn't uncommon among staff. Some of it is justified and some misplaced. The possibility that a kid might become violent is a sobering thought.

Fifty teachers and aides in a special education center listed how they viewed the children and their environment:

- Students have low academic levels
- Students feel the staff is out to get them
- Their communication and processing skills are limited
- Parents' experiences and expectations influence student behavior (academic performance is not stressed)
- The system is out to get you (parent expectations)
- The kids are narcissistic instead of having self-respect
- The students are unprepared; I am expected to supply everything
- They lack manners; they demand things without asking
- They talk out
- They tease each other
- They get in each others' business
- They do not respect each others' personal space
- Hygiene problems
- Foul language
- Debate and challenge everything
- Don't accept responsibility for actions or learning
- Don't try to learn
- Narrow-mindness
- Don't study
- Impulsive
- Students disrespect staff
- Lack of enforcement of school codes on a consistent level

- Students are resistant to change
- Students of a different race automatically label you a racist
- Disrupting classes
- Name-calling
- Negativity
- Impulsive yelling, tattling, temper tantrums, throwing of furniture
- Sleeping—avoidance (?)
- Defiance
- They prevent willing students from learning
- Low self-esteem
- Lack of self-confidence
- No motivation, initiative
- Frustration
- Substance abuse
- Lack of structure
- Lack of self-discipline/self-control

You can see why special education teachers like Anita Majors have to be deeply committed to their profession and their students. Anita is a jolly, overweight African American woman in her twenties who works at a middle school for at-risk children. A frequent adviser at Anytown, she's had a tough life and knows what many of these children are going through. We've seen her work into the night, presenting a program to honor twenty-eight African American children for being good students—twenty-eight kids who stood tall, with their heads up, whose self-esteem soared when they got a certificate accepting them into the STEP (Students Targeted for Educational Performances) program. Dozens of beaming parents and friends were watching them receive the recognition they deserved.

When we met for a youth conference at her school, Anita introduced the man who would substitute for her that day. We would be with sixty other middle school students who were in the dropout prevention program. He left us alone with the students he was supposed to be working with. It was difficult to keep them on task, and no other teachers stopped by to give us any help. It took all our energy to keep them from bolting into the hall and leaving the building.

When the final bell rang we were physically drained. We headed for Anita's classroom as the kids ran to their buses. She opened the door and gasped as we peered in. The place had been trashed. Chairs and tables overturned, supplies strewn around as if a tornado had hit it.

"What happened to your sub?"

"Either he went to sleep or he left!"

Like countless other unsung educational heroes, Anita pushes on to help kids break the cycle of despair that engulfs them. Even without adequate support, she continues to make a difference.

A year later we returned and found the students more cooperative. Henry Barry, a twenty-six-year-old African American AIDS counselor, assisted us, and the Black boys really liked him. The students were only twelve to fourteen years old, but their chatter was laced with sexual innuendo.

We separated the boys from the girls and asked each group to write down the stereotypes they had of one another. Then we brought them together. The boys' list was pretty tame: "Dirty," "Smelly," "Dumb," "Pushy," "Lazy," "Sloppy," "One-track mind," "Sex Crazy."

About what you'd expect from adolescents.

"Why do you always ask us to suck on your meat?" a girl called out. Several boys laughed nervously. Another girl went on, "You know you do. All you care about is blow jobs."

"Don't laugh," shouted the first girl. "It's true," she said, looking at Anita.

"Yup, that's all they care about," affirmed another.

Henry seized the opportunity to launch into his spiel.

"You can get AIDS and STDs from that, too. The worst times of the week for me are Wednesday and Thursday evenings when I have to give the results of their HIV tests to kids like you who thought they'd never get it. I hate that part of my job. I have to lift weights and work out for two hours afterwards to get rid of the tension and depression I feel." They listened, but we didn't know if it changed their behavior.

We spent the next two days with small groups of teachers at Anita's school and shared their students' comments.

"It's not the first time the subject has come up, but it's the first time with middle-schoolers. Something more is going on here. I don't think the boys were involved—you could tell by their reactions. But I wonder if some of the girls are in unhealthy relationships. Studies show that many of the teenagers who become pregnant have partners who are six years older. I think the situation's worth looking into." We don't know if they heeded the advice.

Another unsettling incident happened during lunch in the teachers' lounge on my second day. An aide began complaining, "I don't know what to do with Laquanda. She's not feeling well but I won't let her leave. You know how bad her home is. She's only twelve and she's a nice girl. I don't want her to go back there."

"Where will you take her?" I asked.

"To the juvenile detention center, I guess."

"But she hasn't done anything wrong."

"It's the only place I can think of that will take care of her."

"Why don't you ask the social worker?"

"She's not here today."

"You mean you have a special education center with 450 kids and no full-time social worker?"

"I guess they can't afford it," she said with a shrug. Four months later the state legislature returned $1 billion to residents in a tax rebate.

The possibility of being assaulted at school can weigh heavily on some teachers' minds, especially those in schools for children with behavioral disorders. We were with twenty middle and high school students at such a school. There were 250 students there for a variety of reasons and offenses, in grades K–12. They wore a variety of labels that euphemistically designated their incorrigibility. The stigma cannot be erased from the kids' and teachers' minds.

About half the students were African American. Our group of fifteen was two-thirds Black. As participants straggled in, we heard loud shouting in the hall. A young Black teenager was admonishing a White student for failing to keep his temper under control. He screamed racial epithets at her and another student while two others physically restrained him. The girl became increasingly agitated, shouting threats at him as her friends ushered her into the media center, where she calmed down.

"I'm not gonna lose it over that boy," she said. "I got other things to think about and my son to care for. See?" she whipped out a picture and handed it to me. "His name is Justin, and he's ten months old. Isn't he beautiful?"

At that moment there was another disturbance outside the door. A teacher intervened and ordered the students to go to class, but one barged in on us with the teacher close behind. She asked him to come with her.

"F— you. I'm gonna smack you in your mother-f—ing fat bitch ass. You can go f— yourself."

"What you lookin' at? I'm gonna smack your f—in' ass, too." He started walking toward me. Then, perhaps thinking better of it, he turned, and walked over to a table where two smaller Black boys sat and pushed them in the face.

"I'm gonna kick your asses!"

The teacher seemed to take it in stride and again asked him to leave. He ambled across the room a few feet from me, veered to the right, and went out the door with her.

It was an ominous start to the day, but the other kids didn't seem particularly disturbed. Business as usual. The program continued.

A tall Black youth got up off the floor after filling in his culturegram and turned to another kid.

"Don't laugh. It's true," he said.

"What's the matter?"

"He don't believe me. It asked where you was born, and I put in jail. That's true. My mother was in jail when I was born."

Having eight staff in the room helped keep order, but every once in a while a kid would get up and leave. We weren't sure if they were going to the bathroom or were bored with the workshop. An aide followed each time, and a few minutes later they both returned. The students were not allowed to enjoy even the minimal amounts of freedom permitted at regular schools. Every door was locked and had to be opened with a staff key. The school resource officer stood in the hall most of the day to prevent altercations.

(Today, many middle and high schools have armed police officers on campus. Some of them have good rapport with students, counseling and guiding them. Others spend much of their time arresting them. Many would like to help kids, but can't because they lack the skills or are too busy trying to keep the lid on. Most seem good-natured, although from time to time we get complaints about overzealousness. One officer had a penchant for using pepper spray on students, especially Blacks. The kids complained bitterly, but the administration took no action. He returned to the streets after coming under fire for using excessive force in quelling a brawl. Within a week he was under investigation for harassing a Black man who had been walking through his own neighborhood to get a newspaper—he was a teacher.)

About an hour into the workshop, the young man who had threatened me came in, his head slightly bowed. Without saying a word, he handed me a folded piece of paper and left:

Dear Sir,

Please excuse my bad behavior and my bad language. Sometimes I act and say things I really don't mean. I will try to be better behaved from now on.

Mr. Donald Boylin

We showed a video that presents faces of people from all over the world, and we talked about its meaning. The students picked up on the oneness of humanity. Their eagerness to discuss their views on race relations was striking. Many kids have to be coaxed into such discussions, but not this group. A lanky African American with a modified Afro and a Black comb stuck in it sat across from me at a round table.

"You want to know what I think about White people?" he said in an agitated voice. "A White man killed my father." He looked at me with disgust and continued. "My mother's in jail. I went to visit her two weeks ago and her front teeth were missing. She said a White guard knocked them out. And you want me to like Whites!"

We pointed out that things were not where we wanted them to be, that there is still racism and injustice in our society, but things have improved over the last thirty years.

"You think things have changed!" broke in another young man. He was the president of the multicultural club, an athlete they were trying to return to high school so he could play football and break out of the cycle of despair. "They haven't changed a bit. I been workin' at McDonalds for six months and the other day they hired a White boy and put him on the cash register after I been bustin' my ass. Right off he got a better job and more money than me. Tell me why I can't even walk down the street without bein' hassled by the police. I can't go into a store without someone followin' me around like I'm a criminal. And you say things are gettin' better! No they ain't, not one bit. They ain't never gonna change."

A middle-aged White teacher who had been leaning on a bookcase near the back joined in: "You want things to change? Then you have to make the changes in yourself first. That's where you have to start!"

"I don't have to listen to his kinda shit," said the first young man. "Man, I'm leavin'." We later learned he had had several confrontations with the teacher, who had a reputation for belittling students. After he left we continued talking, disagreeing over the prospects for change. A White teenager, wearing heavy gothic makeup (black lipstick, greenish-black fingernails, long dark hair, and heavy mascara) tried to pull things together.

"I know it isn't right out there, but we have to work together to improve things."

They heard her, but I doubt they concurred.

Though most of the special education centers we visited were well kept, that wasn't always the case. We can't forget giving a workshop at a human warehouse—a private, county-funded facility where kids were stuck until they were placed in foster homes or otherwise "disposed of." It was little more than a holding cell without bars, a place for outcasts—but they are our children.

We can't begin to explain the rage and pain we felt. These kids were supposedly hopeless because they'd been thrown out of school. Many were abandoned by their parents. Living in foster homes, on the street, or anywhere they could, many were already adjudicated and might be sent to jail when they got older for crimes they had already committed. They may not be pleasant to look at and work with, but they didn't deserve to be treated like baggage, shunted from place to place, penned up in a few houses on a busy street in a crime-ridden area. They lived in filthy, crowded conditions, supposedly receiving a public school education from staff who were in some cases barely above their own dysfunctional level.

We came partly out of curiosity and a desire to figure out a way of helping hard-to-reach kids, and partly because Toni, one of my college students, asked for help. She is a twenty-year-old African American who makes seven dollars an hour attempting to give these kids a chance for a better life. Frustration, anger, and desperation are what she feels. She wants to make a difference, but it's hard to get through to the kids—to get them to realize the path they're on leads to deprivation, despair, and even worse.

How do you make them listen and understand when nobody has ever listened to or cared about them? Why should they pay attention when nobody ever taught them civility? Can they respect others when they have no self-respect? Admire others when they despise themselves? They see no reason to defer gratification when they have only known hardship and rejection; to cooperate when they have always had to fend for themselves; to trust when they have been cast out by loved ones; to be understanding and forgiving when they have been abused and neglected.

We arrived ten minutes late after taking a wrong turn. There were teenagers milling around the street and on lawns of four homes that serve as dorms and classrooms. Toni approached with a big smile on her face.

"Let's go over to the house where we're to meet. We'll get the kids in now, and they'll be ready to listen—I hope."

A thirteen-year-old youth came over to scout us out. We greeted him and gave him some materials to carry as we walked across a lawn with more bare spots than grass. We approached the small ranch-style house and followed the kids inside. The place had a dank, stale odor. The lighting was poor, and the room was brimming with children of all shapes and sizes ranging in age from a little crew-cut nine-year-old to a strapping eighteen-year-old.

The kids sat or stood around teasing one another. Almost half were White, several were Latino, and the rest were Black. Three precocious sisters sat in the front row, two of whom were biracial and the other White.

Two Black boys were plugged into Walkmans, headphones blaring into their ears. The sisters were eyeing us, waiting to see if we were worth paying attention to. They could converse—something some of the staff had difficulty doing. A blonde sitting with them was very bright, perhaps even gifted. What have they done to deserve being put here?

We were struck by the dirt—the whole place needed to be cleaned and painted. And the kids were disheveled and dirty. Even some of the teachers could use a little hygiene. When not chasing kids down for unauthorized departure from the room or interceding between potential combatants, they dozed off in their chairs.

The students represented a wide variation in ability and level of functioning. Some were medicated, others probably should have been. Many had learning disabilities, and even more were classified as severely emotionally disturbed. The girls in the front gave several correct answers to my questions and beamed when I commended them. Then an argument broke out. The nine-year-old sat beside a taller boy and grabbed for his cap.

"That's my hat! Give it to me."

"It ain't your hat. It's mine," said the older boy.

"You took that hat from my bunk. Give it back."

"I ain't gonna give you nothin'."

Tearfully, the younger boy said, "I'm gonna tell Mr. Sessel."

"Tell him whatever you want," said the older boy, as he slouched in his chair, sucked a lollipop, and listened to his Walkman.

Moments later a staff member confiscated the contested item and led them away. The other kids barely took notice.

We showed a video about stereotypes. It always evokes laughter because of the slang terms and dialects, but these kids remained emotionless. When we asked for examples of the stereotypes they'd seen, they were silent. We put them into small groups and sent them to different rooms. Seven or eight youths bolted from the house.

"I ain't goin' to do none a this," muttered one as he walked past me.

In the next room a tall boy hassled the smaller kids. Two girls were teasing each other, pushing and shoving. Outside, four male staff milled around aimlessly with the defecting youths. Two fourteen-year-olds checked each other's heads for lice. We returned to the main room (what must have been the master bedroom before it was converted to a classroom) and found the three sisters and their friend engaged in an animated conversation with a young man who hadn't been there before. One of the girls listened while drawing ornate figures on her hand and arm.

"They don't know how to work in groups," said Toni. "They need close supervision and won't open up because they don't trust one another. A lot of them can't read and write very well."

"What kind of classes do they have here?"

"Regular stuff from eight o'clock until two, and then they have scheduled activities. You can't let them run around, or they'll just take off. Maybe they'll come back, otherwise we call the police and they pick them up. They don't have any place to go. Most come from foster homes. They've been neglected by their parents. They need hugs. I'm afraid many of them will end in prison," she said, as we glanced at a slender Black girl, not more than eleven or twelve, standing by the door sucking her thumb.

The center was closed six months later.

We have an aversion to giving anyone labels, especially children. No one ever lives up to his or her full potential, and some children, through no fault of their own, never get a chance to develop their abilities. Our experience with children in special education programs has reinforced our faith in the basic goodness of kids and their resiliency in the face of formidable obstacles. We must never give up on our children, yet that nearly happened at Lennox High when teachers and administrators called for police intervention to quell a riot among a hundred kids who were fighting in classrooms and halls.

It was nearing the new millennium, but the origin of this trouble started long ago in what used to be known as Yugoslavia, and with the war that was ravaging the homeland of these hundred limited-English-proficient students who now called the United States their home. A harried assistant principal at the large multiethnic school that had been receiving scores of refugees from the war-torn country asked for help: "Would you please come over? It's getting out of hand. Last week they were fighting at a convenience store not far from here and a dozen police cars had to be called in to stop it. Today there must have been a hundred of them fighting everywhere. We've got a parents' meeting tonight. It would be great if you could attend and get an idea of what's going on."

I couldn't attend the meeting that evening, but the following morning I spoke with the administrator and learned more about the situation.

"The whole thing started about a year ago when Catholic Charities and Lutheran Services started relocating these refugees from Yugoslavia. There are dozens of families in the area, some from Bosnia, some Serbs and Croats. They hate one another and periodically this stuff spills over into school. Some of these kids have seen things that nobody should have seen and I'm afraid that things could really get out of hand if we don't do something right away."

"How did the parents' meeting go last night?"

"Better than the other ones we've had. Except one of the parents got mad and said if we didn't stop things he was going home to get his gun."

Communication between the school and parents was poor because the translator was distrusted by some parents who came from different ethnic groups. The irony of the situation was that the very internecine struggle that had destroyed their homeland had been transported across the ocean to our community.

It was the week before Thanksgiving. With the help of a street-smart African American young woman on our staff, we met with fifty of these teenagers in an attempt to create a dialogue. In addition to the thirty kids from the former Yugoslavia, there were other students from the Limited English Proficiency program: Vietnam, Palestine/Israel, Mexico, and Central and South American countries as well as African Americans, goths or unconventionals, and Southern culture Whites.

We gathered them into a circle on the floor of the media center. Four teachers and two assistant principals hovered in the background as I began.

"Look, we all know that things aren't going well here. I know what a beautiful country you come from because I visited there in 1979 when Tito was still alive. I drove from Athens to Dubrovnik. I stopped at Kotor, Budva, and ate lunch one day in what used to be called Titograd. What's happened there is terrible, but you're here now. This is a chance for a new beginning. Do we have to repeat the same mistakes?"

"It's a terrible thing, the things that happened to us," said a beautiful auburn-haired girl. "I have tried to get along with them, but they hate us."

"Who's us? What do you mean?"

"Bosnians," she replied.

"Why do you call yourselves Bosnians?" sneered a thin boy. "I come from there. That's my country. I'm Serb."

"Your people murdered my father," she said tearfully. "And tortured my mother."

"How can you say things like that?" shouted a long-haired blonde. "You act like you're the only ones who suffered. My father was also killed—murdered by Muslims like you!"

"Hold it! Can't you see where this is going? Don't you see the similarities? Just listen. Let's go around and tell our stories."

For the next two hours the students took turns recalling their journey from their war-torn home to the United States. Most of their fathers had been killed or were unaccounted for. Some had witnessed firsthand the horrors that daily flashed across our television screens during the war. They spoke from pain and suffering that had been pent up inside for years. All of the teachers and many students were teary-eyed.

When a blond Southern culture boy quipped, "If ya' all liked that place so much, why don't ya' all go home?" A Muslim girl spoke for all:

"We loved our home, but we can't go back there because there's a war. When we went to Germany they made us live in camps and we couldn't go to school. Now we're here in your country. We'd like to go home, but we know we can't. We're trying to learn English and to fit in, but you make fun of us. Do you see the way we dress? Do we look different from you? Why do you bother us and put us down? This place has saved our lives and we know that. Why don't you just leave us alone?"

"I . . . I didn't mean to hurt any of you. My friends and I were only having a little fun."

"You think it's funny to make fun of us?" sobbed a blonde in broken English. "After what we've been through? All we want is to be left alone so we can learn. That's why we came here." When students from other strife-ridden countries began to share similar stories, many in the group realized the common themes that ran through their lives and the futility of unbridled hate.

We made a small breakthrough that day. Many of the Serbs and Muslims still wouldn't talk to one another, but the fighting subsided. And the Southern culture kid vowed to "talk to my friends and tell them to leave ya' all alone."

Over the next two years we met with the group twice a month, for two hours each time. We obtained a grant that enabled us to buy materials for them to work on projects together, and we took them on field trips to a university, a Marine Science Institute, and a folk fair cultural festival. We provided lunch with the help of the school administration, which dedicated four teachers and assistant principals to the project.

We got to know most of the kids and they began to trust us. Our goals were to reduce the conflict among them, improve their grades and increase their graduation rate, and assist them in entering college. Our strategy was to establish the common humanity among them by allowing them to share their experiences.

We improved communication among the disparate cliques and overcame some of their antipathy toward one another by encouraging them to work on projects they designed to combat prejudice among students and staff at their school. Three main groups were formed: one that created posters on an anti-prejudice theme; another that, with the help of college students, developed short videos and public service announcements for the classroom promoting tolerance; and a third that worked on developing a program to mentor incoming ninth-grade students to smooth their transition into high school and reduce conflict among them.

The group wanted to create a presentation for their teachers, who, they believed, lacked an understanding and appreciation of their culture and history. They also wanted to produce a cultural fair and talent show for students at the school. Most of these projects were completed, but there were some rocky times—like the morning we showed them the ABC program *The Land of the Demons*, about the war in their homeland.

The kids from Yugoslavia were transfixed by the footage, while some of the American students chatted obliviously. As the video played, many of the Yugoslavian kids became tearful. One pointed to the screen and gasped, "That's the camp where they took my father! We never heard from him again." When it ended the room was silent.

"I wasn't sure I should show this, but your advisers thought it was OK."

"You did the right thing," said a tall lanky boy. "They should all see what went on there."

"That's right," said a smartly dressed dark-haired girl. "But I didn't like it that some of them were talking while it was going on. That was very disrespectful!"

"Who are you accusing of being disrespectful?" demanded an Asian American girl.

"You know you didn't pay attention to the video. You talked the whole time. We lived through hell over there. Most of us lost fathers and brothers and you don't even care."

"I'm sorry if I offended you. Some of us didn't realize. . . . The video was too impersonal. It's not the same when you tell your story."

At the end of the 2002 school year the fighting among them had ceased. Disciplinary actions decreased. Ten graduated and four went on to college.

There are nearly 5 million limited-English-proficient students in the United States, and 80 percent of them are Latinos. Children like these have stories that need to be told and talents that, if nurtured, will contribute to the great pluralist experiment that has made this nation the land of opportunity and dreams.

# 7

---

## Epilogue: Making a Difference

### HATE HURTS, LOVE HEALS: WHERE DO YOU STAND?

$S$ome people like to work with adults, others with the elderly—but working with children is rewarding because you can never anticipate where their uninhibited exuberance will lead. If you hold the bar high you will not often be disappointed. Throughout this book I have tried to convey the message that teenagers are faced with many problems in and out of school, and the two are intertwined. We need to provide educational opportunities that tap the creative energy and enthusiasm of youth, to empower them, and help them develop a sense of mastery and self-esteem.

For many children, traditional educational strategies are boring and irrelevant, and may even be counterproductive. And the pervasive emphasis on high-stakes standardized testing mandated by NCLB is contributing to a growing disenchantment with schooling among the nation's students. While some youth are able and willing to adapt to these methods, large numbers of them are being alienated, and their potential academic achievement and contributions to our society lost. Here are a few examples of youthful contributions that demonstrate the potential of these untapped human assets.

In 1987 Jack Calhoun of the National Crime Prevention Council (McGruff's "Take a Bite Out of Crime") conceived a program called Youth As Resources (YAR). He believed youth have tremendous potential for making contributions to society. YAR is designed to encourage children and teenagers to engage in community service. Initially funded by a grant from the Lilly Foundation in Indiana, YAR has spread to more than thirty sites around the nation—and even to Poland and Australia. The concept is simple: Help children become responsible, productive citizens by getting them involved.

The National Conference for Community and Justice, Tampa Bay, through a grant from the Children's Board of Hillsborough County, became the host for YAR in 1996. We established a separate board, half youth and half adult, to oversee the program, and hired a coordinator to present this challenge to the area's youth: We believe in you. We know you have the potential to make things happen in your community. Come up with a community service project. Present it to our board and apply for funds. If they like it, we will give you money to do it.

In seven years we awarded over $150,000 to more than one group with more than four thousand children and youth. There were a few hundred strings attached. The kids must conceive of the project and carry it out. They must write the proposal, along with a line-item budget, and present it before the board. They must have an adult to advise them, and a non-profit like a school, house of worship, or civic organization to sponsor them. And they must have a celebration after it's completed.

The first group of kids who came before our board were sixth-, seventh-, and eighth-graders. They asked for $4,000 to pay someone to repair the roof on a church in their neighborhood, which they would make into a community center. The kids on the board said they would give them the money if they got someone to show them how to repair it. They got a volunteer from Habitat for Humanity who showed them how, and they got their community center.

A junior in a rural part of the county had a similar request. He said there was no place for kids to hang out where he lived, so he organized a group that submitted a proposal to convert a derelict building into a coffee house where kids could read, rap, and relax. They did the carpentry, masonry, plumbing, and painting—and now have a place to call their own.

A group of African American teenagers who were members of a Seventh-Day Adventist church drama club in Tampa came to our YAR board with a unique proposal. They recognized that it was difficult for African American children in foster homes to get adopted and wanted to do something about it. They received a grant that enabled them to write, produce, and direct a play about the history of Africans through slavery and contemporary times. They even made the scenery.

They recruited Black foster children for the production, taught them how to act, and performed the play in churches, highlighting them throughout the region. Three children were adopted and there were inquiries on eighty others. The group received a Points of Light Award and were flown to Washington, DC, where they performed the play for dignitaries.

A very strong-willed young woman attended Camp Anytown and didn't know what to make of it at first. As the week went on she got the message of cooperation and peace. Two of her friends had been murdered, and a third was killed in an accident. By the time the camp was over she vowed to make a difference in her community.

She received a YAR grant to create a series of workshops for teens where she lived and formed an organizing committee to help plan the activities and recruit participants. She had to enlist the support of some antagonists, but won them over, including a well-known drug dealer who went straight. She organized a series of workshops on anger management, human sexuality, parenting, and job skills. To entice participants into the workshops, they were guaranteed a place in a basketball tournament. More than 150 teenagers attended workshops and played in the tournament. The YAR board was so impressed that it re-funded the program, which drew an additional three hundred participants.

Shortly after Christmas 1999 another tragedy befell her—a friend was killed in a drive-by shooting. She redoubled her efforts, obtained grants from the Points of Light Foundation and the Tampa Bay Community Foundation, and conducted two daylong workshops for children on peace and African American heritage. More than two hundred children participated in the celebration of African music, dance, and life. She graduated from college and is now a sought-after school consultant.

A group of children living in a rural area with a high population of Mexican American migrant workers applied for a YAR grant to buy toys for underprivileged children. The YAR board suggested they ask the children what they wanted. They were surprised to learn they wanted their own blankets, which they purchased along with the toys—and gave them a party.

Two youth groups obtained YAR grants to create dramatic presentations against gangs and violence. In one, a black-hooded Grim Reaper danced among the troupe, smiting the warring factions until no one was left alive. They performed their work in area schools and churches.

Another project was conducted by a group of middle school students in an area reputed to be rife with gangs. They called themselves the TAG Team—Teens Against Gangs. On a Saturday morning, three hundred of them marched through the neighborhood escorted by police on motorcycles, sirens blaring. When they arrived at a nearby high school they conducted workshops to discourage gangs. They asked teens to sign pledges not to join gangs, and to report gang behavior to the police.

Violence, or the threat of it, weighs heavily on the minds of many children, like the group of sixth-graders who obtained a grant that enabled them to escort first- and second-graders home safely. Several groups got grants to work with nursing home residents. One group of elementary school children made them gifts and visited regularly, reading to them and helping them write letters. Two others planted flower gardens around nursing homes; one even built a greenhouse and joined residents in planting what they raised around the neighborhood. Another built a greenhouse and distributed home-grown fruit and vegetables to area residents.

Kids are limited only by their imaginations. They are not deterred by considerations of liability, risk, and expense. They are far more observant and aware of their community's needs than adults realize. If you want to get your hand on the pulse of the community, ask a kid. Unfortunately, too few adults bother to do that.

Several years ago we created a countywide Youth Congress for high school students to provide leadership training for them. They could learn how public policy is made and serve on boards of directors of corporations and community agencies. It was evident that we needed to train the adults on the boards so they could adapt their regimen and attitudes to accommodate youth. We had students assisting the United Way and participating in decisions on the allocation of funds by a government agency dedicated to children's issues.

In the spring of 1999 the Youth Congress decided they had had enough of name-calling and prejudice that led to tragedies like Columbine. They created a regional anti-bias campaign and called it "Hate Hurts, Love Heals: Where Do You Stand?" The program was supported by Tampa, St. Petersburg, Clearwater, and Hillsborough and Pinellas counties, and the Florida Commission on Human Relations.

They designed posters, pencils, and bumper stickers. One hundred billboards went up around the region, and sixty thousand book covers were distributed in area schools. A local television station assisted the students in making a powerful thirty-second public-service announcement that ran for several months. They created a two-hour anti-prejudice workshop for middle school students, presented it to the Hillsborough School Board, and began implementing it in area schools.

Despite these successes, many children are frustrated because they have been abused or neglected at home, in school, or in the community. They may be violent because they don't know how to cope with anger and lash out at a system that has little tolerance for people who look or act the way they do. Children, especially African Americans and Latinos, suffer from the insults and injuries that are part of their existence as minorities in a White-dominated society. Many feel left out because our educational institutions neither reflect nor adequately acknowledge their heritage, culture, and contributions. They don't have to say anything—you can see it in their faces and sense it in their demeanor.

It was the fall of 1998, at a workshop in a middle school in St. Petersburg, in the heart of the area torn by riots two years before. The sixty students discussed their experiences with prejudice and discrimination, and recounted some vivid examples.

A tall, well-built African American youth began: "It happened three or four years ago. I was ridin' my bike not far from here, and I almost got hit in a drive-by shooting. I could feel the bullet go right by my head. Another shot made me flip my bike. I got scraped up pretty bad. I went home and told my mother what happened, and she called the police.

"Two White policemen came and asked a lot of questions. They didn't believe me, so I took them to where the shooting happened. They looked all over the place for evidence—bullets and shells, but they didn't find anything. They told me I made it all up. 'You know it never happened. You were just doin' somethin' stupid like niggers do and got hurt.' I never told my mama what they said 'cause she would have gotten real mad."

How many other children are walking around with scars from prejudice and discrimination? It is that sometimes real, sometimes imagined reason for getting a low grade, being criticized, not getting promoted, being suspended. Was it racism? Sexism? Anti-Semitism? Favoritism?

There is always a lingering doubt about why we are treated differently. Some call it paranoia; for others it may be reality.

But it is amazing how resilient kids can be if we give them a chance. Three weeks after the St. Petersburg riots in the fall of 1996, we were at a Boys and Girls Club on the south side of the city conducting a dialogue on race relations. The building was woefully small and inadequately equipped. As rain pounded on the tin roof, we wondered how many kids *weren't* being served by this antiquated facility.

During a break we walked around the room checking out posters children had made. There was a handwritten letter stuck on the bulletin board. At the bottom was a silhouette of Dr. Martin Luther King Jr., and coming from his head was a cloud-like shape. Inside it were these carefully printed words:

> I have a dream that it will be peace in the Blacks communities. And that Black on Black crime will stop. We need to work together. White and Black will stick together. And it will not be just a White and Black world it will be a mixed world. We will have no races of Black or White. We will love each other in different ways. I am writing this because I want to finish what Dr. Martin Luther King started. Because I do not care what anyone says because I am willing to stand up for what I believe in.

PRAISE TO THE LORD

AND I'm
JOSEPH
milton
JONES            Age 9

# Appendix: Activities for Making Happier Classrooms

This guide provides teachers with methods and activities they can use to prevent and attenuate interpersonal conflict among students that impedes academic achievement. It is our thesis that schools must become learning communities where students treat one another with dignity and respect. If they are subjected to ridicule, gossip, intimidation, and violence, little substantive learning can occur.

Despite the pressure to master fundamentals of reading, math, and science and make satisfactory annual progress as mandated by federal and state authorities, tens of thousands of students are falling behind. The Black/White achievement gap is not significantly narrowing, and while children of color lag behind White students, the academic performance of White students leaves much to be desired. Many students of all ethnicities are not learning and performing at their grade level and have not mastered fundamentals.

Even more disturbing is the lackluster performance of students who ostensibly master fundamentals but have little grasp of history, geography, civics, and ethics and cannot think critically. For many students, the process of getting an education is an exercise in self-defense and survival. Having a challenging learning environment more often means confronting the jibes, insults, violence, and alienation of a hostile school climate rather than working with friendly and helpful teachers and classmates.

But this situation is amenable to change. Students do not have to endure the verbal and physical attacks that have precipitated tragedies like Columbine. Schools must be made safe so that students can concentrate on curriculum. And while many students do not receive adequate nurturing and supervision at home, they must feel needed and wanted when they are entrusted to schools for supervision and instruction. Yet it is disconcerting to know that large numbers of educators fail to understand or acknowledge the relationship between and importance of creating emotionally safe learning environments and achieving academic success, despite voluminous evidence in support of this assumption. At a time when it is becoming increasingly difficult to integrate "extraneous" material into the curriculum because of the emphasis on standardized NCLB requirements, attention to interpersonal relationships is imperative given the increasing diversity of our students and the cultural differences between them and their teachers and administrators.

This discussion is intended to give educators information that will enable them to create learning environments that are respectful and safe for all—a precondition to learning.

## GETTING TO KNOW YOU: BREAKING DOWN BARRIERS

We've all seen kids square off. It begins with taunts and put-downs and can lead to fighting. Regardless of the source of the hostility, much of the animosity among adolescents can be attenuated by providing them with the tools for de-escalating tension. The first step is to make a commitment that every classroom will become a small community of caring and sharing individuals. Each child must feel part of the community—needed and wanted, with something to contribute. Even if children don't get recognition at home, they must feel at home in your class and be acknowledged as a unique good human being with the potential for greatness.

In order to accomplish this, teachers must provide opportunities for discovering the individual differences and qualities of each child, and children must be given the chance to demonstrate these qualities to their classmates. Seek to establish a climate in each classroom that will permeate the school so students feel part of a community. When students are detached and alienated from one another—when they don't know or care about one another—they are more likely to say and do things that are offensive. If students learn about one another and associate ideas, needs, wants, and feelings with their classmates, they become more accepting and understand the humanness inherent in each individual: more compassionate and less inclined to rudeness and abuse. Teachers can accomplish this by letting students know they are wanted in the classroom.

Hal Urban, author of *Life's Greatest Lessons*, urges teachers to lay the foundation for an amiable relationship with students by greeting them each day at the classroom door in any way they are comfortable: a handshake, hug, high-five, or nod of the head. In more than three decades of teaching, he came to appreciate that kids come from different backgrounds and have different learning styles that must be acknowledged in first encounters, because that sets the tone of classroom interaction.

## ESTABLISH GROUND RULES

On the first day of class, create ground rules. Let students establish them for their behavior. *Do not impose your rules on them.* Ask for two volunteers to help lead the discussion. One will record student responses on the board or a sheet of newsprint, while the other acts as a facilitator. Explain the role of a facilitator as a person who promotes discussion without interjecting his own sentiments—a neutral organizer of the discussion.

The facilitator begins by asking the class to give suggestions for the ground rules that will govern their behavior during the term. It won't take long to get around ten useful rules that correlate with the ones you would have given them, for example, one person speak at a time, no side conversations, raise your hand if you want to talk, no put-downs, and no cursing. The difference is that these are *their* rules. When they are finished, the rules should be prominently displayed. If rules are violated, remind them that they are responsible for adhering to them.

Giving students latitude in setting the classroom climate is a step toward empowering them and demonstrates your trust in their ability to assume adult responsibilities. Treat them fairly and consistently, ask for their input, and create an atmosphere of mutual respect, and you have laid the foundation for a communal learning environment.

## THE ESSENTIALS OF SEATING

I'll never forget where I used to sit in the classroom as a kid—in the back, where I thought I could hide from the glaring eyes of my teachers. I was not a model student. My behavior was atrocious and I was nearly left back in the second grade. I used to get in lots of fights. I was fat and had bright red hair and freckles. When kids would call me Howdy Doody or Fatty, I'd punch them out.

Those were the days before we discovered the concept of hyperactivity. Before Ritalin and Prozac. In those days they just used to call me a "rotten kid," and I did everything I could to live up to that appellation.

We've long known that labeling children has a definite influence on the way they define themselves and their behavior. Social scientists refer to this as a self-fulfilling prophecy—we label children as good or bad, leaders or followers, bright or dull, and treat them accordingly, and they often conform to our definitions of them, or, as in the case of too many children of color, rebel against authority they see as racist, insensitive, or biased.

Research by psychologist Carol Dweck (2002, 2007) and Lisa Blackwell, Kali Trzesniewski, and Dweck (2007) demonstrates that children create mindsets about their ability to learn, and this affects their academic success. Dweck was able to improve the math academic achievement of seventh-graders by teaching them about the brain's capacity to learn, contradicting their negative mindsets, which previously impeded their progress.

Every student should feel comfortable being in school. Regardless of their home environment, or conditions in other classrooms, teachers have the ability to create a climate of understanding and respect in their classroom. *Don't let students become isolated or alienated by sitting in the back. Don't allow a status hierarchy to exist—break up cliques.*

At Anytown, our weeklong residential multicultural leadership experience, we observe students when they arrive to ascertain cliques and affiliations and break them up. We assign students to different dorms and discussion groups, and mandate that they sit with different people every time they eat in the cafeteria. This forces them to meet all of the delegates at the camp and expands their knowledge and appreciation of the diversity there.

Observe where each child sits on the first day of class and ask them to sit in a different seat each day. Ask them to interview the person in front or behind them so they can learn a little about one another. Nothing too personal: things like their name, if they have brothers or sisters, their hobbies, sports, favorite movie, music, or food. They can report what they learned to the rest of the class. It may take a class period, but it helps create a sense of community by building relationships.

It's also good to discuss the concept of confidentiality so students know that what is revealed in class discussions stays in the room. Note that since people sometimes violate this rule, they may not wish to disclose certain things about themselves or their friends and family. However, if they want to discuss confidential things you can arrange for them to see someone. State that you will not divulge information disclosed in class to anyone unless it is associated with abuse or neglect. You must, by law, report that to the authorities.

We are not advocating that you turn your class into a group psychoanalysis session. We recognize that you have a strict timeline for accomplishing curricular objectives and you may lack the professional expertise or even the inclination for such activities. You may be reticent about creating opportunities for students to discuss personal matters because they seem irrelevant or may lead to disclosures you would prefer not to hear. But you must realize that you are working with children who are being exposed to a wide range of violent, sexually explicit messages in the media, in their communities, and at home, and they need to feel part of a safe community before they are willing and able to learn.

## CREATING COMMUNITY THROUGH ICEBREAKERS

An interesting and amusing way of breaking the ice in your classroom is to create charts or culturegrams out of four-foot-long pieces of butcher paper. Across the top, create categories that students can fill in beneath them. Remind them that they do not have to answer if they don't want to. Students can develop their own categories, but it is useful to include the following: name and nickname, place of birth, ethnic heritage, religion, language(s) spoken at home, favorite food, favorite music, hero or heroine, and career plans (or what you'd like to be when you grow up).

Spread the culturegrams on the floor around the room, with several markers at each. Make enough to accommodate ten students on each one. When they are complete, post them around the room. Students can then introduce themselves to their classmates and summarize their responses, observing class rules.

Other categories might include favorite band; favorite movie, television show, or book; hobby; favorite place for having fun; and silly things, like most embarrassing moment. Some responses may evoke laughter or ridicule if they aren't dealt with sensitively. For example, many children do not have a faith tradition and may be reluctant to put "none." You might find atheist, agnostic, or Wiccan listed. This provides an opportunity to educate students about the variety of religious expression. It could also lead to a class investigation of historical, cultural, and political traditions touching numerous substantive curricular issues.

Activities like culturegrams are an attempt to provide students with substantive information about one another. By learning about each other's heritage, likes, and dislikes, they begin to realize that every individual in the class has needs and wants and human qualities. Students comprehend that they have more similarities than differences. Everyone wants to be treated with dignity and respect and needs to be part of a classroom community where they are safe and can learn without being stereotyped, bullied, or ridiculed. (The teacher should also fill in a culturegram.)

Another activity that helps establish rapport among students is Hello Bingo. Ask students to help create a list of twenty-four questions that reveal bits of information about one another, for example, is an only child, is left-handed, is ambidextrous, was born in the same month as you, is the same height as you, likes to swim, likes classical music, likes hip-hop, can sing the alphabet backward, has a unique hobby or pet, or can do twenty pushups. Each question goes into a square on an 8½ x 11 sheet of paper. The center square should read "Your name here."

The object of the game is for students to find people in the class who match each question. A person can only sign one square on another student's sheet, and they should answer truthfully. Some of the fun in this get-acquainted activity is associated with checking the veracity of the answers. This is done after a stipulated time (usually fifteen or twenty minutes), or after three or four people have completed all of the squares on their sheets. You could call out the names of students in some of the boxes to corroborate their responses, and even ask them to demonstrate skills such as singing the alphabet or national anthem, doing pushups, and so on. Sometimes we throw in trick questions like "Can stand on hands for ten seconds." This can be interpreted as either doing a handstand or literally standing on one's hands.

Requiring students to complete all of the boxes (not just horizontally or diagonally) and requiring that each box be signed by a different student forces them to meet everyone in the class. Ask them to introduce themselves to one another before they pop the question. In the beginning they might turn to the students in their immediate vicinity, but they will soon have to move about the room.

You might offer prizes to the first three students with correctly completed sheets. The whole activity takes about thirty-five to forty minutes. It works best with large groups (forty or more), but it is effective with smaller groups, and the number of questions can be reduced to suit the size of your class. It can get pretty raucous, so be prepared for noise. Provide pencils and watch them have fun.

A variation of this game is called Cultural Bingo. It follows the same rules and format, but the squares ask questions that are designed to elicit information about students' ethnicity and culture: for example, likes Vietnamese food; has a relative who lives in Puerto Rico, Mexico, South America, Germany, and so forth; celebrates Passover, Ramadan, Cinco de Mayo, and so on. You can ask questions that tap different holidays, food, music, art, and literature of the students in your class so no one is left out. Each student then becomes a piece of the solution to the game and is a valued, integral part of the activity.

Students may not know what some questions mean, for example, Ramadan or Passover. We usually refrain from explaining questions during the game, forcing participants to discuss possible meanings with one another. When the game is completed we process the activity, allowing students who fit into the categories to explain what they mean. Teachers should be prepared to provide supplementary information or clarify students' responses at the end.

Games like these require the ability to read and write and can be challenging for some students. On more than one occasion we found kids opting out of such activities because they couldn't read the column headings or the questions in the squares. I realized this one day at a middle school with sixth-graders who took an inordinate amount of time filling out their culturegrams. You might read the requested information aloud before beginning.

It's not always a good idea to ask for volunteers to read aloud. Students may have difficulty reading and can become the object of jokes and ridicule after stumbling in front of peers. Sometimes, despite their deficits, they will volunteer in an attempt to please you. I'll never forget the time I asked an attorney at Anytown, who was on our volunteer staff, to read a chart. As she stumbled painfully over monosyllabic words, I quickly asked another person to continue. Later, she disclosed that she was dyslexic.

The idea behind these games is to create opportunities that are enlightening and inclusive. Try not to employ skills or questions that will exclude or alienate students, or make them uneasy. We suggest that teachers participate along with students. You have to assume the same risk as they do by divulging some personal information, but no one should be forced to answer questions that make them uncomfortable.

We're not suggesting that teachers attempt to become students' best friends, although as the nonprofit youth alliance America's Promise contends, many children would benefit from having at least one caring adult in their lives. We are asking teachers to consider establishing rapport by breaking down barriers arising from different ethnic, sociocultural, and economic backgrounds. Reducing the impact that differences can have between and among students and teachers facilitates interaction and communication that creates harmonious intergroup relations. If students and teachers are anxious and suspicious about one another, this can affect their relationships, attitudes, classroom and school climate, and, ultimately, academic success.

## HOW TO USE AND CREATE DIALOGUES

Recent court decisions lifting school busing desegregation orders that had been in effect for thirty years have been a mixed blessing. Now, school choice plans facilitating neighborhood schools are resegregating public education. As the proportion of minority students rises, so may racial tension, which manifests itself in the formation of cliques and activities by White students who feel threatened by the influx of Blacks and Latinos, for example, by wearing and displaying the Confederate battle flag.

I am often called in to alleviate tension before it escalates. On one occasion a reporter inquired, "What are you going to tell the students when you get there?" I responded, "That's the problem. Too many adults try to tell kids what to do. I'm not going to tell them anything. I'm going to listen and let them talk to one another. It's their school and they have to work it out among themselves."

Time and again we observed how the use of student dialogues diminished the level of animosity. While we were credited for achieving a breakthrough in human relations, it was the students who deserved the commendation. We were merely the catalyst, creating the environment that enabled them to defuse the situation.

## The Art of Dialogue

Why not create classrooms that challenge and inspire all the students? If we kindled the desire to learn in every child and afforded children the opportunity to demonstrate their uniqueness to their classmates, this would create a bond of shared experiences, challenges, and curiosity. To create such an environment, teachers must be willing to relinquish power and control, and encourage students to participate in planning and delivering curricular materials so they become active learners instead of passive receptacles.

Dialogues are the key to the empowerment process. The first step in creating a dialogue is to arrange the seats in a circle so each student can see his or her peers. All the chairs must be on the same plane—no one can sit in front of or behind the circle. This configuration also creates a sense of equality. There's no place to hide. The only dilemma may be how to arrange the chairs in overcrowded rooms. In such situations you might consider making two circles—an inner and outer ring.

It's important to have a discussion about the differences between dialogue and debate. Help students understand that a dialogue is a discussion intended to educate and inform. A debate is designed to convince others that your point of view is superior. A dialogue presents different points of view for the participants, who are left to decide which perspective they find most attractive. A debate focuses on demonstrating the rectitude of one's position to the exclusion of others'. The tone of a dialogue is cordial, while debate often heightens tension and is adversarial.

Some students find it difficult to hold their opinions and emotions in check during dialogues. They want to be the center of attention (often because they don't get any elsewhere or because they are used to monopolizing the conversation). Others think they can bully adversaries into submission through verbal intimidation, much like what they've witnessed among friends or at home.

Many kids haven't had much experience in civil discourse. They're used to blurting their responses out whenever they please, interrupting and cutting off others at will. Without proper preparation, emotions may triumph over reason and leave hurt feelings and escalated tension. Recent research (Wallis 2004; NIMH 2001) explains some of their impulsiveness. Physiological changes in adolescents' and young adults' brains occur through their mid-twenties. Decision making skills are not yet fully developed, at times leading to impulsiveness and poor decision making.

Nevertheless, the value of dialogue in schools as a method for improving understanding and reducing tension has been proven, and this process can be undertaken with appropriate planning. Shortly after Columbine, two of my staff assisted the principal of a high school that had similar demographics as the Colorado school. He confided to us that he feared something similar could happen there. He was aware of the stress that many of his middle-class White students were under and observed the increasing tension between some of them and the small but increasing number of African American students on campus.

We tailored a program to meet the school's needs. The students had an extended homeroom every Thursday, which gave us forty minutes. We trained 140 students in dialogue facilitation, two per room. They received three hours of instruction on the philosophy, techniques, and methods for conducting dialogues, and they had practice discussions to familiarize them with the process. For three months every class in the school spent each Thursday morning in a discussion of students' own choice.

The principal asked me to address his faculty and explain the process because he recognized the need for their support of the project. After I finished my presentation, he voiced his strong support for the program: "I expect every one of you to help. You'll be in the room to monitor what goes on, but you're not to lead the discussion, just observe and help avoid disciplinary problems. They may discuss anything they choose. I don't care if it's sex, drugs, or whatever. You'll be like a fly on the wall. I don't want you to report any of their discussion to me or to Officer Jones [the school resource officer] unless it's about abuse or neglect. These kids have to have an outlet for their problems and this will give them a chance to talk things out. You will do this. And I will be in the halls to check on you."

The program was somewhat successful. Students were surveyed and reported that for the most part they enjoyed and benefited from the discussions. Teachers gave mixed reviews about the ability of some student facilitators. In some rooms we observed business as usual—teachers leading and monopolizing the discussion. In others, students tried in vain to facilitate while disinterested teachers and classmates zoned out or dozed off. But many classes conducted spirited discussions and looked forward to the day when they could share their thoughts. In the end, the principal credited the program for reducing tension and changing the climate of the school.

## Rules for Dialogue

It is imperative to establish ground rules to avoid problems. In their exuberance to enter a dialogue, students may say or do something that offends their peers. Without rules, the discussion can become a shouting match.

As with ground rules for your class, it's best to let students establish them. A good set of rules should include the concept that sharing is voluntary—you don't have to participate, but listen and try to understand the other person's point of view. Even if you think they're off base, remember that their perception of reality is reality for them and they believe and act on this. Participants must practice active listening, that is, not only paying attention but trying to understand one another's positions. Making eye contact is also a sign of respect in some cultures.

Active listening also includes the right to ask clarifying questions to elicit more information or requesting that the speaker restate her position. Sometimes it is useful for listeners to offer support or encouragement for the speaker, especially when emotional or sensitive points have been made. This affirming action demonstrates that the listener(s) comprehend the essential points being made. But clapping and other signs of approval should be avoided because it conveys support for one position or person over another and this may slant, distort, or impede the conciliatory atmosphere of the discussion.

Several caveats should be made. To avoid students blurting out responses to positions they don't agree with, it is useful to employ the eraser rule. This rule stipulates that only the person with the eraser can speak. Even though students' rules may stipulate that one person speaks at a time, or you must raise your hand to be recognized, you may need to employ this rule until your class becomes comfortable with one another and respectful of the process. Also, to avoid misunderstanding and facilitate active listening, you might invoke a rule that requires every speaker to summarize the previous person's point. You won't have to utilize this for long.

Another good rule is to require everyone to use "I" statements. They should speak from their own experiences and avoid generalizing about a whole group or become accusatory by saying "you, you, you." When people use accusatory statements, that puts others on the defensive. They withdraw or become antagonistic, blocking effective communication. Students need to practice using "I" statements to defuse anger and conflict in and out of class. For example, instead of saying "You said that" or "You did that," they could say "I feel bad when someone says or does that." It displaces the blame, is less antagonistic, and makes the point without escalating emotions.

Students should try to be nonjudgmental by avoiding negative facial expressions and body language, verbal put-downs, or sounds that show disapproval. (This will take a lot of practice, but the group norms will eventually prevail.) Participants must commit to the process and with it acknowledge that they will take risks, make mistakes, agree to learn, and move on. Another imperative rule is that no one can stand up or leave during the dialogue. We learned this the hard way. Emotions may run high and you don't want kids getting to their feet and making menacing moves toward one another.

Leaving the room is an inadequate method for alleviating stress. It prevents the student from hearing different, albeit sometimes disquieting, perspectives that may challenge their belief system. It may temporarily reduce tension, but it denies participants the opportunity to hear about and learn different opinions and reconcile divergent points of view. They haven't learned anything except avoidance of unpleasant issues.

Another important rule that must be stressed in dialogues is confidentiality. Every person in the group must understand that "what's said here, stays here." Participants must feel safe expressing their views and sharing experiences.

Children need to learn how to engage in conversation to defuse tension. Dialogues should become a regular method of enriching the classroom, making students active listeners and learners.

Many dialogues are self-facilitated. This works well when participants observe the ground rules. To increase successful outcomes, teach participants about the role of the facilitator. Remember, the idea is to empower students so they assume greater responsibility for themselves in the process. Understanding the function and importance of an objective discussion leader provides them with valuable insight and skills, and demonstrates that you have confidence in their character, skill, and maturity to assume an adult responsibility. While not all students are capable of assuming this role, they all benefit from learning about the process and having an opportunity to volunteer as a facilitator. You may be surprised to find how many students would like a chance to lead the discussion, and setting the bar high helps create an atmosphere of trust.

While books have been written about conducting dialogue and facilitating, here are a few ideas you might find useful. Since many students are shy or reticent about taking on the responsibility of being a facilitator, ask for two students to co-facilitate. They can support one another in leading the discussion and adherence to the ground rules. It's also helpful to ask for a volunteer to record important points made during the discussion. Before the dialogue ends, another volunteer can summarize the main points and students can clarify or embellish their position.

Facilitators must remain neutral while they guide the discussion. The adage that less is more holds true with respect to facilitating. Some student facilitators have a difficult time restraining themselves. Remind them of the importance of their role of neutrality in creating an objective dialogue. They will have a chance to participate in the discussion another time.

Facilitators should begin by asking each participant to state their name and other relevant information, for example, grade level. When utilized for conflict resolution, participants should say why they're in the dialogue and what they hope to achieve by it. That's often enough to occupy the group for several hours, since it leads to a discussion of what caused the conflict. In class dialogues about social or curricular topics, the group might be led by facilitators in a discussion of historical, philosophical, political, sociological, or theoretical aspects of an issue.

Facilitators should know that the group might be silent at times and they should also remain silent until someone resumes the discussion. This phenomenon can be a source of consternation for exuberant facilitators who feel that they or the group have failed if the discussion isn't always animated. They should be patient and let the group process ideas and proceed at its own pace. Of course, facilitators can offer leading questions to rejuvenate the discussion, but this should be a strategy of last resort.

Without being overbearing, facilitators must regulate the interaction of participants. One of the greatest challenges is preventing someone from monopolizing the conversation or intimidating other participants. The ground rules can be cited when necessary. A few tactful words like "That's good, Jamie, and now let's see what Ronnie has to say about this" can help shift the conversation to other people.

The Study Circles Research Center (www.studycircles.org), a leader in promoting dialogues around the nation, contends that facilitators should occasionally feed the content of the discussion back to the group by saying something like, "Let me see if I'm hearing you correctly." A skilled facilitator also learns to use body language, eye contact, and verbal and nonverbal cues to encourage or discourage participants.

Being informed about the issue at hand and knowing the participants may be assets for facilitators. And while one might question the ability or maturity of teenagers to engage in dialogue, we have had notable success with students from the fourth grade through high school. For example, a large school district in Florida obtained a federal Safe Schools/Healthy Students grant that incorporated the concept of dialogues. Students were recruited to engage in after-school discussions about issues ranging from teenage pregnancy to violence in school and the community.

They created a slogan: "Raise your standards not your fists—You've Got the Power to Stop the Violence!" Over three years their slogans and messages were placed on billboards in the community and on posters in schools. Students made public-service announcements on commercial television and conducted teach-ins in middle and high schools. The program was credited with reducing conflict in schools and the community.

The bottom line is that kids need to have the opportunity to contribute to their school and community in a meaningful way. They need to share their views about one another and issues that affect their lives in a safe, respectful environment. Why not afford them the opportunity in the classroom? Isn't that where learning is supposed to occur?

# References

Adams, Lorraine, and Dale Russakoff. (1999). "Athletes vs. Outcasts." *St. Petersburg Times*, June 27, D1.

Advancement Project and the Civil Rights Project of Harvard University. (2000). "Opportunities Suspended: The Devastating Consequences of Zero Tolerance and School Discipline." Report for a National Summit on Zero Tolerance, Washington, DC, June 15–16. http://www.civilrightsproject.harvard.edu/research/discipline/discipline_gen.php.

Alliance for Excellent Education. (2005, August). "Teacher Attrition: A Costly Loss to the Nation and States." Issue Brief, Washington, DC. http://www.all4ed.org/publications/TeacherAttrition.pdf.

American Bar Association. (2001). "Zero Tolerance Policy Report." http://www.abanet.org/crimjust/juvjus/zerotolreport.html (retrieved December 17, 2005).

American Federation of Teachers. (2006, July). "Smart Testing: Let's Get It Right." Policy Brief No. 19.

Annie E. Casey Foundation. (2005). "Teens Not Attending School and Not Working, by Race: Percent." KIDS COUNT State-Level Data Online. http://www.kidscount.org/sld/compare_results.jsp?1=121.

Aronson, Elliot. (2000). *Nobody Left to Hate: Teaching Compassion after Columbine*. New York: Worth.

Associated Press. (2006). "Parents, Teachers Divided on Education." *St. Petersburg Times*, February 9, 8A.

Ave, Melanie. (2006). "Pen Still Mightier Than E-Mail." *St. Petersburg Times*, December 24, B1, B6.

Baer, Justin D., Andrea Cook, and Stephanie Baldi. (2006, January). *The Literacy of America's College Students*. Washington, DC: American Institutes for Research.

Ball, Deborah, Heather Hill, and Hyman Bass. (2005). "Knowing Mathematics for Teaching," *American Educator* 29, no. 3: 14–23, 43–46.

Ballenger, C. (1992). "Because You Like Us: The Language of Control." *Harvard Educational Review* 62, no. 2: 199–208.

Blackwell, Lisa S., Kali H. Trzesniewski, and Carol S. Dweck. (2007). "Implicit Theories of Intelligence Predict Achievement Across Adolescent Transition: A Longitudinal Study and an Intervention." *Child Development* 78: 246–63.

Banks, J. A., and C. A. M. Banks, eds. (2001). *Multicultural Education: Issues and Perspectives*. 4th ed. New York: Wiley/Jossey Bass Education.

Barnes, Annie S. (2000). *Everyday Racism.* Naperville, IL: Sourcebooks.

Bloom, B., and A. N. Dey. (2006). "Summary of Health Statistics for U.S. Children: National Health Interview Survey 2004." *Vital Health Statistics* 10, no. 227.

Cartledge, G., and J. F. Milbrun. (1996). *Cultural Diversity and Social Skill Instruction: Understanding Ethnic and Gender Differences*. Champaign, IL: Research Press.

Civil Rights Project. (1999, August). "Civil Right Alert. Testing: The Needs and Dangers." Cambridge, MA: Civil Rights Project of Harvard University.

———. (2005, May). "Confronting the Graduation Rate Crisis in the South." Cambridge, MA: Civil Rights Project of Harvard University.

Clark, Kenneth B., and Maime P. Clark. (1950). "Emotional Factors in Racial Identity and Preference in Negro Children." *Journal of Negro Education* 19: 341–50.

Cole, Yoji. (2002). "America's Diverse Future Sits in Kindergarten and Elementary Schools." *Diversity Inc.* October 22: 68.

Coleman, Arthur. (2000). "None of the Above." *Education Week*, August 2.

Cooper, P. M. (2002). "Does Race Matter? A Comparison of Effective Black and White," 47–66. In *African American Teachers and Their Culturally Specific Classroom Practice*. New York: Pelgrave.

De Villier, Paul. (2003). "High-Stakes Testing—Florida Comprehensive Assessment: A True Measure of Acquired Skills or a Political Ruse?" *ERIC*, June: 15.

Dell'Angela, Tracy. (2005). "Dakota Indians Say Kids Trapped in School-to-Prison Pipeline." *Chicago Tribune*, November 29.

Demmert, W. G., Jr., and Towner, J. C. (2003). "A Review of the Research Literature on the Influences of Culturally Based Education on the Academic Performance of Native American Students." Portland, OR: Northwest Regional Educational Laboratory. http://www.nwrel.org/indianed/cbe.

Dillon, Sam. (2006). "Schools Slow in Closing Gaps Between Races." *New York Times*, November 20. http://www.nytimes.com/2006/11/20/education/20gap .html.

Doherty, R. W., et al. (2003). "Five Standards and Student Achievement." *NABE Journal of Research and Practice* 1: 1–24.

Donovan, S., and C. Cross. (2002). *Minority Students in Special and Gifted Education*. Washington, DC: National Academy Press.

Dweck, Carol S. (2002). "Messages that Motivate: How Praise Molds Students' Beliefs, Motivation, and Performance (In Surprising Ways)." In J. Aronson, ed., *Improving Academic Achievement*. New York: Academic Press.

——. (2007). *Mindset*. New York: Random House.

Dwyer, Kevin. (2000). "The School Shooter: A Threat Assessment Perspective." Quantico, VA: National Center for the Analysis of Violent Crime.

*Education Week*. (2006, June 22). "Diplomas Count: An Essential Guide to Graduation Policy and Rates." http://www.edweek.org/dc06.

Elias, Marilyn. (2006). "At Schools, Less Tolerance for 'Zero Tolerance.'" *USA Today*, August 10, 6D.

Farkas, Steve, Jean Johnson, and Ann Duffett. (2003). "Stand By Me: What Teachers Really Think about Unions, Merit Pay and Other Professional Matters." New York: Public Agenda.

Fischer, Kent, and Geoff Dougherty. (1999). "A Lesson in Grading Schools." *St. Petersburg Times*, March 21, A1, A14.

Florida Department of Education. (2001, Fall). "Moving to Florida/School District Data." Education Information and Accountability Services.

Frankenberg, Erica. (2006). "The Segregation of American Teachers." Cambridge, MA: Civil Rights Project of Harvard University.

Frankenberg, Erica, and Chungmei Lee. (2002, August). "Race in American Public Schools: Rapidly Resegregating School Districts." Cambridge, MA: Civil Rights Project of Harvard University.

Galinsky, Ellen, and Kimberlee Salmond. (2002). "Youth and Violence: Students Speak Out for a More Civil Society." New York: Families and Work Institute and the Colorado Trust.

Gay, G. (2000). *Culturally Responsive Teaching: Theory, Research, and Practice*. New York: Teachers College Press.

Gay, Lesbian and Straight Education Network. (1997). *Staff Development on Homophobia Issues*. New York: GLSEN.

——. (2004). *State of the States 2004: A Policy Analysis of Lesbian, Gay, Bisexual and Transgender (LGBT) Safer Schools Issues*. New York: GLSEN.

Ginsberg, M. B., and R. J. Wlodkowski. (2000). *Creating Highly Motivating Classrooms for All Students: A Schoolwide Approach to Powerful Teaching with Diverse Learners*. San Francisco: Jossey-Bass.

Glickman, Carl, ed. (2004). *Letters to the Next President: What We Can Do about the Real Crisis in Public Education*. New York: Teachers College, Columbia University.

Greene, Jay P., and Marcus Winters. (2002, November). "Public School Graduation Rates in the U.S." Manhattan Institute Study, Civic Report No. 31.

Guerino, P., et al. (2007). "Discipline and Safety in U. S. Public Schools: Findings from the School Survey on Crime and Safety: 2003–04." (NLES 2007–302) U.S. Department of Education, National Center for Education Statistics. Washington, DC: U.S. Government Printing Office.

Hacker, Andrew. (1995). *Two Nations*. New York: Ballantine.

Hall, Daria. (2005). "Getting Honest about Grad Rates: How States Play the Numbers and Students Lose." *Education Trust*, June: 1–15.

Hall, Daria, and Shana Kennedy. (2006). "Primary Progress, Secondary Challenge: A State-by-State Look at Student Achievement Patterns." *Education Trust*, March.

Harry, B., and J. Klingner. (2006). *Why Are So Many Minority Students in Special Education?* New York: Teachers College Press.

Hegarty, Stephen. (2002). "Florida Dead Last in Graduation Study." *St. Petersburg Times*, November 21, 5b.

———. (2003). "Teachers Not Buying State's Performance Bonus Program." *St. Petersburg Times*, April 3.

Hoberman, John. (1997). *Darwin's Athletes*. Boston: Houghton Mifflin.

Howard, Gary. (1999). *We Can't Teach What We Don't Know: White Teachers, Multiracial Schools*. New York: Teachers College, Columbia University.

Indiana University Media Relations. (2007). "Students Are Bored, Many Skip School, Lack Adult Support," February 28, 2007. http://newsinfo.iu.edu/news/page/normal/4948.html.

Ingersoll, Richard. (2004). "Revolving Doors and Leaky Buckets," 141–47. In Carl Glickman, ed., *Letters to the Next President*. New York: Teachers College, Columbia University.

Intercollegiate Studies Institute. (2006). "The Coming Crisis in Citizenship: Higher Education's Failure to Teach America's History and Institutions." National Civic Literacy Board. http://www.americancivicliteracy.org/report/summary.html.

Jarrell, Anne. (2000). "Sex in 7th Grade." *St. Petersburg Times*, April 9, F1, F6.

Johnson, Jean, and Ann Duffett. (2003). *Where We Are Now: A Digest of a Decade of Survey Research*. New York: Public Agenda.

Johnson, Susan Moore. (2006). "Why New Teachers Stay," *American Educator* 30, no. 2: 8, 13–15, 18–21, 45.

Jussim, L., J. Eccles, and S. Madon. (1996). "Social Perception, Social Stereotypes, and Teacher Expectations: Accuracy and the Quest for the Powerful Self-Fulfilling Prophesy," 28: 2281–2388. In M. P. Zanna, ed., *Advances in Experimental Social Psychology*. New York: Academic Press.

Kilman, Carrie. (2006, Fall). "Learning Lakota." *Teaching Tolerance* 30: 28–35.

Klump, Jennifer, and Gwen McNeir. (2005, June). "Culturally Responsive Practices for Student Success: A Regional Sampler." Northwest Regional Educational Laboratory, Portland, OR.

Kosciw, Joseph G. (2004). *The 2003 National School Climate Survey: The School-Related Experiences of Our Nation's Lesbian, Gay, Bisexual and Transgender Youth*. New York: GLSEN.

Kosciw, Joseph G., and Elizabeth M. Diaz. (2006). *The 2005 National School Climate Survey: The Experiences of Lesbian, Gay, and Bisexual and Transgender Youth in Our Schools*. New York: GLSEN.

Kozol, Jonathan. (1991). *Savage Inequalities: Children in America's Schools*. New York: Harper Perennial.

Ladson-Billings, G. (1994). *The Dreamkeepers: Successful Teachers of African American Children*. San Francisco: Jossey-Bass.

Landsman, Julie. (2001). *A White Teacher Talks about Race*. Lanham, MD: Scarecrow Press.

Lee, Jaekyung. (2006, June). "Tracking Achievement Gaps and Assessing the Impact of NCLB on the Gaps: An In-depth Look into National and State Reading and Math Outcome Trends." Cambridge, MA: Civil Rights Project of Harvard University.

Lee, O. (2003). "Equity for Linguistically and Culturally Diverse Students in Science Education: A Research Agenda." *Teachers College Record* 105: 465–489.

Levine, Arthur. (2005). *Educating School Leaders*. New York: Education Schools Project.

Losen, Dan, and Gary Orfield, eds. (2002). *Racial Inequity in Special Education*. Cambridge, MA: Harvard Education Press.

Lush, Tamara. (2004). "Floridians Oppose Gay Marriage," *St. Petersburg Times*, March 8, A1.

Maholmes, Valerie. (2002). "What School Is All About." *Education Week*, October: 23.

Marshall, Tom. (2007). "Blessing for FCAT Success Raises Ruckus." *St. Petersburg Times*, February 22, 4B.

McIntosh, Peggy. (1990). "White Privilege: Unpacking the Invisible Knapsack." *Independent School*, Winter: 31–36.

Mishel, Laurence, and Joydeep Roy. (2006). *Rethinking High School Graduation Rates and Trends*. Washington, DC: Economic Policy Institute.

"More High School Seniors Pass Advanced Placement Tests in 2005." (2006). *St. Petersburg Times*, February 8, 7A.

National Assessment of Educational Progress. (2007). *The Nation's Report Card: America's High School Graduates*. Washington, DC: National Center for Education Statistics.

National Association of School Psychologists. (2003). "Position Statement: Student Grade Retention and Social Promotion." http://www.nasponline.org/about _nasp/pospaper_graderetent.aspx.

National Center for Education Statistics. (2002). "Indicators of School Crime and Safety Report of 2001." Institute of Education Sciences, U.S. Department of Education. NCES 2002-113/NCJ-190075.

———. (2005, November). "Indicators of School Crime and Safety: 2005." U.S. Department of Education.

———. (2006). "The Condition of Education." Institute of Education Sciences, U.S. Department of Education, NCES 2006–073.

National Center for Lesbian Rights. (2003). "Gay/Straight Alliances: Q&A." http://www.nclrights.org/publications/gsaqa0703.htm.

National Center for the Analysis of Violent Crime. (2003). "The School Shooter: A Threat Assessment Perspective." http://www.fbi.gov/publications/school/ school2.pdf (retrieved May 29, 2007).

National Education Association. (2007, January). "NCLB/ESEA: It's Time for a Change!" Report of the National Education Association. For additional stories go to http://www.nea.org/esea/nclbstories/index.html.

NIMH (2001). "Teenage Brain: A Work in Progress." http://www.nimh.nih.gov/ publicat/teenbrain.cfm (retrieved December 27, 2005).

Orfield, Gary, and Johanna Wald. (2000). "Testing, Testing." *Nation*, June 5.

Perry, Mark. (2000). *Walking the Color Line: The Art and Practice of Anti-Racist Teaching*. New York: Teachers College Press.

Price, S. L. (1997). "What Ever Happened to the White Athlete?" *Sports Illustrated*, December 8: 32–51.

Salemi, Anna Torrens, and Kelly McCormack Brown. (2004). "School Phobia: Implications for School Health Educators." *Journal of Health Education* 34, no. 4: 199–205.

Seastrom, Marilyn, et al. (2003). "Qualifications of the Public School Teacher Workforce: Prevalence of Out-of-Field Teaching 1987–88 to 1999–2000." *Education Statistics Quarterly*, July.

*St. Petersburg Times.* (2003). "A's No Measure of FCAT Success." January 21, A4.

———. (2006a). "More Schools Missing No Child Mark," May 10, 3A.

———. (2006b). "No States Meet Teacher Goal of No Child Law," May 13, 3A.

———. (2006c). "Report: States Lag in Teacher Quality," August 17, 3A.

Starfield, Barbara, Judy Robertson, and Anne Riley. (2002). "Social Class Gradients and Health in Childhood." *Ambulatory Pediatrics* 2, no. 4: 238–46.

Steele, Claude M. (1999, August). "Thin Ice: 'Stereotype Threat' and Black College Students." *Atlantic Monthly* 284: 44–54.

Stein, Letitia. (2006). "School Newspaper Censored." *St. Petersburg Times*, October 24, A1.

Stiefel, Leanna, Ross Rubenstein, and Amy Ellen Schwartz. (2004). "From Districts to Schools: The Distribution of Resources Across Schools in Big City School Districts." http://www.emsc.nysed.gov/csl/resources/from_districts_to _schools.pdf.

Tatum, Beverly Daniel. (1997). *"Why Do All the Black Kids Sit Together in the Cafeteria?" and Other Conversations about Race*. New York: BasicBooks.

Tobin, Thomas C., and Melanie Ave. (2006). "Teachers Troubled with Job, Poll Says." *St. Petersburg Times*, May 14, 1A, 6A.

Urban, Hal. (2005). *Life's Greatest Lessons*. New York: Fireside.

U.S. Department of Commerce. (2000, October). *Current Population Survey*. U.S. Bureau of the Census.

U.S. Department of Education. (2006, February). "Expanding the Advanced Placement Incentive Program." http://www.ed.gov/print/about/inits/ed/competitive ness/expanding-apip.html (retrieved September 16, 2006).

U.S. Department of Health and Human Services. "National Youth Risk Behavior Survey: 1991–2005." Centers for Disease Control and Prevention. http://www .cdc.gov/yrbss.

Venezia, Andrea, Michael W. Kirst, and Anthony L. Antonio. (2003). "Betraying the College Dream: How Disconnected K-12 Post-Secondary Education Systems Undermine Student Aspirations." Stanford, CA: Stanford Institute for Higher Education Research.

Waddell, Lynn. (2005). "Florida County Ending Official Support of Gay Events." *New York Times*, June 25, 17.

Wallis, Claudia. (2004). "What Makes Teens Tick?" *Time*, May 10.

Winchester, Donna. (2006). "Students in Need of Civics Lesson." *St. Petersburg Times*, March 26, 1A, 13A.

Wineburg, Sam. (2005). "Don't Know Much about History? Then Don't Teach It!" *St. Petersburg Times*, March 8.

Wiseman, Roslind. (2007). "How to Fight the New Bullies." *Parade*, February 25: 6–8.

# Index

# About the Author

**H. Roy Kaplan** is associate professor in the Department of Africana Studies at the University of South Florida in Tampa. He previously served as executive director of the National Conference for Community and Justice (formerly, The National Conference of Christians and Jews)—Tampa Bay Region. He received his PhD in sociology from the University of Massachusetts, Amherst, in 1971 and was a professor for twenty years, teaching at the State University of New York at Buffalo and the Florida Institute of Technology.

In December 1998 Dr. Kaplan was one of only ten individuals to receive the Education Heroes Award, granted by the U.S. Department of Education, for his exceptional contribution to Florida's future through its students, and "extraordinary efforts in providing students with alternatives to racial, cultural, and personal injustice."

Dr. Kaplan served as an adviser on the President's Commission on Race Relations, One America. He has received numerous civil rights awards and has authored numerous articles and two books: *American Minorities and Economic Opportunity* (1977) and *Lottery Winners* (1978). He has appeared on numerous radio and television shows, including *Phil Donahue*, *The Today Show*, *Good Morning America*, *CBS Evening News*, *NBC Nightly News*, and *Prime Time Live*.